LIVING YOUR LEGACY OF GREATNESS

Discovering Within the Image and Likeness of God

Volume One

Markeithia Lavon Silver

Copyright © 2004, 2021, 2024 Markeithia Lavon Silver

All rights reserved.

No part of this book may be reproduced, stored in a retrieval system, or transmitted by any means, electronic, mechanical, photocopying, recording, or otherwise, without written permission from the author. This Book series may not be copied or reprinted for commercial gain or profit. Brief quotations in critical articles or reviews or occasional page copying for personal or group study are permitted and encouraged. Permission will be granted upon request.

ISBN:

Unless otherwise indicated, all Scripture quotations are taken from the Holy Bible, King James Version, Public Domain.

Fair Use Notice: Limited portions of this book may contain short excerpts of copyrighted material within the bounds of fair use as permitted under United States copyright law (Title 17 §107 U.S. Code) for purposes such as commentary, criticism, comparison, news reporting, research, and education. This book's author and publisher make no claims regarding the copyright status of any work quoted herein.

Unless otherwise noted, Biblical definitions are taken from *Strong's Exhaustive Concordance of the Bible*, by James Strong, Copyright ©1890, Hendrick Publishing, Public Domain.

The following Bible Lexicons, Dictionary, and other religious and academic texts are also used:

The Brown-Driver-Briggs Hebrew and English Lexicon, by Francis Brown, Samuel R. Driver, and Charles A. Briggs, Copyright ©1906, Oxford, Clarendon Press, Public Domain.

Thayer's Greek-English Lexicon of the New Testament by Joseph Henry Thayer, Copyright ©1886, 1889, New York American Book Co., Public Domain.

Vine's Complete Expository Dictionary of Old and New Testament Words by W. E. Vine, Merrill Unger, William White Jr., Copyright ©1940, originally published by Thomas Nelson Publishing. All Rights Reserved. Used by permission of HarperCollins Christian Publishing. www.harpercollinschristian.com.

Disciplines of the Spirit by Howard Thurman, First Edition, tenth printing, Copyright ©1963, 1977, 2003, Friends United Press, Fair Use.

Thoughts Are Things by Ernest S. Holmes, First Edition, Copyright © 1967, Devorss & Co., Fair Use.

In-Tune with the Infinite by Ralph Waldo Trine, Copyright © 1933, The Bobbs-Merrill Company, Fair Use.

Morning B.R.E.W. by Dr. Kirk Byron Jones, Copyright © 2005, Augsburg Fortress Publishers, Fair Use.

The English Translation of the Message of the Holy Qur'an, Third Edition, Second printing, Translated by Professor (Dr.) Syed Vickar Ahamed, Copyright ©2007, Book of Signs Foundation, All Rights Reserved, Used by permission.

The Sunnah, and Second Hadith, The Fourth Volume of al-Bukhari's Collection of Authentic Hadiths, Bukhārī, Muḥammad Ibn Ismāʿīl, 810-870 Compiler. The Fourth Volume of al-Bukhari's Collection of Authentic Hadiths. [Place of Publication Not Identified: Publisher Not Identified, to 1175, 1174] Pdf. https://www.loc.gov/item/2021667384/, Public Domain.

God Talks with Arjuna, THE BHAGAVAD GITA: Royal Science of God-Realization by Paramahansa Yogananda, Copyright © 1995, 1999, Second edition, 1999. Reprinted 2002, All Rights Reserved. Used by permission.

Al-Ghazzali On Discipling the Self by Seyyed Hossein Nasr, Ed. Translated by Muhammad Nur Abdus Salam, Copyright © 2002, 2003 14th Edition 2010, Kazi Publications, Inc., Fair Use.

Dictionary quotations taken from *The Complete Word Study Dictionary of the Old Testament, Copyright ©* 2003, and The Complete Word Study Dictionary *New Testament* by Dr. Spiros Zodhiates, Dr. Warren Baker, and Dr. Eugene Carpenter, Copyright © 1992, AMG Publishers International, Inc. All Rights Reserved. Used by permission.

George Herbert Mead on Social Psychology by George Herbert Mead, Copyright © 1934, 1936, 1938, 1956, 1964, and 1977 by Phoenix Books/The University of Chicago, Fair Use.

The Roots of Social Knowledge. *American Journal of Sociology* by Charles Horton Cooley, https://doi.org/10.1086/214025, Copyright ©1926. This article was reprinted by The University of Chicago Press in October 1998 and falls under the "fair use" guidelines.

"The Social Self – 1. The Meaning of 'I'", Chapter 5 in *Human Nature and the Social Order (Revised Edition)*. New York: Charles Scribner's Sons by Charles Horton Cooley, Copyright ©1922. This article was reprinted by The University of Chicago Press in October 1998 and falls under the "fair use" guidelines.

The author has made every effort to trace the ownership of all quotes. If a question arises from the use of a quote, she regrets any error made, and she will be pleased to correct it in future printings and editions of this series.

ISBN (Paperback): 979-8-9904362-5-1
ISBN (Hardback): 979-8-9904362-6-8
ISBN (ebook): 979-8-9904362-4-4

The "Living Your Legacy of Greatness" series deals with several sensitive issues people struggle with daily. People often need more assistance than a book or literature can offer. **THIS BOOK DOES NOT REPLACE REAL THERAPY.** *This book is for informational purposes only and should* **NOT BE CONSIDERED THERAPY OR ANY FORM OF TREATMENT.**

The author cannot respond to specific questions or comments about personal situations, appropriate diagnosis or treatment, or otherwise provide any clinical opinions. **IF YOU THINK YOU NEED IMMEDIATE ASSISTANCE, CALL YOUR LOCAL EMERGENCY NUMBER OR THE MENTAL HEALTH CRISIS HOTLINE LISTED IN YOUR LOCAL PHONEBOOK OR STATE'S GOVERNMENT PAGE.**

The resources in this book are provided for informational purposes only. Readers **SHOULD NOT USE THIS BOOK TO REPLACE THE SPECIALIZED TRAINING AND PROFESSIONAL JUDGMENT OF A HEALTH CARE OR MENTAL HEALTH CARE PROFESSIONAL.**

The advice and strategies found within may not be suitable for every situation. This work is sold with the understanding that neither the author nor the publisher is held responsible for the results accrued from the advice in this book. Where applicable, you should consult with a lawyer, health care or mental health professional, financial advisor, or other health care professionals where appropriate for further details and future actions.

DEDICATION

This, the first volume of the *Living Your Legacy of Greatness series: Discovering within the Image and Likeness of God*, is dedicated to my children, Kasia Lavon and Anthony George, whom I love from the deepest part of me. May you always remember that you were created by greatness to *be* great! Be faithful to that greatness, mighty in Spirit, and no matter what you do or where you go, do not forget about God! He is our Source and Sustainer and Sovereign over *all* matters! Never forget that He always has the last say in *every* situation! When He speaks, say, "Amen," because He has a plan and a purpose for His decision. Trust Him all the way! Love always, Mom.

ACKNOWLEDGEMENTS

In my appreciation and deep gratitude for all those who have provided inspiration, support, and encouragement over my lifetime and to keep moving forward with this publication, I wish to thank the following:

First and foremost, I give God *all* the glory for allowing me to be a conduit and for manifesting this publication in its fullness. I could not have done it without Him. Next, I would like to thank my dad, the late Melvin T. Silver, my stepdad, the late Delmon B. Glasco, and my mom, Jacqueline Hines-Glasco, for birthing me and giving me layers of consciousness that have made me who I am today.

I also honor all my other mothers who impacted my spiritual growth, especially my grandmothers and great-grandmothers, Hattie-Mae Fitts (God is blessing me big-grandma), Myrtle B. Fitts (I remember everything you told me and held them in my spiritual pocketbook!), Laura Williams (Thank you for teaching me the meaning of respecting my elders!), and Mayolia Silver-Wilkerson (Grandma, I am still telling the Lord about it and "Him is fixing it every time"!). To my grandfathers, the late Jimmy L. Hines and the late Lonzo Silver, who provided strength and direction for my life's journey.

To my spiritual/God mothers who encouraged me to be humble and always stay at the feet of Jesus, the late Mother Mary Livingston-Foxworth, who had a hug that made you feel you were on a cloud. Your love for God would permeate my being each time you embraced me. I shall never forget what you whispered in my ear! To the late Evangelist Bessie Reed-Williams, who stretched me in ways I did not know I had and taught me the power of walking in faith and how to hold my "ice-water." The late Sis. Mary Reed for always being there when I needed a friend. The late Dorothy Mumford-Walker, thank you for grafting me into your family and exhibiting the true meaning of Christ's love! The late Mother Bessie Blackwell, thank you for showing me the strength of unity and family. To the late Ruby Lee Jackson-Mitchell, thank you for all the songs you would sing to me that warmed my soul and kept me grounded in God's love! The late Betty Davis, thank you for your loving arms and care for my family! To the late Beulah Tara Hollins-Bussey, thank you for your strength, kind words, and tasty meals! To the late Estelle Roberts and Katherine "Kitty" Hodge, thank you both for keeping us neighborhood children in line and showing us what self-respect for ourselves and others looked like. Mother Mari Adams, thank you for loving me from the moment you met me. For supporting my education and believing I could accomplish anything I set my mind too! To Mother Adella R. Quinn, thank you for all the long talks and discussions—you are an encouragement!

Elder Anna L. James, thank you for all the lessons on seeking out God's Word for the answers because they are there for the asking, knocking, and seeking! I am grateful for the many times I heard you praying for those you love in the midnight hour—the power of prayer! To Lilly-Mae Bryant, who always has a word of encouragement. Thank you for allowing me to be daughter number three! Mother Elva Nesbit, Pastor Gillian Ezedi, and the entire ASAH Temple family thank you for your prayers during one of the most trying times in my life. To be sure, it was God and the fervent prayers of the righteous who brought me through! I am forever grateful! To Pastor LaVanya and the entire Ladies, Can We Talk Ministry, thank you for *all* your support, prayers, and words of encouragement! I would not have made it this far without you. I am forever grateful! Last but certainly not least is my mom, in every sense of the word, Mother Josephine Selby, one of the most formidable women I know. Thank you for all you do! Thank you for teaching me the meaning of "putting it in God's hands" and leaving it there! Thank you for being my mom and a grandmother to my children! I love you with all my heart!

To my aunts who stood in the gap and made up the hedge on many occasions, the late Ardelia M. Bowers, who gave me many of my firsts and instilled in me that I was of a royal priesthood set apart to be used for His glory, the late Aldonia Williams who stood firm in the face of every trial. Thank you for your unyielding support and family dinners and for modeling the power of God's strength in adversity! Last but certainly not least, my mother/auntie, Mother Novella Silver-Davis, was the first to teach me how to eat table food. I so enjoy our talks about the Lord and the wisdom you bestow upon me as your niece and spiritual daughter. Love you much! Thank you to my aunts, Delores Dunbar, Kendra Saunders-Bey, and Renee Montgomery, for your encouragement throughout the years!

To my spiritual fathers who planted and watered the Word of God into my spirit, the late Reverend William L. Cooper of Metropolitan Baptist Church, who lovingly made all the Sunday school children memorize Scripture in large portions. My love for God's word began in that little Sunday school room—Thank you, Sister Higginbottom! To the late Bishop A. Foxworth Sr. of Grace Community Church Pentecostal Household of Faith, who loved me as a daughter and strengthened me with just a look! Thank you for being that rock to so many of the young people! My Archbishop

A.L. Foxworth Jr. of Grace Church of All Nations taught me to walk in the spirit of excellence, search out God's word for myself, and grow-up in grace. I could not understand it then, but now I see! When I explain a word or phrase, I often see your impact on my life. Thank you for watering the seed of righteousness within my spirit! To Apostle Willie Hartman of Unity Tabernacle for encouraging me to step out. Thank you for being that bridge in times of trouble. I am forever grateful! To the late Deacon Hurley "Whistle" Williams, thank you for letting me know I mattered! To Loman McClinton, thank you for being a mentor and godfather and encouraging me to push forward no matter what!

To Apostle Dr. Lord Michael Hunt and the SAKAL Global Ministries family, thank you for all the prayer and fasting symposiums that have allowed all those who partook to hear the voice of God and govern ourselves accordingly. Thank you for all the teachings that pricked us to reach higher and prepare for our quantum! To my Apostle Steven F. Thomas of ASAH Global Ministries, thank you for seeing greatness in me and following God's leading to cultivate that greatness! This book series is a nod to your declaration over my life in 2004. I am *forever* grateful! Finally, to my daddy/uncle, the Right-Reverend Saint Joseph Silver. What can I say except that I love you with *all* my heart! You stood in place of my father when he could not. I am forever grateful! You empowered me from a young age to reach for the stars and go after that which others thought I could not reach. I love you *always*!

To my sisters who were willing to read and catch mistakes, offer encouragement, and extend a listening ear as I navigated through this process. It took a while, but I am finally here! Thank you, Juannetta "Niecy" Silver, Valerie Harris, Bunnie Jones, Venetia Lewis, and Shirley Green! To my brother in Christ, whose heart leaped with reading the manuscript. Thank you, Elder James D. Watkins, for being my brother and friend for over forty years! I love you much! To my big brothers from another mother, Elijah Foster Jr., and Antonio "Tony" Hobbs, thank you both for always looking out for me! To Deacon Carlton "Chris" and Sis. Prophetess Donna "Pat" Gayle, you all are such an encouragement. Thank you for exemplifying a calm, cool, and collected demeanor in the face of trying times, sending those daily Scriptures, and for your prayers and unwavering support! I love you very much!

I would also like to thank Mr. Sooraj Mathew of the ArtCat for assisting me in catching the vision of my book cover. To my writing mentor, brother, and friend, Rev. Dr. Kirk B. Jones. Thank you for believing in me *and* my writing! I am forever grateful for your unwavering friendship and professional support, for leaving Mondays open to hone my skills, and for encouraging me to "keep writing" even when no one else thought I could. I am *eternally* grateful!

To the late Daniel K Pai, Sifu Clarence "June Bug" Cooper, and the entire Pai Lum White Dragon King-Fu Organization for the many years of discipline and training. Professor Tierney of Eastern Nazarene College in Quincy, MA, thank you for marking up *all* my papers and challenging me to be a better writer. Professor Gregory Johnson of Vermont Law and Graduate School, thank you for all those office hours and suggestions to make me a better writer. I still hear you when I complete a sentence, "Keep the subject as close to the beginning. Writing is rewriting!" Thank you! Last but certainly not least, Professors and mentors Nelson P. Lande, Emeritus of Philosophy Lawrence Blum, Emeritus of Sociology Glen Jacobs, Sociology of Religion Jorge Capetillo, and Emeritus of African Studies Dr. Robert Johnson, all of the University of Massachusetts, Boston, thank you all for your guidance, insight, and encouragement as a student. I am *eternally* grateful! To my elementary and middle school teachers, Mr. Rich and Mr. Morris, who cultivated a spirit of excellence in me. I will never forget you! Thank you for seeing what I could not see in myself! To Jean McGuire and the METCO program, which empowered its students to stand firm in the face of challenging times! To the Boston Police Department and its academy staff for solidifying the importance of discipline and training. To Maryann Connolly and Blaine Henry, thank you for showing me the importance of integrity and a respectable work ethic.

Thank you to the Dana Farber Cancer Institute for caring tenderly for me during my treatment. I am forever grateful to you and your impeccable staff, nurses, physicians, phlebotomists, and social workers.

Finally, I thank Genesis Publishing House and the entire publishing team for a job well done! Last but certainly not least, I would like to thank Apostle Mary Lafayette, who spoke prophetically concerning my life and what the Lord had in store for me in creating this very project. Thank you for your obedience, prayers, and support!

"Now I say that the heir, as long as s/he is a child, differeth nothing from a servant, though s/he be lord of all; But is under tutors and governors until the time appointed of the Father" ~ Galatians 4:1-2 (Emphasis mine). His timing is perfect! Thank you *everyone*!

In Love, grace, and growth,
Evangelist Markeithia Silver

TABLE OF CONTENTS

Dedication v

Acknowledgements vii

Foreword xv

Preface xix

Chapters One: A Life Worth Living 1
    Things I Am Telling Myself. 8
    The Power of God's Light. 37

Chapters Two: Expect to Do More 39
    Kingdom Terms Defined 43
    It Can Be Done If You Trust and Believe 54
    The Proclamation 61

Chapters Three: You Are Part of the
Unified Consciousness 63
    My Dual Consciousness 78
    A Place Like No Other 87

Chapters Four: Living With the Mind of God 89
    When You Know You Are Covered, You Are Fearless!..... 103
    The Rod in My Hand! 107
    Longing 109

Chapters Five: Transformation: A Necessary Process of Growth 111
Amazing Grace 126
My Testimony 129
Motives of the Heart 139
Surrender.. 147

Chapters Six: Be Aware of Who You Are 149
My Place 171

Chapters Seven: No-Thing to Fear 173
Wholeness Defined 185
Quiet, Please; I am Trying to Hear Myself Think.............. 207

Chapters Eight: The Process of Discerning and Creating God's Will (Reality) for Your Life 209
Creating the Right Formula 220
My Dreams.. 222
What Are You Speaking to Yourself?................ 232
Discovering Me... 235

Chapters Nine: A New Me 237
I Am Free 249
Declaration of Independence 250

Daily Affirmations 251

Footnotes/Bibliography 255

FOREWORD
By
Rev. Dr. Kirk Byron Jones, Ph.D.

*L*iving *Your Legacy of Greatness* is an essential book. We are living in times of unequaled complexity, stress, and strain. Rushing to keep up with ever-increasing demands often leaves us drained and doubtful about the overall contribution of our overdoing. Yet, when we attempt to slow down and smell the roses, we are haunted by feelings of guilt and negligence. Something other than driven-ness and guilty respites is needed to meet the challenge of our modern morass. That something is a transformation from within, of such endearing and enduring quality, inspires continual human flourishing—God's dream for each one of us.

Markeithia Lavon Silver provides a compelling prescription for inner change in her first book series, Living Your Legacy of Greatness. With the care of a pastor and the precision of a surgeon, she surveys a myriad of emotional and spiritual challenges that we all face. She then offers us biblically-based principles and life-tested practices to confront them like never before.

Living Your Legacy of Greatness is a layered blessing. The author's learned theological, philosophical, and sociological analysis is one rich layer. A second layer is her particular wording of formidable teachings that call us past our bitterness to our better and beyond our ever-expanding best through their soundness and sounding. Sample these treats of truth:

Imagination, faith, godly wisdom, and knowledge of God's Word create the pulsating power necessary to manifest your dreams and visions.

Fear is a dream stealer!

We must dare to dream and dream big, so much so that it takes our breath away.

Forgiveness is the act that removes the veil so you can see your future clearly.

Finally, there is a magnificent third layer. Some writers are poets who can speak to our minds and hearts and sing to our souls. Markeithia Lavon Silver can sing words on paper and does so at the conclusion of each chapter. One of her beautiful word songs is *My Place*:

I hear Sweet, Melodic harmonies from heaven softly raining and resting upon the garden of my mind. This calm drizzle soothes my innermost being.

My garden is arrayed with beautiful flowers whispering a scent of uniqueness. The tulips, daffodils, and roses all delight in the melody sung by the gentle Wind. They respond with a score directed by the Light.

I, too, like the hummingbird, seek to express my destiny's sweet, pure calling. I am one with the "Us" Spirit God. In sacred silence, I receive a cup of loving grace.

Nearby, I see the oasis of restoration. This sanctuary is where I dwell. My Refuge is always accessible to me. I look within, and it is there that I bathe and receive my soul's massaging grace. Whenever weary, I travel to My Place of rest and dive into its waters' tender, serene warmth. Here, all I do is drink; all I do is drink...

I began by telling you that *Living Your Legacy of Greatness* was essential. You must already suspect that I did not tell you the complete truth. *Living Your Legacy of Greatness: Discovering Within the Image and Likeness of God* is an important and *enchanting* book. Join me in learning from it and experiencing its captivating quality.

PREFACE

Imagine yourself effortlessly entering beyond a door with endless possibilities of abundance and wholeness—a harmonious balance of mind, body, and spirit. You joyfully grasp infinite gems of Love, Harmony, Health, Happiness, Dominion, Power, Success, and more in this place. Envision, as a child captivated by the beautiful array of colors hanging over its sleeping bed, reaches out in joy at the enchanting mobile display with discoveries in its new world.

Living Your Legacy of Greatness Volume One: Discovering Within the Image and Likeness of God is about freedom to be who God created you to be. This book underscores the self-determination that empowers you to liberate yourself from certain habits of thought about yourself and the world, ideas that decree and govern how you see yourself, others, and, ultimately, God. This writing invites self-reflection to propel you towards liberty that evolves you and the world to an elevated wholeness. This book was birthed out of questions I sought answers to from our Most High God concerning our legacy as Christ's followers. I asked the Creator and Sustainer of all things, "Did You not say through Jesus, 'Greater works shall we do'? Why are we not doing more wondrous work? What precludes us from doing what You prophesied and spoke into our lives? From Jesus's statement, should we not presuppose that

You predestined humanity on a designated trajectory of greatness through Christ Jesus?"

God's response was as thought-provoking as it was enlightening. What God allowed me to discover confronted me, leaving me no choice. I needed to align the "self" with what God permitted me to uncover. As the principles of living the legacy God bequeathed unto humanity manifested in my psyche, I knew that change was inevitable for me and the world, should I apply what He imparted. It set me ablaze inside. I wanted to lay hold of my spiritual birthright! I realized I was walking in ignorance as a King's child and living like a pauper. From wanting to grasp the notion of kingship emerged the necessity of confronting myself with the words of the Lord, "What doest thou here?" ~ 1 Kings 19:9,13. If I could get myself out of the way, I would see the Lord…and the "train of the Lord would fill [my] temple." ~ Isaiah 6:1.

Discovering Within the Image and Likeness of God is dedicated to elucidating the spiritual image and likeness of the Lord within everyone, to impart illumination to the intellect, prepare and empower humanity's collective will to seek the Good, for the achievement of greatness, bequeathed to us from the foundation of the world. This message is for lovers of El-Shaddai/Elohim/God's righteousness, who created the Universe and reigns supreme. This work is for those seeking after the heart of God, His truth, justice, and mercy, which elevates one to a place of abundance and legacy of greatness. This writing inspires hope of unity in the Spirit— modeling Christ's oneness as He is one in the Father. It is my earnest expectation as the writer to invoke and evoke interest and attention that will motivate you to strive for change in your mind (psyche), your spirit (character/behavior/temperament), and your conduct (behavior/personality).

This inspiration shall be the cause of summoning the Fruits of the Spirit: Love, Joy, and Peace. Moreover, the priority is to flame the desire to seek out the essence of who God is and His Power, which alters and exalts the believer's life destined for greatness. Once you know the Divine Light that dwells within God's temple (called body), overcome obstacles of fear and doubt, and use a disciplined mind, you will be prepared and propelled, like Peter, to strengthen your sisters and brothers.

Allow me to share prose that I penned in July 1999, entitled *Freedom Arrived*:

Freedom Arrived Today by Air Express Overnight Delivery.

As I opened this nicely wrapped package, five smaller bundles (representing the grace of El-Shaddai) were inside the box. Like a child receiving a gift, I was excited! Who thought enough of me to send me a present? I looked at the return address: From the Most-High, Heaven, Eternity, 12345. I opened them individually; the spiritual truths revealed elevated me spiritually.

One package said, "Spend some time with Me."

Another revealed, "I love you with an everlasting, unconditional love. Rest upon My wings and soar beyond your wildest dreams."

The third package implored me, "Do not fear; I am with you! Be free from the opinions and definitions of who others think you to be! ...Including yourself!"

As I meditated upon these few packages, I began to weep and leap for joy. An awakening immediately occurred within my Spirit. Simultaneously, a breaking within my soul began to free me. Words from the gift elevated me from this world's bondage—from the subjugation of my self's preconceived notions.

As I hastened to open the fourth package, the gift revealed, "There are no limitations to your greatness, so soar, soar, soar!"

I took a deep breath in anticipation and opened the last package. It reminded me, "My grace is sufficient for you. Plunge into the well of My grace, and receive, from My bosom, a well that will never run dry!"

I began the journey of freedom; will you travel along?

This book intends to show you, gentle reader, that no matter your situation, you are entitled, by eternal law, to live a life of greatness. As a citizen of the Kingdom, as a son/daughter of Zion, you will understand that greatness is a birthright and obtainable by ALL who believe! Although there is a prerequisite of a disciplined mind, if you are teachable, possess the simple desire to be, and envision being great, you will grasp God's intended position for humanity. Further, The Law of Cause and Effect will step you into your space of greatness without fear, posturing the joy of whom God destined you to be—great!

Chapter One, *A Life Worth Living,* discusses the notion of Jesus's coming so that we might lay hold to everlasting life and enjoy it more abundantly. Not only did Jesus create the Door for us to walk through, but He also created the Door for us to emulate. Our imagination, moreover, is instrumental in laying hold of our abundance. Specifically, I will discuss Paul's admonishment in bringing that very imagination under subjection to God's promises in our lives and how wielding that authority makes us fit for the Master's use. Once we discover our God's Power, His role in our lives as Lord and Savior, and the subconscious mind's function, the vehicle of a disciplined and trained mind, we will perform great exploits!

Chapter Two, *Expect to Do More,* emphasizes the importance of focusing beyond your present state—creating a reality to present to the Master of the Universe for manifestation. The chapter highlights the importance of obtaining the concept of faith, discussed in Hebrews 11, "For without faith it is impossible to please Him…S/he that comes to God must first believe that He *is,* and a rewarder of them that diligently seek Him." Moreover, *Expect to Do More* reiterate the presence of expectation, ancillary to the engagement of most, if not all, of our affairs. Without a minimum level of hope and belief, our present state persists. Accordingly, we experience

xxii

sinking into our sea of problems, allowing our circumstances to overwhelm us and draw us into the deep waters of despair instead of conquering them—just as Peter did when he walked on water. Correspondingly, as long as Peter's focus was Christ-like, he walked above his storms and circumstances.

Conversely, when Peter began to deviate from the prescribed formula of greatness, he began to falter. However, thanks to El-Shaddai, Jesus was there to save him. Following Peter's encounter with nearly drowning, Jesus admonished Peter about his lack of faith. "Oh, ye of little faith" describes an inward belief system deriving from or relying upon what you *think* about yourself and your situation. When you consider yourself unworthy and your circumstances too huge to surmount, you will miss the opportunity to evolve into an excellent faith level each time the occasion emerges to level up. Going against everything you believe about yourself may challenge you, "but hope thou in God!" Expectation and Hope are the parents of desire. Lose one, and you stop dead in your tracks. Finally, we discuss faith and its importance in maintaining your expectations of more. We need the harmony of all three: expectation, hope, and imagination focused on retaining and growing your faith, which facilitates your progression from faith to faith and glory to glory.

Chapter Three, *You Are A Part of the Unified Consciousness*, emphasizes Jesus's concept of oneness. His words, "We are one with Him as He and the Father are one," depict a unity within the body of Christ, designed to empower the believer. This concept provides security and assures believers of their connection to Christ as they rest in the notion of "as Jesus is, so are we in this earth." Furthermore, our oneness with the Christ-Spirit spills over into our oneness with the Father. This principle is essential in understanding how we create our ability to live beyond our wildest dreams for the good of others and ourselves. We must, moreover, be able to "think big." Once you grasp that you are a part of God, God is a part of you; you shall generate what you say according to His Word, and living your God-given right to the things of the Kingdom will become like second nature. In fact, it will *be* your nature because you will discover *who* you are and what that determination entitles you to receive.

Chapter Four, *Living with God's Mind*, explains the importance of discovering your oneness with God. Once you grasp the notion that you are one with God and will accomplish the necessary exploits as sons and daughters of the Most High God, you will "be strong in the Lord and *in* the power of His might." Rediscovering and uncovering God's mind (the willpower to do His good pleasure) within you allows you to think and move, like the Light in which you are a mirrored reflection. We are God's Children, and that gives us Kingdom privileges. David's appeal, "[Did I not tell you], you are gods, and children of the Most High, but we shall die like men?" provides insight and warnings as to why we must resist thinking and living by the flesh and so, walk in the Spirit.

Similarly, Paul instructed us in *I Thessalonians* 2:12, *Ephesians* 4:1, and *Colossians* 1:10, "To walk worthy of the vocation wherewith God calls you." Once the Christ Spirit permeates your being, you will heal the sick, mend the brokenhearted, open deaf ears, and free the captives. These are only a few. Remember, Jesus said, "Greater works shall you do!" Finally, living with a Christ-like mind will create affluence, provide insight beyond measure, and cause you to become a mighty force in God's plan of righteousness, truth, and justice.

Chapter Five, *Transformation: A Necessary Process of Growth*, highlights that everything we say and do begins in our minds as thoughts and imagery. Paul admonishes us to "Be transformed by the renewing of our mind." If we want to change, it must first begin in our minds. Accordingly, before our circumstances change, we must pause to make a conscious, purposeful decision within our minds. Once we decide to change, we bring about that conversion by renewing (reframing, transforming) our minds. Converting our minds may entail reminding ourselves of truths we learned that we need to reacquaint ourselves with and changing our thought patterns and focus, aligning them with what the Lord and Kingdom intelligence say. Suppose we introspectively discern that the same results keep manifesting in our lives. Then, it becomes clear that we need a different course of action and focus on yielding a different result. If conforming to the thought process of lack frustrates you, be free from lack by entrusting yourself to the thought process of plenty, and you will see a difference once you alter your perspective.

Change is not an overnight process. You did not manifest your situations overnight; they will not change suddenly. Nevertheless, God is merciful, and the inevitability of transformation will occur when you change your thoughts and images within your mind. Patience in enduring behavior modification will yield a great harvest. Ideas, moreover, produce representations within the mind, creating reference points that govern our perceptive abilities. Our precepts and concepts, in turn, control how we see the world and others, even ourselves. We must change our minds' illustrations to alter how we see others and ourselves. You accomplish this formula by engaging the mind in a disciplined, purposeful thought-power process. If disunity bothers you, refresh your mind with different images of those around you—change the reference points hidden within the crevices of your mind and watch how your vistas inevitably change.

Chapter Six, *Being Aware of Who You Are,* conveys a spiritual awareness of who you are in God. This consciousness fortifies you to function in greatness and perform great exploits. The Bible says, "They that know their God shall be strong and do great exploits." Mindfulness precedes one's ability to change. Knowledge comes before action. It would be best if you had both for sustainable change. When you become aware of where you are and accept responsibility for being where you are, you make the necessary adjustments. Self-awareness is essential in catapulting you from one end of the spectrum to the other. Of course, this awareness also implies a choice to choose greatness. Once you become aware of who you are and regain your identity, you must *decide* to be great. You must elect to accept your crown of prince or princess in the Kingdom. In short, understanding the powerful gift of God to choose from is always available.

Moreover, the ability to will the self, one way or another, is power in and of itself. Use it wisely! Protecting that authority of choice and taking control of your options will ensure you walk a path of purpose, freedom, and greatness. Accordingly, the Bible tells us we must opt for unity in the Spirit, for Christ died for all and is *in all* that believe. Further, the more knowledge you gain about change, the more rooted you become in striving for others' betterment and that of yourself. This inner awareness that El-Shaddai, God resides in the room with you is more than just saying, "God is omnipresent." *Knowing it* empowers your stance, character, and voice, emboldening everything in your daily life and circumstances. You *become* fearless in the Lord!

Chapter Seven, *No-Thing to Fear,* is a mindset that tunes us into the reception of God's Power and Wisdom, which informs us in every circumstance. Throughout the Bible's sacred pages, the Word emboldens us to walk in a posture of Power, Love, and a Sound Mind—fearing nothing. In the Old Testament, El-Shaddai tells Joshua, "Fear not. As I was with Moses, so *shall* I be with you." ~ Joshua 1:5. In the New Testament, Paul advises and inspires us with the knowledge that the Power of God resides in us so that fear cannot dwell. ~ II Timothy 1:7. More importantly, Jesus says, "Let not your heart be troubled, neither let it *be* afraid." ~ John 14:27.

Fear has no place in the hearts and minds of God's Children. We should not allow anything to cause fear. Fear impedes your growth and precludes you from being who you are. Moreover, fear can become an idol/pseudo-god if not adequately evaluated.

This pseudo-god's fear of a thing supplants the True and Living El-Shaddai, God, the Infinite Wisdom, and Creator of all things. Thus, you no longer worship the Creator who made you in the likeness and image of the "Us" Spirit; you worship the fear, creating desolation and isolation from God. Specifically, fear causes separation from the One who can and does sustain, secure, and provide for you. This disconnection unfolds in the story of Adam and Eve in the Garden. If you want to stop a child from running free, tell them a monster will catch them and eat them up. The child will most likely stop running because of the fear of the beast eating them. This notion of crippling fear is what happens to us as adult Godchildren. Our experiences distort the image and likeness of the Infinite Power within us. Society deceives us into thinking conversely to God's promises through socially constructed views. We believe that the monster of poverty, sickness, lack of x, y, and z, or anything contrary to God's promises for our lives, will eat us up if we run free (destroy the yoke, think big, or be whom God called us to be). However, when you choose to believe Jesus, who tells us, "Whom the Son has set free (Mind, Body, and Spirit), is free indeed (free to explore, free to create, free to be who you are)," you know it, and you are free.

What will you choose? If you no longer want to see through the glass dimly as you gaze at the image and likeness God created in you by the "Us" Spirit, choose freedom. Elect to be released from what you tell yourself, the bondage of pain scribed upon your heart that you must accept, the chains of your past telling you that you must believe, free from anger, lack, unforgiveness, and anything that "exalts itself against the knowledge of God." Dear gentle reader, be WHOLE and be F-R-E-E!

Chapter Eight, *The Process of Discerning and Creating God's Will (Reality) for Your Life*, discusses faith and its importance in creating reality related to living your legacy. What we focus on (in our mind) will expand. "Now, *faith* is the substance of things hoped for, the evidence of things not seen." ~ Hebrews 11:1. Often, we talk about the substance of faith and the evidence of the same. Still, we never magnify an essential aspect of constructing faith's outward manifestation, which begins in your imagination. Within the creative ability, we enjoy the capacity to receive knowledge, wisdom, understanding, and skill and reflect upon what we obtain and experience. Our imagination allows our minds to expand and contract ideas.

Nevertheless, we must be discriminatory in what our minds will accept. We must ask ourselves if what we are ingesting is illuminating ~ II Timothy 2:15. Ask, does what I am holding on to give meaning or opportunities to change my life? We fill our minds with so much stuff. If we are not careful, we can corrupt our visions and thoughts, which impede our growth in God. We must remove those things that restrict us from laying hold of our destiny of greatness. Specifically, we must be willing to alter our mindset—change how we view things, process things, and impress upon ourselves what the truth is to cash in on the abilities of the mental vision of our greatness in God *through* Christ Jesus.

Imagination, faith, godly wisdom, and knowledge of God's Word create the pulsating power necessary to manifest your dreams and visions. This process eludes us because we are underdeveloped in our imaginations. We must dare to dream and dream big, so much so that it takes our breath away. "Is there anything too hard for God" ~ Jeremiah 32:17, 27? The answer is no! Nothing is too hard for God to assist us in creating our masterpiece to His glory! Also, we must consider the wisdom of disciplining our minds to focus on what we need. "As a man or woman thinks in her/his heart, so is s/he." ~ Proverbs 23:7.

Moreover, "Without a vision (and the Law of God's words to build upon), the person will perish." ~ Proverbs 29:18. This disciplined thinking process refers to the coined phrases "thought-catching" and "vision-building." As we focus on what we are thinking and monitor what objects are at the crux of our vision, we will notice that everything around us begins to resemble our thoughts and concepts. However, a disciplined mind will prepare and propel you into a realm of endless possibilities fit for the Master's use. ~ II Timothy 2:21.

Chapter Nine, *A New Me,* underscores discovering that your life is worth living; God's Word and Power endow you to expect more. Walking in oneness with God, living daily with the Mind of God, transforming the inner and manifesting on the outer, will bring you peace that passes all understanding. Living in your space, posturing whom you are as a Godchild, fearing nothing. Additionally, by monitoring your thoughts and visions, you will inevitably become transformed into the image of His Son, the son/daughter God created you to be from the beginning. Mahatma Gandhi said, "If you want to see a change in the world, start with yourself, and healing will multiply." Jesus said, "You are the salt of the earth." Creating a new you will also change the world as we know it.

Creating a new mind is synonymous with creating a new body. When you want to lose weight or build muscle, you go to the gym, hire a personal trainer, or begin walking daily. The point is that you make a change to acquire your desire. Once, I received an email that went something like this: "Discipline is the difference between desire and acquisition." You create a new pattern of eating and exercising to construct a new body or desired weight. However, to acquire it, you must act upon what you know. You can do the same with the mind. If we form fresh thoughts, we produce a new reality by acting upon those thoughts one day at a time. Thought-catching (a confrontation of your "self"), affirmations and declarations, embracing the art of change, and bringing yourself into a state of newness (in constant awe of the condition of becoming) are all a part of that process. Can it be done? Beloved, "The world yet groans for the manifestation of the sons/daughters of God." Yes, it can!

WHAT ARE YOU WAITING FOR, BELOVED? COME ON! LET US BEGIN!

This volume intends to inspire the reader to look beyond the religious dogma, race, and socio-economic status and see that God gave humanity when the heavenly breath whooshed into Adam's nostrils—a legacy of greatness. Moreover, God's legacy for us is still being spoken and offered by the Creator to the believer, awaiting our engagement to lay hold of that inheritance. This birthright, pronounced from the beginning of time, endows humankind with the inalienable right to co-create their reality to God's glory and honor. It is an extraordinary endowment to learn that the Universe, as we perceive it to be, is under divine order to give us what we ask. That reality, however created, can be a treasure to some and a curse to others.

Nonetheless, it is your reality. I challenge you, gentle reader, to venture to create the best possible circumstance to better yourself and humanity, live in a world absent of fear, full of peace and harmony, and a fertile consciousness for consistent prosperity in El-Shaddai, God. I wish you freedom, healing, wholeness, and tranquility deep within the crevices of your soul mind.

In Love, Joy, Peace, and Happiness,
Markeithia Lavon Silver

CHAPTER ONE

A LIFE WORTH LIVING

"I come that [you] might have LIFE and that [you] might have it MORE ABUNDANTLY." ~ John 10:10b (Emphasis mine).

—Jesus

"What we are is God's gift to us. What we become is our gift to God. [Therefore, present your best self!]."

—Eleanor Powell

What does life mean to you? Is it merely to feel the "blood running warm in your body," or that all your twelve systems and seventy-eight organs are working correctly? Jesus was not referring to just the physical existence on this earth. His declaration spoke of something beyond the physical presence of humanity. If you are willing and desire to conceive the notion of life outside of the norm of abundance, keep reading. Presupposing Jesus's ministry in theory and practice was based on engaging life with vigor and tenacity under the guise of a heart of service. In accordance with the laws of El-Shaddai, God leads one to suspect Jesus spoke of life beyond this earthly realm. Jesus passionately healed the sick, cast out demons, and fed the hungry. He called those things that were not as they were and told us we could and would do the same and more. Jesus's life and ministry were not an example of mere existence; they illustrated active participation within society and living life to the fullest under the auspices of Kingdom laws: precepts, concepts, thoughts, and visions. More importantly, you observe Jesus mending relationships and walking in the epitome of "repairer of the breach" for humanity.

Specifically, he didactically spoke to a nation (Israel) that evolved more broadly, reaching its outermost parts. Jesus was inclusive and not exclusive. As *Yēšûa*'s (Jesus) ministry unfolds, one cannot help but notice God's loving plan and His redemption of humanity back to His bosom. I find it remarkable that his ministry's subtle nuances entailed social issues, and the ills of his time are still prevalent today. For instance, the woman considered a "dog" by Jewish tradition displayed great faith in her daughter's healing, earning a place in our sacred Scriptures as an example of how to move God's hand even if the world attempts to convey that you do not belong. Another illustration is the Samaritan woman. Jesus reconciles the relationship with the Samaritans after he talks with a woman at Jacob's well. Jewish history places them at odds with one another. Nonetheless, Jesus goes against the grain, displaying the Father's eternal love toward all humanity.

He, moreover, tells us that we shall do more wondrous work! We shall walk in the Spirit and Truth, displaying God's righteousness and justice among all people. I postulate that this concept is why Jesus added the more abundantly clause. Not only did he come to empower us to live and create, but to be alive and to design overflowingly—beyond whatever we could conceive or perceive for the betterment of all humanity. Jesus's use of the word abundantly in Greek is *perissos. Strong's Concordance* defines this word as superabundant (in quantity) or superior (in quality) and, by implication, excessive. Jesus came so we might

Living Your Legacy Of Greatness

live a life superabundant in quantity and superior in quality. Jesus also desires us to surpass measure or rank—to be pre-eminent in all situations.[1] Who would not want to live in a world like that? Not only did He, but El-Shaddai also fashioned the Door for us to walk through. He emulated the Door for us to replicate. Our imaginations are instrumental in laying hold to that abundance. God provided reconciliation back into His presence and furnished a prototype to pursue our way to greatness. We *can* replicate *Yēšûa* (Jesus) through imagination, turning thought into action. Jesus postures this notion of being free and detached from the bondage of wrongful thinking: things contrary to Kingdom thinking.

Kingdom intelligence is not a new concept. In Luke 9:1-2, Jesus gave the Apostles Power and Authority over all devils and the ability to cure the sick before sending out the Disciples. Also, he commissioned them to *preach* the Kingdom: *the greatness of the Kingdom resides in you.* ~ St Luke 17:21. The *art of reframing your thinking triggers the ability to recognize the King's presence on the earth and the Kingdom within, allowing you to operate from a position of power in Christ Jesus.* This miracle of mastering and reframing your thinking will lead you to unity in the Spirit, freedom from fear, peace of mind, love in abundance, joy overflowing, and fearlessness. "For I (God) did not give you the spirit of fear, but of power, love, and a sound mind; in His presence, there is fullness of joy, and at His right hand, pleasures forevermore." ~ II Timothy 1:7 and Psalms 16:11, respectively. You can accomplish swimming in the waters of fearlessness, joy, and pleasures by first seeing it.

Interestingly, social theorists conclude that imagination is integral to our development. The ability to reflect, redefine, and perfect our thinking, behavior, and conceptualization power is found in our minds' ingenuity. Social theorist Charles Horton Cooley found, "In a [substantial] and interesting class of cases, the social reference takes the form of a somewhat definite imagination of how one's self...appears in a particular mind. [The] kind of self-feeling one has is *determined by* the attitude toward what [we] attributed to that other's mind."[2] What does he mean by this statement?

Charles Horton Cooley referred to this social process of creating the self as "The Looking-Glass Self."[3] Coined by Cooley to describe how the self emerges, Cooley purports that the notion of the "self" develops from the interaction with others. The "looking glass self" concept reflects upon (introspectively) who we are and who *we perceive* others think we are. The self is our concept of who we are. In Cooley's analysis, the self-idea has "three principal elements: the *imagination of our appearance to the other person*; the imagination of their judgment of that appearance, and some self-feeling… (Emphasis mine)."[4] In other words, we imagine how we appear to those around us. We vicariously enter the other's mind through the imagination to perceive how they will judge our actions. We interpret others' reactions to our efforts, assuming how they perceive us, thereby developing a self-concept based on how we perceive others to evaluate us. If the evaluation, within our mind, is favorable (a feeling of joy), we continue the conduct.

Conversely, if we think the projected perception is unfavorable (agony, fear, doubt), we discontinue the perceived poor conduct. If unchecked, we may miss God's move when an opportunity arises, contrary to how we feel about ourselves. *We must be open to the fact that we misinterpret our assessment of ourselves, creating a self-perception detrimental to the self and its advancements in the Kingdom of God.*

Therefore, our perception of how others appraise our behavior and emotions determines how we respond. Accordingly, our identity is not out of our consciousness's reach but socially constructed by our imagination and social belief systems. The formation of the self is fundamentally a social process based on the interaction that people coordinate with one another, intermingled with self-reflection. Fascinatingly, the famous poet Johann Wolfgang von

Living Your Legacy Of Greatness

Goethe said, "Treat a wo/man as s/he appears to be, and you make them worse. Conversely, treat a wo/man as if s/he was what s/he potentially could be, and you make them what s/he should be." Well, gentle reader, I perceive you to be great; therefore, I recommend you treat yourself great if you can imagine!

Cooley's description of imagination in harmony with the self-feeling (emotions/mental precepts) creates the social "I." In the formation of the social "I," "directly or indirectly [our] imaginations of how we appear to others [and the emotional force behind those thoughts] are a controlling force of normal minds."[5] The social self's underpinnings are the knowledge obtained through our phenomenological (subjective experiences) perceptions and how others view us. "The social self is simply an idea, or a system of ideas, drawn from the communicative life, that the mind cherishes as its own [i.e., vision-building]. Self-feeling has its chief scope within the [public] life, not outside of it...reflected [upon] by a world of personal impressions [within the mind]."[6] How we perceive others recognize us is crucial to the idea of the "looking glass." In seeing ourselves in the mirror of others, we respond to the expectations of others. Further, when we experience life: hurt, pain, rejections, and the like, *we create a dialogue that generates determined perceptions.* By doing this, we design a self that may be contrary to and alien from God's original image without catching what we are doing.

Specifically, these images may tear away our self-esteem's fabric—creating ridges and impressions, as Cooley says, within the mind. We dim the flame of the very image and likeness created through the perceptive mind because of the mental scripts we create for ourselves or based on our concepts. This mental script is what psychologists refer to as "qualia," which, in turn, creates an archetypical exemplar as a reference point to make sense of the world. This exemplar is a mechanism used within the reflective mind in understanding and empathizing with others. Further, these

Markeithia Lavon Silver

images allow our psychological intelligence to associate images by anticipating how others may feel about themselves and exchanging ideas regarding those images and perceptive phenomenological experiences.

Moreover, the impressions unseen by the naked eye creates a determined result in our reality. Our self-perceptions bring us to an expected end. Furthermore, when you continue piling it on, creating ridges unlike the original god-self or allowing persons, places, and things from your encounters to perpetuate your past pain, you will eventually be unable to move effectively in who God created you to be. More importantly, if communally viewed by a group, these images emerge as a collective consciousness. David said, "Ye *are* gods; all of you *are* children of the Most High. But ye shall die like men, and fall like one of the princes" ~ Psalms 82:6-7. Why? Because they will not *see* themselves as God sees them! You will behave feebly in your stance if you see yourself as feeble ~ Numbers 13: 25-33.

For instance, on the one hand, some look at themselves, failing to *see* an ability to stand erect and overcome any obstacle; they *see* less than, not enough, not worthy of, why even try, I cannot win, no one likes me, I want to be accepted, and on and on. On the other hand, some base these feelings upon the images they constructed in response to others and what someone told them in their childhood or how someone treats them in their workplace or other spaces. Thus, low self-esteem dictates that they are not worth having more than what they presently possess within the mirrored reflection of their alien selves ~ Matthew 7:1-5. Our thoughts trigger the Law of Attraction: The Internal Energy that attracts our attention to people, places, and things, self-fulfilling the impressions within us. I am not just speaking of material wealth. I am more concerned about spiritual prowess and its effect on the physical world. Here, the most critical step is recognizing the dialogue, which creates the concept of the "self." This discourse governs how we see ourselves

Living Your Legacy Of Greatness

and not necessarily how God created us in the image and likeness of the "Us" Spirit.

"By a single process [within the imagination], we increase our understanding of persons, society, and ourselves."[7] Furthermore, social psychologists show the correlation between how we conceive and perceive God and our concepts and precepts of our natural father. My godmother, the late Evangelist Williams, would say, "My father died before I was born. However, my mother would tell me how much my father loved me and how good a father he would be if he lived. The idea of my father's love filled my mind, so I could not think of anything else. The Love of the Father was easy to understand because of what my mother told me about *my* father."

Consequently, some people's notion of a father's love is challenging. Some cannot get beyond the trauma and encounter a tough time accepting the Father's love because of their natural father's absence or abusive presence. Accordingly, they must rethink that kind of love. In Luke 11:11-13, Jesus lets us know God will go beyond what earthly fathers do. To be sure, the Father's Love will love us beyond our pain if we only let Him into our broken spaces.

Cooley maintains that language and the interpretation of that dialectal exchange, by which we complete this process, determines how we approach our subsequent exchanges. He asserts that the influence is predicated upon "the very fact that the word, and the idea it stands for, are phenomena of language and the communicative life...impressed upon us by our contact with people. When there is no communication, there can be no nomenclature and no developed thought...What is called 'me'... [A] part whose interest arises from the fact that it is both general and individual."[8] In other words, *what you say to yourself and the meaning those words hold in your imagination facilitate creating self-images*. Your interaction with others develops and defines your vocabulary, describing yourself and creating grooves and patterns within the psyche. Telling yourself that you are small will project smallness to others; in turn, others will treat you according to how you treat yourself (with what measure you use, it shall be measured to you again ~ Matthew 7:1-5). In other words, if you reject you, others will treat you in kind. Likewise, if you tell yourself that God loves you and greatness resides in you, that you are "accepted in the beloved," you will create a world of love, excellence, and acceptance ~ Ephesians 1:6.

Grab your journal, and let us review the narratives you created concerning yourself, others, and God. Entitle this exercise: *Things I Am Telling Myself.*

Things I Am Telling Myself.

WHAT ARE YOU WHISPERING TO YOUR INNER-SELF ABOUT YOUR "SELF"?

We will take a moment and write down everything you tell your inner self about your "self." Entitle the paper *Things I Am Telling Myself Chart* and divide it into three columns. One column should be what you desire for yourself. A second column should entail what you believe and repeat daily to yourself; the final column is the new thought pattern. Take a few minutes and reflect upon what you bought into about yourself, including things your parents said, good, bad, or indifferent. Write down what your teachers or employers said. If you are honest, you will begin uncovering, discovering, and recovering who you are. By revealing these inner thoughts and visions, you find out what you are saying to yourself, so you can judge whether to keep repeating them to yourself, continually pouring be-life into them, and by choice, allowing them to exist. If you discover you should eliminate them from your

Living Your Legacy Of Greatness

life, stop reciting them, and you will sever their life source (faith and focus), and they will die.

This exercise is essential. Why, might you ask? The heart is at the crux of all that is important—salvation, freedom from fear and doubt, and acceptance. The fall of humanity deeply affected our position in God and our hearts and minds. Moreover, the human heart's condition is more pervasive as it clouds who we are far beyond what we can comprehend ~ I Samuel 16:7. *See also* Psalms 44:21, 139: 2-23, Jeremiah 20:12. Jesus said, "Out of the abundance of the heart, the mouth speaketh" ~ Luke 6:45. *See also* Mark 7: 21-23. Jesus also spoke about staying away from a troubled heart ~ John 14:1-3. A troubled heart flows from its lack, rejection, inadequacy, not enough, fear and doubt, depression, stagnation, and anything contrary to the greatness God designed for us from the beginning. On the other hand, a grateful heart flows from the banks of abundance, acceptance, freedom, prosperity, godly wisdom, knowledge, and understanding—a soil fertile for planting the righteousness of God.

Therefore, looking at the origin of our issues, and not just their manifestation, uncovers our serious matters. Our dilemma springs from the heart—one needs to address what is inside, hidden deep within. We identify them and seek the Lord for cleansing with hyssop, a washing white as snow, creating a clean heart to prepare Rivers of Living Water to flow. For out of your heart spring (belly) shall flow Rivers of Living Waters ~ John 7:37-39. From this heart space, the Holy Spirit dwells, and the seven characteristics of the Holy Spirit Operate. In contrast, the things of the flesh stammer the workings of the Spirit, and thus, you must eradicate them. The paper should look something like this:

Things I Am Telling Myself Chart

Things I desire	What I Think About What I Desire.	The New Thought Pattern
I am a nice person.	No one likes me; I do not experience meaningful friendships. I am always left out and alone.	The Spirit of Love flows through me richly; I am liked and accepted by all; I enjoy plenty of friends.
I am a writer.	I am not an adequate speller; my writing will look terrible, and no one will read it.	The Spirit of Inspiration, Wisdom, Knowledge, Understanding, and Skill flows from the Source of *All* Things; I joyfully receive and write as the Spirit leads. Nations will read and enjoy God's work, experience deliverance, and grow in their relationship with God!
I am prosperous.	I do not own any money; I am always broke. Money eludes me, and I struggle to make ends meet.	In Him, I live, move, and acquire my being. God meets all my needs. I live in abundance! I am surrounded by abundance! I am blessed that I might be a blessing.
I am successful in business, ministry, parenthood, marriage, etc.	I do not ever get new clients. No one wants me to speak at their function. People ignore my ideas. Most people disregard *my* feelings. My children never listen to what I say. They will not assist me with everyday chores or help the household. My wife/husband never listens to me. They do not understand my feelings.	I seek God *first* and, thus, attract all that is good. My client list is overflowing. My engagements are continuous. I and my feelings matter; even if it appears no one is listening, God is *always* listening. My children are a blessing to me. I enjoy them. They are courteous, sensitive to the household's needs, and willing to help. I commit my marriage and family unto the Lord—My wife/husband listens to me with their heart. God bestows upon their understanding and hearing of my inner desires. They display love and compassion toward me. The Infinite Power of El-Shaddai flows freely without inhibition through my ministry, my family, and my life.

I am healed from my infirmity.	I cannot get out of bed. I am in pain from arthritis, lupus, cancer, high blood pressure, or any disease.	I consecrate my life unto the Lord daily and Command and Decree the twelve systems of my body to fall subject to the Word of God—my body receives God's loving touch each day. Say, "I am one with Christ as He is one with the Father." The Love of El-Shaddai is perfected in me. Fear, death, and disease cannot dwell in this body. I openly receive the healing Power of God. The Infinite Power of El-Shaddai, God knows all my organs, muscles, veins, sinews, cartilages, and every area of my being; I decree Healing Virtue to the 12 Systems of my body, healing me back to my original state of wholeness in my mind, body, and spirit—I am operating at an optimum level according to the Word of God.

Then, as you reframe your thinking, you will begin the process of recovering what the Infinite Power of God spoke about you: You are His most precious gift. God already accepts you as you are (shrouded in the precious blood of Christ) and whom you will become (son/daughter) by the grace and mercies of God. If you write "I am a nice person" in one column, tell what you believe in the other. Listen in the silence as you pray what you tell yourself. Unraveling and becoming aware of your self-narrative is essential to the transformation process. Then, utilize what God says to drown out those things opposing His legacy for you. This exercise may take a few days, even weeks, to complete; however, you may continue reading after several minutes if you are stuck.

Keep your journal handy and refer to it as you read this book. This tool of writing down what you are saying to yourself will help you transform growth, transcend your belief about yourself,

Markeithia Lavon Silver

and trust in God in troubled times. Your life will change as you synchronize your thinking with what the Lord says about you. Let us continue with what Cooley says regarding the attaining of knowledge.

Cooley asserts that obtaining knowledge by which we increase our understanding is "both behavioristic and sympathetic: the perception, or imagination of external trait, is accompanied by sympathy with the feeling, sentiment, or idea that goes with it… To have human value, the word, and the inner experience [a feeling of happiness or sadness—the emotional state of mind] that interprets it must go together."[9] In short, our process of learning who we are from the inside out coincides with how we perceive other people's feelings about us (*and not God who "knows the thoughts He has toward us"*). This social learning process allows the mind to recall and reflect on our experiences. This recollection shows us that "we not only keep a record of our inner life, but we also work up the data into definite conceptions and perceptions, which we can pass on to others by the aid of the common symbol—[language]."[10] This reflection ability is instrumental in Cooley's socialization process. Scripture cautions us to be mindful of our thinking and not let it get out of control ~ Proverbs 23:7, Philippians 4:8, and II Corinthians 10:5, respectively. Our value, moreover, is not determined by the words of others but by the worth God places on us ~ John 3:16, Jeremiah 31:3, John 15:13.

Furthermore, it is critical to note that we keep these impressions as reference points for future encounters within the subconscious mind. These reference points create grooves in the subconscious mind predetermining our courses in life. To alter those sequences, we must change the impressions within the neurological synapses by changing how we think and feel about ourselves and others. Cooley provides a natural way of obtaining knowledge. However, as believers, the beginning of wisdom and knowledge is in our reverence (fear) of the Lord ~ Proverbs 9:10, 14:26-27, 15:33, and

Living Your Legacy Of Greatness

19:23. James tells us that we can obtain insight by merely inquiring of the Lord. He gives freely upon request ~ James 3:5. First, however, we must seek God's forgiveness for placing our stock in those things we created and images built of ourselves contrary to God's vision designed for us and then seek Him for deliverance. ~ Numbers 33:52, Deuteronomy 12:2. Ralph Waldo Emerson, I think, captures this notion of becoming whom you idolize when he wrote: "We must be cautious about what we worship because what we worship, we become."

There are compelling reasons to suppose that while searching for a repeated response from those they hold in high regard, a person concomitantly looks at their behavior and the reactions of individuals they desire to please. Thus, "the [individual] learns to be different things to different people, showing that s/he [has] apprehended [a perceptive] personality and foresee its operation."[11] This definition is what Cooley refers to as "introspection." This theory reveals the myriad of thought processes that go into visions of rejection, lack, poverty, success, and other thoughts contrary to Kingdom thinking.

More importantly, if you derive a perceived response of dismissal, deficiency, and the like through self-examination, you look for those reactions, continually solidifying your thoughts and sinking deeper into a state of worthlessness. I postulate that this type of responsive behavior is at our nation's crux of racial injustice. Suppose the notion of superiority and inferiority are socially constructed concepts. In that case, we surmise certain racial groups will never escape the perpetuated culture of feeling less than others unless those symbols and the meaning behind them change. Likewise, when we do not modify the symbols and meanings of those symbols concerning how we feel about ourselves, *we will remain enslaved to those thoughts, contrary to Kingdom principles of greatness.*

Markeithia Lavon Silver

The complexity of ideas that go into building a dream typifies the artful expertise of a home designer. The designer comes to your home, takes measurements, maps out a space plan, chooses furniture according to your specific design style, and sketches a plan before presenting it to you. In essence, they are counting the cost before building your space. The beauty is that you can tweak the project until you are overjoyed aesthetically. We, too, must be purposeful about the visions we build. Ultimately, your image is the totality of the thoughts focused upon and the seeds you planted in your mental garden. Those thoughts' sources (seeds) are primarily based on your internal aesthetic. What shall we say, then, concerning God's vision toward us? Trusting God entails believing He knows what is in our best interest ~ Jeremiah 29:11. He created us with wisdom, knowledge, and understanding ~ Psalms 104:24, Proverbs 24:3. More importantly, when He breathed into us, giving us His spiritual DNA, indicates to us, He designed us for greatness. Thus, no false visions we create should supplant God's intention for us based on others' opinions. However, our fear and doubt can falter our resting and accomplishing God's will in our lives ~ Read the story of Abraham, Sarah, and Haggai and the confusion that still exists today surrounding the two sons of Abraham. *See also* St. John 10:8-19 (Gabriel silences Zachariah's speaking ability because of his lack of trust).

Interestingly, Cooley asserts that an individual's behavior (outside) and consciousness (inside) "mutually complement each other [perpetuating the social process]."[12] This practice is pretentious. One can unconsciously behave without noticing their actions or placing imprints upon their minds, which govern how they act in the future. Unbeknownst to the individual, their responses render a determined result from the reference points and narrative created. This recognition of the mental process is beneficial when following a road map from point A to point B, allowing you to discern the best travel direction. However, assuming we desire

Living Your Legacy Of Greatness

greatness, we must consciously opt into the contemplative method of halting our thoughts. In that case, we must thought-catch the seeds we plant into the atmosphere and monitor the visions we build in our imagination, lest the tare (negative thinking) choke the fruit we are attempting to grow. We must "keep it real," as my daughter would say. Shakespeare's medieval quote, advocating truth over deception, captures it nicely, "Above all, to thine own self be true."

What does all this information mean for me, you might ask? Society is a living organism. As citizens of a society, we are affected by the adaptations and assimilations that drive, shape, or change the organism, whether we are conscious of it or not. As an organism, intuitive tools, like the *looking-glass self*, are used to make sense of the world. According to social theorists, we utilize the "Looking-Glass Self" to learn how to behave and think.

Additionally, once behavior embeds itself within our minds, we meaningfully pass on those images and perceptions to others. We, then, house them within the subconscious mind as a proverbial lighthouse, drawing like-minded people into our space and creating a tribal collective consciousness. They refer to this conveyance of communication as the "socialization process." Further, behavioral socialists believe that the inner self envisions the other person's appearance, simultaneously visualizing the result of that appearance perpetuated by the feelings behind that vision and judgment. By vicariously entering the mind of the other, perceiving how they will distinguish us, we create within our psyche an interpretation, or image, of how others see us and how we see ourselves based upon the alleged understanding of another.

If I were to extrapolate from Scripture, I would venture to say that David imagined himself in the mind of God, interpreting how God sees us, thus rendering his many typologies of God and us as little g's. David *went after* God's heart to (1) dwell in the house of the Lord all the days of his life, (2) behold the beauty of the Lord, and (3) inquire in His temple ~ Psalms 27:4. David participated in Kingdom socialization by *seeking* to dwell, behold, and inquire of the Lord. *David's communication with God was such an elevated level of exchange that it now enables us to see God as David saw Him!* This illumination of David's relationship with God should stir you deep in your inward parts! We, too, can reach God's heart if we so dare.

Our emotions, moreover, come into play based on the intensity of the experience. When the desired evaluation is to our liking, we continue developing concepts and archetypes that we store within the mind as a positive stimulus. Clearly, David enjoyed God. Once he tasted the Lord's sweetness, he did not turn back ~ Psalms 19:7-10, 34:8. Conversely, if our feelings convey unfavorable occurrences, we stow them in our memory as negative stimuli, discontinuing the behavior. Accordingly, *we attach a thought process, a narrative, and a stored voluntary subconscious reaction that dictates our future responses.* Thus, by past practices, your acuity determines how you will approach and respond, or not, to every situation. Likewise, how you define the word and the inner feeling must go together. *The challenge, then, becomes aligning ourselves with what the Creator says we are, discarding what the world says we are.* WHAT WORDS ARE YOU USING TO DEFINE YOUR "SELF"? To be sure, discarding what the world says about you is not an endorsement to forgo submitting to leadership, maintaining an intimate relationship with God, and seeking education in the Word of God. It underscores humanity's weight on others' perceptions and guidance outside God's counsel ~ Psalms 1.

Additionally, we create a system of ideas, which I refer to as *Vision-Building*, devised from the knowledge we acquire through our perceptions. Vision Building is a concept that is the driving force in our lives—the compilation of thoughts and ideas that determine our life's courses. Psychologists refer to them as

Living Your Legacy Of Greatness

"reference points," discussed briefly above, as unconscious acts. We draw from these reference points when faced with life's issues, guaranteeing or predetermining the results. Has someone you hold in high esteem ever told you, "If you follow this advice, I guarantee this result will occur?" You adhere to their instructions precisely, and the outcomes discussed follow. Likewise, the effect is the same as our perceptions and reference points. If we obey the reference points exactly, we receive what our perceptions told us we would—a self-fulfilling prophecy. Thank goodness we can change and rearrange our perceptions to get different results when the outcome is unfavorable.

Nonetheless, we must understand and grasp that a particular set of perceptions *can* predetermine our results. We can change the outcome if we are willing to upend and uproot those perceptions that immobilize our growth. The enemy bullies us in this place of self-deception (the lies we tell ourselves). Why? Because he understands that godly discernment and socially constructed perceptions are two different things. The former leads you on God's path for your life ~ Psalms 16:11. The latter is a hit or miss and may lead you to death ~ Proverbs 16:25. The accuser understands this process and attacks us in various areas that stem out like branches on a tree. In our weaknesses, we find it difficult to trust God. We find it challenging to acknowledge that we are loved, cared for, and accepted. When we do not rely upon God to walk us through our encounters, the enemy throws us around like a ship without a sail. However, when we trust God in our limitations and abandon deceptive images and reference points that decry our greatness, our life will change dramatically because, in our vulnerability, He is strong ~ II Corinthians 12:19.

This imbalance of ideas and their consequences is why Paul implores us to follow Jesus—a way to bring us peace ~ Philippians 4:8-9. Jesus guarantees our outcomes if we follow him: living a life of abundance, the ability to heal from hurt, mend, and deliver

Markeithia Lavon Silver

the captives, and oneness in the Most-High God through *Yēšûa* the Christ. This declaration of unity in the Spirit does not say we become the Infinite Power of Creation. It is to say that within our spirit, manifested within the earthly realm, we stand heirs and joint-heirs to the Power and privileges of the Crown of Glory through *Yēšûa* (Jesus) Christ—the Great "Us" Spirit of the Universe. As our knowledge of God unfolds, the more apparent the meaning of Acts 17:28, "In Him, we live, move, and [acquire] our being," becomes evident, and the more accustomed we become to the notion of maturing into sonship and doing more wondrous works. One day, I heard the Spirit say, "Child of God, I see My reflection in you… Go forth and live, love, dream, and create in abundance. Let shine your beautiful self I created." Likewise, I urge you, gentle reader, to go forth and live your legacy of greatness!

For a moment, consider all that the social theorist Cooley has said. In short, we utilize a mirror image, perceived thoughts in others' minds, in determining how we feel and think about ourselves. Therefore, we conceptualize the self by gaining knowledge (experience) from these mirrored images. We predicate our identity, then, on what we think others think. If we accept this premise as accurate, why not replace the incisive images of what others think about us with Christ-Spirit's corresponding image, determining how we feel about ourselves by reflecting upon Jesus and his actions? God gave us a Mirror Image when He sent His Word made flesh. ~ Hebrews 1:3. who came in the volume of the Book. Jesus epitomizes oneness in the Infinite Power of El-Shaddai. He postures his communion, dominion, and oneness with the Father/Creator, living to the fullest with all power in his hands. Unapologetically, Jesus\Yēšûa lived within the space of that greatness. More importantly, Jesus told us who we are by saying, "The Kingdom (of God) is *within* you." When we supplant others' images with the image of Jesus (the Christ-Spirit), fear will dissipate, lack will disintegrate, and brokenness will dissolve. Doubt would

Living Your Legacy Of Greatness

no longer receive the procreation of fear, thus aborting the babies of failure. We would, then, see ourselves as God sees us— whole, free, and great! In fact, that, my friend, is a life worth living!

We are to hold fast to the notion of oneness in Christ at all costs, as Word-made flesh is one with El-Shaddai, God of the Universe. Jesus is the express image of His person ~ Hebrews 1:1-3. We are heirs and joint heirs with Christ. As such, we by proxy are the express image of Christ in the earth ~ I John 4:17. Let us look at some examples to substantiate our claim. On the one hand, if we supplant society with Jesus as the Mirror of our reflection, we will respond to the expectations God intended for us: oneness, wholeness, and greatness. However, remaining in our state of human frailty, a mental state of limitation, brokenness, fear, and failure, we will not evolve into God's sons and daughters ~ St. John 1:12. Apostle Paul prays that the "Father of glory gives us the Spirit of Wisdom and Revelation in the knowledge of Him." He prays "that our eyes of understanding, being enlightened, [that we] may know what the hope of His calling and what is the richness of the glory of His inheritance in the saints, and what is the exceeding greatness of His power" ~ Ephesians 1:17-19.

What is the hope of His calling, the richness of the glory of His inheritance in the saints, and the exceeding greatness of His power? First, we must align our minds with what God says about us: God made us in the image and likeness of the "Us" Spirit. Our God is awesome! He reigns supreme and is Sovereign! *See* Isaiah 40:22-31. God's redemption plan uncovers the hope for humanity's reconciliation back to the bosom of God. This substratum is the knowledge of our greatness and power—the ability to grow, the capability to become great, the power to become the sons and daughters of Zion in Christ Jesus ~ St. John 1:12. Lay hold of it today! Second, Jesus "blotted out the handwriting of ordinances against us, contrary to us, took it out of the way, nailing it to the cross…He spoiled principalities and powers, he made a show of

Markeithia Lavon Silver

them openly, triumphing over them" ~ Colossians 2:14-15. We are heirs and joint heirs with Christ ~ Romans 8:17. As He is, so are we in this earth ~ I John 4:17. Finally, we stand in Power through Jesus Christ, who sits on the Father's right hand! What a position!

In the Old Testament, Job bore testing beyond the measure of most of God's servants. Job endured all his family killed, his possessions stripped, and his health challenged. Nevertheless, Job withstood his wife and friends' ridicule because he trusted God. He never once gave in or gave up. Why? Have you ever asked yourself, "How did Job survive?" Many people focus on Job's patience and long-suffering. This observance is necessary when the vision is tarrying. However, the question becomes, what undergirded his fruits of the spirit? ~ Galatians 5:22-23, Ephesians 5:9-11. God also commanded that his life would not be touched, but *Job did not know that*. When Life and vision are in you and running through you, you can survive anything. I will say that again! You can survive anything when you possess Life *IN* and *THROUGH* you!

Moreover, Life will speak to your spirit, telling you, "You shall not die, but live, and declare the [good] works of the Lord ~ Psalms 118:17." Often, rendered motionless by our thoughts of despair, we tell ourselves the exact opposite, which spawns defeat and not victory. Stop telling yourself you are a failure! Begin telling yourself, "You are a victor in all that you say and do in Christ Jesus," no matter what it looks like, beloved. Too often, we get caught up in the weeds of what the situation appears to convey. Challenge yourself to stop focusing on what you perceive is occurring and counteract what you see with God's ruling. If the Lord be for you, it is more than the world against you! ~ II Kings 6: 16-17. Tell the devil that the Spirit of Life dwells in me, and I am no longer a slave to the yoke of sin ~ *See* Romans 8. Amen!

I sat still and asked the One who had all the answers, "How did Job survive?" I heard this in my Spirit: Job was, in fact, strong in his faith in God. He went unbelievably into the realm of knowing. Job declares, "Though He slays me, *yet will I trust Him!*" ~ Job 13:15. (Emphasis mine). He let everyone know he was holding fast to the vision of greatness. He not only had faith and patience, but as a backdrop of that faith, he *knew* in his spirit that God would bring his vision to pass (wholeness and freedom). *The joy and love for God that he stored within transcended his circumstances.* Job followed the Law of Righteousness by works and sought to understand it by faith ~ Romans 9: 32-22. As Job submitted himself unto God's righteousness, God could take him through that stumbling block to the other side of his experience ~ Romans 10:3. He held fast to the vision of reaching beyond the break *within* his mind!

Moreover, he had the joy of knowing who he was in God's sight within his emotions. Job could see beyond himself and his situation into the realm of understanding. I will talk more about Job and his encounter with God, what he endured, and the purpose of his trial in *Volume Two, Exiting the Cave: The Journey of Restoration*, but let us focus on Job's vision. Can you see beyond yourself and your circumstances into a place of knowing? Job aligns himself with what he knew: I am a Godchild—my reward is the manifestation of that greatness. How Job acquired his spiritual alignment entailed the removal of pride. God deemed Job a righteous man. However, in His infinite wisdom, He knew Job possessed a subtlety of pride lurking, awaiting the moment to overtake and destroy his inner righteousness. Outwardly, he was righteous. Inwardly, the potentiality of worshiping the work of his hands stood at the threshold of his heart, threatening his greatness in God. ~ Job 16:30. Given God's vested interest in Job, it becomes evident why God allowed satan's test of Job. He needed to eradicate the subtlety of pride that would inevitably encroach upon his legacy of greatness ~ Micah 5. *See also* Ezekiel 28: 13-18 (Lucifer's beauty corrupted his wisdom). Accordingly, Job understood, in the end, the change that God required to occur in his life ~ Job 42:1-6. As a result of his humility, God rewarded him double for his trouble ~ Job 42: 10-17.

Markeithia Lavon Silver

Job cried out in a jubilant way to the world as an example of trusting the transformation process, saying, "I will *wait* until my change comes!" Can you endure the process until your change comes? Can you tolerate God's necessary pruning? Can you trust that He knows precisely what to do to get you to your place of greatness? Job portrays his excellence in refusing to throw in the towel, and he lives in the space provided for him as a prince of the Kingdom. He even went as far as to curse the day he was born. Some say Job displayed his actions outwardly, what he felt inward—a pity party. I believe what he conveyed to the onlookers: "I will not allow the moment I came into the world to alter God's vision for my life." I imagine the enemy whispering in Job's ear, "If you had been born on another day, these occurrences would happen to someone else." However, his emotions were in line with his vision of greatness. He was not letting go for any reason—not his wife or friends. Job chose "to live and not die and declare the [good] works of the Lord in theory and practice." He elected to endure the process to the end! He bears the development of God's pruning ~ St. John 15:1-2. For that, God awarded him double for his trouble! Good-God Almighty! I am empowered just by typing these words, are you?

Another excellent example of abundant life in action is the story of Lazarus. Lazarus was a friend of Jesus. Lazarus died while Jesus attended to the will of the Father in Samaria. His family wrapped Lazarus in the funeral's clothing and buried him several days prior. When Jesus arrived, Lazarus's sister, Martha, met him at the entrance to the cemetery. She proclaims that Lazarus would be alive if he (Jesus) had been there before her brother's death. Jesus, in reply to her, said, "Did I not say to you, if thou would believe, thou should see the glory of God?" ~ John 11:40. He challenged her to change her vision from death to life within her mind. If she held onto her interpretation of what was occurring and continually spoke energy to the definition of the word (death) into her mind, the reality would still live and miss the manifestation of God's glory. Conversely, if she stopped speaking life to her notion of God's glory (being the false god she created and focused on (death)), it would open a new door: her brother's resurrection and the revealed glory of the True and Living God.

What a fantastic display of the Infinite power of El-Shaddai, God in action! Specifically, Jesus displayed incredible confidence when he spoke those words to Martha. The manifestation of that Power, IN and THROUGH him, exemplifies the oneness of their relationship!

Talk about miraculous power! If she had the will to believe, she should reveal the glory of God in her life! This mind-altering concept is an extraordinary statement of greatness to the children of God. "As a wo/man thinks in their heart, so is s/he." With focused thought of our weaknesses, we embed in our subconscious mind a potential idol/pseudo god that is the collective ideals of our thinking when not rooted in God and His word. If we are not careful, these unholy alliances will create a reality that will fail us. Gentle reader, trust not in chariots or Egypt's fame ~ Psalms 20:7 *See also* Isaiah 30:2-5, 31:1. More importantly, if you make despair, worry, lack, I am not good enough, everyone rejects me, I feel abandoned, and the like, your focus (idol/pseudo god) becomes your object of worship. This form of worship allows the enemy to systematically design as an obstacle that jams you up everywhere you turn ~ Revelations 2:1-7.

More importantly, this hindrance deceptively keeps you from the legacy God created for you. Your creative energy/focus brings those things before you as expressions of your creative reality— your earthly glory. Instead of eating strong meat from God's word and training our senses to discern good from evil, we remain in our infant state, never manifesting into full-grown sons/daughters of God ~ Hebrews 5:14. We should pray each day that the Lord causes us to surrender our senses to Him for His glory. When your focus/

Markeithia Lavon Silver

thoughts are of the Infinite One, All-Knowing, and Powerful God (thoughts of abundance, life, the Kingdom of God, God accepts me in the beloved, I am not alone for the Lord thy God is with me), you (your thought seeds) will manifest after their kind—God's glory. "Seek you first the Kingdom of God and all His righteousness, and all other things will be added unto you" ~ Matthew 6:33. Your words and thoughts focus on God, and His Kingdom laws and precepts divulge all of His promises towards you. Because *"life and death are in the tongue, and when you love what you speak, you shall eat the fruit thereof"* ~ Proverbs 18:21. Good God from Zion! Seek first the Kingdom, and the rest will come. When you begin to practice purposeful renewing of your mind, transforming your reference points into Kingdom points, you engage in the mind's spiritual alchemy. You will change the old (idol/pseudo gods) into the True and Living God of endless possibilities. You will replace despair with joy, lack with abundance, fear with courage, inadequacy with more than a conqueror, abandonment with acceptance, and the like. Isaiah 61:3 tells us the same. The conduit by which you WILL do this is the imagination, thought focus, and the energy of your emotion.

When I asked the Lord what was undermining my progress, He showed me how I had created a garrison designed to protect me from being hurt. The wall represented my way of protecting myself from past experiences repeating themselves. Little did I know, this practice was a form of looking back. The issue is that the stronghold became my god as I trusted it to protect me, not the True and Living God. These barracks, moreover, kept God out as well. This caveat is not saying we should not use discernment or test the Spirit, whether they are of God, or create healthy boundaries ~ I John 4:1. God does not instruct us to engage in situations without guarding our hearts ~ Proverbs 24:3. It is to say, anything that is not God is an idol and in need of you destroying it! ~ II Chronicles 31:1 *See also* II Kings 23: 1-20.

Living Your Legacy Of Greatness

More importantly, we are admonished not to look back when God calls us forward—because it will destroy us ~ Genesis 19:26. We can enumerate the reasons we lock ourselves in due to past hurts and anticipated harm. Introspectively, where does it take us, and what do we accomplish? We are still spiritually creating an anti-God system systematically designed to thwart God's will for us. Moreover, we place that practice before God. We must destroy them and exalt Him lest we be destroyed by our mode of pseudo-protections ~ Isaiah 2:17-18. Put not your trust in chariots and horses but trust thou in God ~ Psalms 42:11. He is an ever-present help and our *Good Shepherd* who shall supply all our needs ~ Philippians 4:19. He is our bulwark, banner, and fortress! ~ Psalms 18:2, 91:2, and Exodus 17:15.

Next, in the story of Lazarus, Jesus blows the minds of the onlookers by telling them, "My Father *always* listens and hears my voice—my inner desires to bring them into fruition!" "Father, I thank You that Thou has heard me. [Furthermore], I *Know* that Thou hears me *ALWAYS*." ~ John 11:41-42. (Emphasis mine). What an excellent declaration for the children of God! Not only does the Father *hear* us, but He also hears us *ALWAYS*. Knowing that He always hears you gives you the power to trust, create, grow, expand, resurrect yourself, and serve. If you cannot hang your hat on that, I do not know what else you can count on, beloved.

Ask yourself, "What does Jesus believe? No, *what does he know before He arrives at the gravesite?*" Sometimes, the little things empower you to move beyond the break and give you what you need to move forward. *Knowing* that God listens, understands, and acts on behalf of those who call upon His name will do wonders for your psyche. Jesus walked onto that gravesite as if he owned the place, and he did. He proffered the position of his oneness and greatness within the Father. He wanted the same for those standing

Markeithia Lavon Silver

around. Jesus's posture of transcendence and oneness with the Father was motivational *and* empowering. The anticipation of revealing God's glory was moving from breast to breast. God designed the whole story to enable the believer from start to finish! ~ St. John 1:12-14. The atmosphere gradually changed until it was overflowing and oozing with the glory of God. Suddenly, he says in a resounding voice, "Lazarus, come forth!" His unyielding thought that God, the Father, had his back and that the Universe was under divine order to give him what he asked for undergirded his power. He more than believed; he *knew* what he was asking for—with joy did Jesus offer it up, trusting God would fulfill what he promised him, giving him the desire and hope of his heart, and with delight did he receive. You, too, can operate within this same vein! YOU ONLY NEED TO BELIEVE and TRUST GOD ALL THE WAY THROUGH!

Let us break down the word belief to clarify where I am going. Jesus came that we might lay hold to abundant life. If you rearrange the word belief, you produce BE-LIFE. "I have come that you might have life (be-life) and have it more abundantly (overflowing)." Each time God spoke a portion of the world into existence, He would say, "Let there *be*..." and it was! ~ Genesis 1. I will briefly mention the emotional force behind what we think here. However, we will go over this notion of belief in-depth in chapter seven: *There is No-Thing to Fear*. BE-LIFE or beliefs are your thoughts revealed. Does the statement "I can show you better than I can tell you," ring a bell? These thoughts govern your reality. When you think of an idea with the same force that God thought the world into existence, you are essentially telling your thoughts, as God did to BE-LIFE, or as the Bible proclaims, "Let there be!" And it was! The Hebrew word for "be" is *hâyâh*. The word *hâyâh* is a primitive word meaning to exist, be or become, come to pass, be (-come, accomplished, committed, like), and continue. In other words, when God spoke, "Let there be...," He called *it*

Living Your Legacy Of Greatness

into existence and commanded *it* to come to pass, become, *and continue*. God is still speaking what He spoke in the beginning. If He stopped pronouncing this world's functions and systems, the light would cease, the firmament would no longer divide, the water and the earth would end, the land would no longer yield seed, and the world as we know it would not exist. Accordingly, *the thoughts that created the cosmos are still in the mind of God and continue to this day.* Likewise, we declare things to ourselves, and they persist if we continue to utter them and hold them in our minds. If you find that the same results occur, please check your narrative. Discern what you say to yourself, revise your self-speech, change the story, and look out for a change!

So, what are the implications of the events that unfolded at the graveside? We discern at least three critical findings. First, *what we say to ourselves matters*! More importantly, our narrative governs our reality. Second, Jesus talked with the Father *before* coming to the gravesite. However, there is no dialogue mentioned in the Scriptures. This untold finding suggests *the importance of maintaining a continuous intimate relationship with the Father*.

Nonetheless, we can conclude that he spoke Lazarus's life into existence and envisioned the resurrection *before* arriving at the gravesite. Likewise, Jesus displays the same formula in the Garden of Gethsemane. We find it chronicled in Scripture that He conquered the cross through prayer in the garden. ~ St Luke 22:42. Jesus was poised for the crucifixion when he left the garden. Isaiah tells us that He never uttered one word of complaint but asked the Father to forgive them, for they knew not what they were doing— but Scripture needed fulfilling for our sakes. ~ Isaiah 53:7 and St Luke 22:34, respectively. Thus, he was obedient unto death, even on the cross. ~ Philippians 2:8. Finally, he purposed in his heart that *his actions would glorify his Father*.

The emotional forces behind his thoughts exhibit his complete trust in the Power that worked in him despite the doubt of the

Markeithia Lavon Silver

onlookers. The Word of God, a heart full of grace, and a readiness to serve and glorify God put us on the trajectory of greatness. We, too, share the same capabilities as Jesus. He said as much. "Greater works shall you do!" Aligning ourselves with God's meaning of His Word with our feelings (as the socialist suggests we do when being socialized into a community), we will take on God's image of greatness—creating an identity instrumental in executing confidence in ourselves as sons and daughters of God. Then, we inevitably posture greatness and live in the space of affluence in our lives. We, too, shall say, "Thank you, Father, for hearing me! For I know that you hear me always!" This proclamation, my brothers, and sisters, is a life worth living.

Utilizing our imagination to emulate Christ is one of the steps to greatness. Paul admonishes that our imaginations can get the best of us if we do not create a structured and disciplined strategy according to Kingdom living. As previously stated, we cannot leave our minds to run amuck. We must be purposeful in attaining knowledge conducive to Kingdom living. It must give us more than just information; it must be illuminating and revelatory. When our thoughts do not meet the illumination criteria, we must discard them. We must leave our minds open to the newness of God ~ Proverbs 4:7. In *II Corinthians* 10:5, Paul informs us that our imagination will go contrary to God's word because it is capricious and arbitrary. We must immediately align our thoughts with what God says about the situation when this happens. For example, if we lack, we must remind ourselves, I enjoy all I need. Furthermore, "we are the head and not the tail, we are blessed in the city and blessed in the field, and our basket is blessed" ~ Deuteronomy 28:3. If our thoughts oppose what God says, we must come against that opposition with a declaration and an affirmation fueled with faith. As Job learned, we must *know* that God has the last say in *every* matter.

Living Your Legacy Of Greatness

Simultaneously, our passion for the matter plays an intricate part in manifesting our desires. A harmonious relationship exists between our visions, thoughts, and emotional force in creating God's reality for us ~ Proverbs 23:7. Imagine decreeing the affirmation of being blessed. However, you continue to focus (the mind/vision) on lack, posturing anger, impatience, grief, or otherwise contrary to what you declare within yourself. What results from this imbalance are chaos and frustration. In that case, you are out of alignment and impotent, and your inner expressions will tarry and even die. If fear enters your thought process, it will postpone your vision. If doubt hovers in your thoughts, it will delay what you envision for yourself until further notice from your faith. We are encouraged to visualize what we want joyfully, just as Jesus displayed with thanksgiving. The moment anything divergent enters, we must excavate it from our minds, thoughts, and emotions, replacing it with what the Most-High God says concerning the matter.

Many of us become discouraged about how our lives are "turning out." We never take the time to consider what thoughts brought us to this place of disappointment. When we investigate our lives, frame by frame, seeking out the reference points that systematically determine our outcome, we conclude and realize that there is something greater than our current state or circumstance. That motivation invokes our creativity to change for the better. The power of choice is a great gift. Please do not take it for granted, but honor and guard it. It is hard to swallow when we take responsibility for our thoughts and visions because of those beliefs, but accept that we must if we desire a different outcome. When we hold ourselves accountable for our focus and thought processes, we place ourselves in the position of deliverance from the old way of thinking, opening the door to affluence (Kingdom Living).

As a young girl, I recall that I was horrible at spelling. In grade school, I learned how to spell phonetically. This means of teaching is excellent for reading and not writing. Memorization, however, is

Markeithia Lavon Silver

for writing and spelling. I love to read, and it comes easy; however, spelling has always been challenging. It was not until a dear friend who read some of my poetry encouraged me to write more that I began to look at my thoughts and visions about writing. I could not fathom being an inspirational writer, although I desired/dreamed of being exactly that. I bought into the things said about my spelling ability *and* me. This feeling of inadequacy tore away at the very fabric of my self-esteem (faith in the ability to move in my gifts and talents). I did not think myself astute enough to author a book of poetry, let alone a best seller outlining the application of living your legacy of greatness. I say this in anticipation of God's promise to do exceeding and abundantly above all I ask or think.

I began to reframe my thinking. I traced back to the root cause of my feelings of inadequacy and imperfection and began to tell myself, "You can do this by God's grace! Walk in your gifts and grace! With God, nothing is impossible! You can do all things through Christ who strengthens you! Thank God for technology and spell check! You hold something unique to offer the world… God created you in the image and likeness of the "Us Spirit." Go forth and design well! You are who God says you are in the now!" ~ I Peter 1:16. As I repeated these things, the shame began to lift, and the inspiration started to flow. Before I knew it, a book was forming. I relied upon the things I had been writing for years prior, even in my childhood. You, gentle reader, are a part of divine destiny manifested in words written on these pages. One day, I heard the Spirit say,

> *Child of God: the trials of life can be, oh, so painful. It may appear that your song is no longer worth playing. Do not allow the challenges of this life to stop you from playing your song. If you permit the toils and snares to break the strings of your violin or crack the reed of your saxophone, your heart will not sing, and the world will*

Living Your Legacy Of Greatness

never hear the beauty of your song—unique like no other. Your past does not define you! Forgive the vision of the past, embrace where you are now, join the Great Symphony of the Infinite Power I placed within you, and sing your song! It is morning! Choose to embrace the day with Love, Happiness, and Kindness. Allow the balm of the One who created you to moisten your reed, strengthen your strings, and Sing, Sing! Play, Play, Play! Soar, Soar, Soar!

Thus, as you can see...I am singing and playing my song, soaring to the glory and honor of the One who created me! Will you choose to do the same? I hope you do!

Similarly, you see this fear and inadequacy exhibited in Peter's life. Peter was once in a place where he did not trust his vision. Fear reigned in his life. Do you recall Jesus went to them, walking on water? The Disciples thought that Jesus was a ghost. At the same time, encouraging them to be joyful and not to fear that it was Jesus. Peter, still unsure (doubt), asked Jesus to come out on the water with him. Jesus granted his request (as it always is regarding God's children). I must interject that the Lord is in the business of blessing without inhibiting. He joyfully blesses His creation continually. He maketh rich and add no sorrow! ~ Proverbs 10:22.

We are the ones who need to get in a position to receive all that He has for us—we do this by utilizing our thought power/focus, our vision/imagination, and the joy/emotional stance of our thoughts and visions. We must also mortify the things of the flesh—hatred, jealousy, envy, and the like ~ Roman 8:13. *See also* Colossians 3: 5-25 and Ephesians 4:31. The things of the flesh are hindrances to God's plan for our lives. They are nourishments to tares and not wheat. Dare to let them go!

Once Jesus assured Peter, Peter trusted his vision and "also walked on water." However, when Peter saw the mighty wind, he was afraid and began to sink. Jesus was there to save him, bearing

Markeithia Lavon Silver

him up and returning him to the boat where he came. Can you envision the tortuous anxiety that befell Peter as he begins to sink into the water? He was overwhelmed by the boisterous winds and waves. I imagine they were coming at him fast and furious. Water entered his nose and mouth, and he likely thought he was drowning. It is important to note that one will revert to the lower self when operating from a place and space of gripping fear. *The narratives scripted within the subconscious guide the actions of the individual.* They rely upon self-doubt, anxiety, and little faith in creating images of defeat.

Nevertheless, Jesus lovingly spoke to him about his little faith, or better yet, his abundance of doubt. Interestingly, when we do not pass the test to the next level of faith, we return to our previous state. Our faith informs our visions. When we increase our faith, we die at the present level of belief and are reborn into the next level of faith. Accordingly, Paul informs us that we must forget those things behind us and reach for the things before us, the "high calling of God in Christ Jesus." If we cling to mental images of past things, we remain mentally in the past. Then, we are unable to move forward into our greatness. More importantly, if we do not strive to operate from our higher selves (a place of knowing—the Christ-Spirit), doubt and fear will continue to prevail, manifesting lack, inadequacy, and failure. On the other hand, when we allow God's perfected love in our lives, fear, disappointment, and doubt cannot dwell in our presence ~ St. John 14. It may attempt to knock at the door of your mind; however, it will be cast down, stumble, and fall, as David states in Psalms 37.

Take a moment to reflect on your past and discover what things you are holding on to prohibit you from laying hold of your legacy of greatness. Is it abandonment? Let it go. How about loneliness? Let it go. Broken relationships? God can heal; let it go. He will do a new thing in you—let it go. Do you continuously ponder on not enough? Let it go. Abusive relationships? Let them go, too.

Living Your Legacy Of Greatness

What did my parents do? Let it go. Sickness in your body? See it leaving. Single parents with no help from the father/mother? Trust God, and let it go! He is the sustainer of all life—call Him on it. He will not disappoint. He hovers over His word, ready to perform it! ~ Jeremiah 1:12. Whatever contradicts God's promises for your life, LET IT GO! Let go of all the stuff! If you need to cry, cry. Stumble if you must, but get your footing. Once you do, dance, frolic, and sing joyfully in your space of diligence and deliverance. Be gentle with yourself while you are espousing the flipping of the situation from weakness to strength. Love yourself; tell yourself you are loved and accepted by El-Shaddai and all of God's creation ~ Ephesians 1:6. Your wife does not seem to understand. Let it go! You are doing your best, which goes unnoticed or appreciated. Let it go. God notices, and He will reward you. Please take a deep breath and let it all go…God has something better; you will *see* that your life is worth living. God will take your testimony and cause you to bless someone if you trust Him! My spirit is shouting GLORY! I see yokes destroyed and the burdens lifted as I type these words. Hallelujah! Glory to the Most High God that reigns forever! God cares, and He will uphold you with the strength of His right hand. Seek Him and His power ~ I Chronicles 16:11, Psalms 105:4. David said, "My foot *almost* slipped." Almost blundering is not slipping. It did not, because God was there to uphold him ~ Psalms 73:2 and 94:18, respectively. Feel the Power of God uplifting you and embracing you with Everlasting Love, and underneath are the Everlasting Arms. Fear not, for God is with you! Do not allow sorrow to cast down your soul but hope thou in God! ~ Psalms 42: 11.

Do not live in a space of terror when sitting in silence, looking at who you are. Who you are is beautiful in the sight of God! Do you know the story of the silversmith? Each day, the silversmith boils the silver to cause the contaminations to rise to the top. The silversmith skims the impurities off the top, leaving the pure silver in the pot. As the silversmith gazes upon the silver in the barrel, s/he sees their reflection in the silver. God is the Great Silversmith, and we are the silver. God desires to see the "Us" reflection in us. This desire is the hope of Jesus's calling! By self-examining your life and bringing those things to the forefront of your awareness, you cause the filth to rise to your mind's surface, where the Lord can remove them if you allow. In the words of Socrates, "An unexamined life is a life not worth living." Remember, oh gentle reader, introspection is the key to deliverance. You do not want to exist merely as a pauper; you want to live life more abundantly as a son and daughter of the True and Living God, as has been endowed by Jesus. Be purposeful in discovering, recovering, and uncovering yourself. Unveil the self you are becoming and the one God created you to be, and live life fully in Christ.

There is much to glean from this story. Peter becomes the rock, where Jesus proclaims, "Upon this rock, I will build my church, and the very gates of hell will not prevail against it." He also said, "The enemy desires to sift him as wheat, but he prayed that his faith would not fail him." However, when he overcame his tests, trials, and the enemy stretching him in all directions, he was to "strengthen his brethren" ~ Luke 22:32. Therefore, we know that this state was not the final status of Peter. He had something to look forward to—his greatness, ability to stand erect in Christ, and, more importantly, to strengthen others.

Your present circumstance and situation are not your final destination. I look forward to overcoming it all. Although Peter had to go through a process to reach his greatness, *he became so comfortable in who he was in God that his very shadow would heal people as he passed by.* ~ Acts 5:12-16. Good God from Zion! *The gates of hell could not prevail against him because he was confident in the Power that resided in him. He endured his challenges; he aligned his thoughts with Kingdom thinking and walked in his godness.* This disposition is how you posture greatness: in humility, a harmonious chord of focused thinking, joyful passion, and confidence in the Power upholding you without fear or doubt. Do you desire the Holy Spirit's fullness to be operational in your life so that you might manifest as a son/daughter of God? Release the fear in your life and give meaning (be-life) to what Jesus said, "Greater works shall you do!"

Let us converse about the process for a moment. Peter first allowed fear and doubt to reign in his life because he did not *know* who he was. Once you remove fear from the equation, doubt will surface. He did not hold faith in his vision. His emotional state of mind was not in alignment with his vision. His circumstances overshadowed his joyous passion. He knew it was Jesus walking on water. He even walked on water until he allowed fear and doubt to reign in his psyche. That is right! *He made a conscious choice to fear.* Read the text! The moment he saw the wind, he became afraid. Consider what happened. The Bible says, "When he saw the boisterous wind, he was afraid and began to sink." Thus, Peter revisited the fear that Jesus had removed just moments before. Peter's loss of focus on greatness reverted to a state of weakness, which he obtained through fear and doubt. In his moment of analysis, he chose tunnel vision. Fear and doubt foiled his image of walking on water with Jesus.

Additionally, he lost his vision of greatness in the face of life's circumstances. He was unable to see beyond his situation. Life thwarted his plan to accompany Jesus's walking on water. He lost his footing and returned to his previous state of mind by doing so. I commend Peter, though; he did not stay there! The rest of the story and Jesus's declaration of his life corroborate that.

Now, what can we learn from Peter's experience? First, we discover that knowing God is with us, we do not need to fear any obstacle. Second, be joyful when engaging in life and its circumstances. Hold fast to your vision, and do not let it go. Third, be-life to your image of greatness by looking beyond yourself

Markeithia Lavon Silver

and your circumstances, harvesting good thoughts, joy, and thanksgiving. Fourth, please do not focus on life's issues so that they take your eyes off Christ and divert you from your course of action. Fifth, align your emotions and thoughts with your desire (envision). Finally, if you feel overwhelmed by the storms of life and their twists and turns, call out to the One waiting to answer your every call. The Infinite Power of El-Shaddai will save and uplift you with the strength of His right hand.

To take on this new way of thought-catching and vision-building, one must be willing to take on the responsibility of mastering the alchemy of the mind. This commitment requires a plan, discipline, and a desire to change. Awareness precedes action, just as faith precedes substance. Knowledge is the substratum of your performance. Faith is the substratum of your anticipated object. Still, it would be best if you did your due diligence. Faith must accompany works, and knowledge must pave the way to the right action. Accepting accountability for your thoughts and visions attached to your beliefs/feelings embraces the power of becoming much more than you now appear to be. Specifically, striving to be purposeful and disciplined in what you think and envision would be best in the transformation process. This disciplined process lays the foundation for heightened joy, peace, love, and happiness. This mindset prepares and propels you into a bearer of creativity ~ *See* Proverbs 4: 4-9 and 9:10, respectively. As your mindset changes, it will give new meaning to the phrase, "Old things are passed away, behold *ALL* things *BECOME* new" ~ *II Corinthians* 5:17.

I will end this chapter with a nursery rhyme I am sure we all remember and prose entitled *The Power of the Light*: "Row, Row, Row your boat gently down the stream. Merrily, merrily, merrily, merrily life is but a dream...." How we live is how we dream; the way we desire is how we live...Choose to live larger, go big in the space bequeathed to you as prince and princess of God's Kingdom. Live life always expecting more than what you see in this temporal world, expecting more than what you see from your circumstances, and expecting your change to come. The Will of God is declared, and your entitlement awaits you!

The Power of God's Light

When you think you are at your wit's end, do not give up or give in, but reach deep within and allow the Light to shine forth and repel the darkness (dreariness, sadness, misery, gloom) you are feeling in your soul.

David said, "The Lord is my Light and my Salvation, whom shall I fear."

The Power of the Light will never let you down. If you lean on It, It will never let you fall (drop, be taken by force). Isaiah 59:19 says, "When the enemy comes in like a flood, God will lift a standard...." That standard is the Light within you breaking forth as the noonday.

You do not need to fear the Light because He oversees the light and holds you in His warm embrace.

Stop crying and wondering what you are going to do. Dry your tears. Allow the balm of rejuvenation to heal your wounded heart.

Discipline your soul to reach within and release the Light. Sound the trumpet of jubilee (liberty, freedom) and rejoice, for your answer has come. Draw from the sacred well of Living water that shall never lack or run dry. The Light is cheering you on; do not you hear It as It reverberates in your soul?

"You can lean on Me!" "Trust Me! I will never forsake (abandon, give up on, disown) you."

Take (claim, posture strength to, or able to bear) hold of the Light, feel it prepare you, propel you into an endless adventure, and position you for greatness. As you soar through the clouds, feel the warmness of His love upon your face. Allow the torch of excellence to burn in you richly.

CHAPTER TWO

EXPECT TO DO MORE

"He is able to do <u>exceeding abundantly</u> above all that we ask or think <u>according to the power that works in us</u>." ~ Ephesians 3:20. (Emphasis mine).

—Paul

"This book of the law SHALL NOT depart out of thy mouth (heart and mind), but thou shall meditate (think upon and align yourself with) therein day and night that thou may <u>observe to do (act like, follow after) according to all that is written therein</u>; for then thou <u>shall make (cause to happen, create to happen, effect or act upon, compel to happen, attain) thy way</u> prosperous, and then <u>thou shall have good success</u>." ~ Joshua 1:8. (Emphasis mine).

—Joshua

"Verily, verily I say unto you, <u>He</u> that believeth on me, <u>the works that I do shall he also do; and greater works than these shall he do</u>." ~ St. John 14:12. (Emphasis mine).

—Jesus

Markeithia Lavon Silver

I was ambivalent about which quote to reference first when beginning this chapter. I settled on reciting Jesus last because I noticed something for the first time. I read the Bible many times. The point I will make eluded me each time I reviewed the Scriptures. Once I bring this point to your attention, you will be as excited as I was reading Jesus's words.

First, Paul informs us that God can do more than whatever we ask or think through the Holy Spirit's inspiration and guidance. Can you fathom exceeding (more than, beyond) abundance? If you are able, envision anything in extravagance. Then, allow yourself to go above, broader, and more profound beyond what you envisage. God can do it for us if we *see* more than what we formulate. "O, the depth of the riches, both of the wisdom and knowledge of God! *How unsearchable are His judgments and His ways past finding out*!" ~ Romans 11:33. (Emphasis mine). This Scripture says it all! He blesses us beyond what we may ask or think. However, the wisdom, knowledge, and judgment of that blessing are unsearchable and undiscoverable! What a mighty God we serve!

The abundance provision is lavish enough; however, notice the contingency clause: "according to the power which works in us." What is God telling us through Paul? When we ask God for something, God will exceed the request, do more than we desire, and manifest more than we perceive. However, He performs only to the extent of the power working within us. Okay, that seems reasonable. What is this "power" that is working in us? We will consult Jesus for the answer. He tells us, "According to your faith, be it unto you" ~ Matthew 9:29. Paul's doxology (praise, to speak in honor of the Almighty) gives us insight into the vastness of God's grace, mercy, and power. This power is best understood from the context of salvation and the Blood Covenant of Christ Jesus. "There is an inexhaustible fullness of grace and mercy in God, which the saints' prayers can never draw dry. Whatever we may ask or think to ask,

Living Your Legacy Of Greatness

God can still do more, abundantly more, exceedingly abundantly more." When we operate from this spiritual seat of power, we are strong, fearless, valiant (courageous), and bold by God's grace and mercies in Christ Jesus. Although available and freely given through the power of the Holy Ghost to every son/daughter of God, we can grieve the Spirit hindering our performance against the enemy, principalities, powers, and spiritual wickedness in high places ~ Ephesians 4:30.

By looking at the Apostle Paul's enumerated causes before and following his exhortation to the saints, he defines the grounds of what hinders the Holy Spirit: the presence of sin inwardly and outwardly. Therefore, our power is more prominent and significant as we yield our bodies to the Holy Spirit's leading. More importantly, our spiritual advantage over the enemy is predicated on total surrender unto the Lord. When we suppress our pain and past traumas, we hinder our growth and grieve the Holy Spirit, which retards our ability to merge as one with the Lord and obfuscates or clouds our expectation of more. According to the Apostle, God desires for us to *know* "what *is* the breadth, and length, and depth, and height (of the manifold wisdom of God); And to know the love of Christ, which passes knowledge, that ye might be filled with all the fullness of God ~ Ephesians 3: 10, 18-19. Wow! Did you read that?! God *wants* us to *know* the vastness of His wisdom! The Greek word for manifold is *Polupoikilos,* meaning much variegated, multifarious. In other words, God's wisdom is multilayered, having great diversity or variety. He wants us to understand it from *all* aspects (in 4-D) so that He might fill us with "all the fullness of God." My God! Oh, that we might comprehend, grasp, and hold on to how much God loves us!

Additionally, John tells us in *I John* 4:13 that "we dwell in Him, and He has given us His Spirit." You must understand that your definition of power and abundance differs from the next person's. However, we aim to align our connotations, values, principles, beliefs, opinions, ideologies, and meanings with the Kingdom's definitions. Remember that the word's representation and feelings toward it must be equivalent to creating the concept. Clarity and distinction are imperative for Kingdom affluence. As I mentioned in chapter one, if we place Jesus in the forefront of our imagination, we respond by doing Kingdom social living and not earthly social existence. I concede that this is a challenge. Nonetheless, you can accomplish this place *in* God with trust, belief, and due diligence.

We must first focus beyond our circumstances and align our thoughts with God's to achieve this place in God. Then, we must forget what we "think we know" or what others declared over us as the truth and embrace the expectation of more. We must be open to expanding our perceptions and minds to create new ones. We must release the views that cloud or retard our imagination of ourselves. No vision—no manifestation. We must continuously redefine the definitions that shape our thoughts, focus, and perceptions until we reach our goal of kingdom thinking. Finally, we must trust the promises of the Lord in our lives and, thus, be willing to stand up and go after what God has in store for us.

I would like you to take a moment and define some terms: more abundantly, affluence, acceptance, prosperity, and success. The reason for this exercise is for you to realize your definition compared to the Kingdom's meaning. Reflection upon what you believe and hold dear must enter the Light of God's Kingdom to recreate the precept and concept of these things. You must learn and act upon the exact definition, or there will be a conflict and a delay in the ascent into the notion of Kingdom thinking. Grab your journal and entitle this next page, *Kingdom Terms Defined*.

Living Your Legacy Of Greatness

Kingdom Terms Defined

Term	Your Definition	Kingdom's Definition
More Abundantly		**I Corinthians 2:9** – "Eye has not seen, nor ear heard, neither has it entered the heart of humanity the things God has prepared for them that Love Him." I see Beyond my perception of the object of my affection. "Pressed down, shaken together shall man pour unto your bosom." Exceeding my expectations.
Affluence		**3 John 1:2** – "Beloved, I wish above all things that you prosper and be in good health, even as your soul prospers."
Acceptance		**Ephesians 1:3-7** – "Blessed be the God and Father of our Lord Jesus Christ, who hath blessed us with all spiritual blessings in heavenly places in Christ: According as He hath chosen us in Him before the foundation of the world, that we should be holy and without blame before him in love: Having predestinated us unto the adoption of children by Jesus Christ to himself, according to the good pleasure of his will, To the praise of the glory of his grace, wherein *He hath made us accepted in the beloved.* In whom we enjoy redemption through his blood, the forgiveness of sins, according to the riches of his grace."
Prosperity		**Deuteronomy 8** – "I am blessed in the city and blessed in the field; my basket is always full. I always possess what I need. God is my Good Shepherd, and He supplies all my needs." If there is a need, God shall meet it ~ **Phil 4:19.**

Success		Joshua 1:8 – "Meditate upon the Law (Kingdom Thinking) day and night that you might do ACCORDING to all that is written. Then, you shall MAKE your way prosperous, and you shall experience GOOD success." Psalms 1:2-3 – "Delight in the Law of the Lord (His way of thinking), meditate day and night. You shall be like a tree planted by the rivers of waters (God will sustain you in all things) that brings forth fruit (plenty, successful without stopping) his leaf also shall NOT wither; *and,* Whatsoever you put your hands to do will prosper." "The blessings of the LORD, it maketh rich, and he addeth no sorrow with it" ~ Prov 10:22.
Wisdom, knowledge, understanding, and skill of any kind		Wisdom and might are His: And He changeth the times and the seasons: He removeth kings, and setteth up kings: He giveth wisdom unto the wise, and knowledge to them that know understanding: He revealeth the deep and secret things: He knoweth what *is* in the darkness, and the light dwelleth with him. ~ Dan 1: 17, 2:21-22. If any of you lack wisdom, let him ask of God, that giveth to all *men* liberally, and upbraideth not; and it shall be given him. ~ James 1:5.

Your thoughts must align with what the Lord says about these terms. If they differ, immediately alter your definition to fit God's description of the word or concept. Remember, rising to the level of wealth consciousness is not merely about securing financial wealth; it is about knowing God and that He shall supply all your needs "according to His riches in glory" ~ Philippians 4:19. *Knowing* that if there is a need, *He shall meet it*! Again, it is beyond faith (be-life that informs your vision of what God shall do).

Moreover, meditating and aligning your thinking with God's word will make your way prosperous and successful. Trust what the Lord is speaking over your life! Recall, He "declares the end from the beginning and from ancient times the things that are not yet done, saying, My counsel shall stand, and I will do all my pleasure... I have spoken it, and I will also bring it to pass; I have purposed it, I will also do it." ~ Isaiah 46:10-11. If He establishes it, He will surely bring it to pass for His glory ~Genesis 41:32. Beloved, God set provision before you (from the beginning) and is awaiting your choice to grab hold and declare the works of the Lord! ~ Isaiah 57:12. *See also* Psalms 118:17.

Let us investigate what will occur when thoughts align with Kingdom thinking. Interestingly enough, in-sync and harmonious thinking and vision-building can work for something as simple as deciding to patronize a new restaurant in your neighborhood. You drive by every day on your way to and from work. You smell the sweet aroma of good cooking and say to yourself, "I am going to dine there one evening." This form of affirmation is the beginning process of expectation and vision-building. We bring to bear this level of expectation in all that we do. We fall short only when we cannot imagine an outcome. After the desire, we must conceptualize it and align the thoughts that cultivate the vision until it manifests. Okay, let us return to the example of the "eating place." Your family loves steak and potatoes. You smell the potential steak and potatoes when you drive by this establishment. In your mind, you begin to imagine the steak's juiciness and the potatoes' fluffiness; you envision yourself and your family sitting at the table and having an enjoyable evening.

It never crosses your mind that you will enjoy anything but a wonderful night at this eatery. You look beyond your present circumstances. Right? The process seems easy enough. You then pass on this potential good evening to your family members and friends. One day, it goes from the potential to eat at this steakhouse to eating there. You made it happen with something as small as eating at a restaurant. You had vision, joy, and thoughts supporting your idea of eventually eating there. Your images and views activated the Law of Belief (thought focus gives me what I believe). The Law of Correspondence (my dreams correspond with my thoughts and beliefs/values), and the Law of Attraction (I attract people, places, and things that I seed to plant into my thought focus/mind), bringing it into fruition. We do it repeatedly; however, we do not realize it. Therefore, we attract things we do not want because we previously thought about them intensely. We consistently speak this conversation or narrative to our inner selves.

Fundamentally, our reality is pure potentiality; our visions are our chosen possibilities. The Universe is under divine order to give us what we ask. The earth assists us in our endeavors ~ Revelation 12:16. It has no respect for persons; it does not discriminate nor play favorites. Furthermore, the Laws of Nature produce the hidden forces of thought and imagery we present unto God (Source of all Power) to manifest our reality. I cannot emphasize the importance within our minds, the visions built from those thoughts, and how we must monitor what we think. We must first discipline our minds to focus on God's Word and reject anything contrary to His promises. God incorporates our inheritance, and His glory shines forth, as we discipline our mind ~ Colossians 1:12, 3:24, Hebrews 9:15, I Peter 1:4. We must watch and pay attention to the narratives we create, the private conversations we have with ourselves ~ Matthew 26:41. If necessary, we must remove the things that served us yesterday but are of no use today due to those thoughts' predetermined results. If we desire to move in the direction of greatness, we must frame our ideas in kind lest we fall into temptation ~ *Id. See also* Mark 14:38.

In contrast, if you begin creating the vision of dining out but then think about money, you may weaken the fruition of your

Living Your Legacy Of Greatness

vision. You may abort your dream if you focus on your lack of financial wiggle room. Suppose you cannot hold together a picture of incorporating the things you like with your current lifestyle. In that case, you may feel despair, fear, frustration, and unhappiness, concluding that "we never get to do anything nice because of lack." As a result, you are disappointed by your expectations and their failure to come to fruition. What has happened is that you disharmonized your vision with thorns and thistles, placing a delay or even canceling what you wanted. You fell into the thorn category in the Parable of the Sower told by Jesus in Mark 4:3-20.

However, if the outcome is favorable, we now possess a faith experience worthy of applying to other areas of our lives, undergirded by God's faithfulness, boldness, and surety (*See* James 1:2-4, Romans 5:3-5, and Philippians 1:13-15, respectively). Why do we not apply this same practice to every area of our lives? We maintain a level of expectation in all that we do. Just as we can expect to provide an enjoyable family evening, we can predict with confidence through our faith in knowing to live our legacy of greatness handed to us by The Most-High, blessed be He from before the foundation of the world.

Children of the Creator can accomplish anything if we only trust and believe—allowing the Power of God to dwell in us richly!

A perfect example of how powerful the mind is over the body came in the story of Paula Deen, a celebrity in an Entertainment Tonight (ET) interview. While on the show, she shared that she developed agoraphobia, the fear of open spaces or exposure to unidentified dangers. When asked how it came about, she responded, "It began with my father's death; [he] was my hero. Then, my beautiful mother died four years later. I was so afraid of death, my body would tense up, and I felt like I had a heart attack." Now, her mindset would bring on a particular set of responses in the body. This outcome is no surprise. Our bodies respond daily to our thoughts—good, bad, or indifferent. When we tell ourselves

Markeithia Lavon Silver

we do not feel up to working, our body responds with sluggishness or sickness. We can empower our bodies to function optimally by speaking to them and relying upon the grace and strength of God ~ II Samuel 22:33, Psalms 18:1-2, 32, Habakkuk 3:19, II Corinthians 12:19. To be sure, and this assertion does not discount a healthy lifestyle of eating and exercising but emphasizing *what we think matters.*

Let us peruse the word of God to see if my assertion is correct. One of Israel's sons, Judah, received a blessing on his father's deathbed. It goes something like this:

> *Judah, you are the one that the brethren shall praise:* **thy hand shall be around the neck of thine enemies;** *thy father's children shall bow down before thee. Judah is a lion's whelp…* **The scepter shall not depart from Judah, nor a lawgiver between his feet…and unto him shall the gathering of the people be** *…Binding his foal unto the vine, and his ass's colt unto the choice vine; he washed his garments in wine and his clothes in the blood of grapes: His eyes shall be red with wine, and his teeth white with milk ~ Genesis 49:8-12.* (Emphasis mine).

Some know this blessing was prophetic, foretelling Christ, the Messiah. Let us fast forward to the House of Jesse. God chose Jesse's youngest son, David, to be king of Israel. Before David was appointed king, he was a shepherd's boy. He attended to his father's sheep. As we delve into a portion of David's life before God anointed him as king, remember the blessing foretold of Judah's tribe.

As David attended to his father's sheep, he could (as social theorist Herbert Mead refers to) "take on the role of the other"—the other being El-Shaddai/Elohim/God. How do we know this? When we read the 23rd Psalms, we observe David referring to God as his

Living Your Legacy Of Greatness

Shepherd. Not only was David able, by way of his imagination, to vicariously perceive God as an overseer of his soul, but he was also able to see God in every aspect of his life as a shepherd over his father's flock. David spoke metaphorically about his life, typifying God in every facet of his life. He perceived and comprehended God as a sustenance provider and peacekeeper, a restorer of his soul, a spiritual guide, a protector, a blanket of confidence, and a robe of security. After all of that, David did not stop there. He recognized God as more. I will not replace David's words with mine because his words speak for themselves: "Thou preparest a table before me…Thou anointest my head with oil; *my cup runneth over*." He then declares with confidence from this vision, "Surely goodness and mercy shall follow me *all the days of my life…*" ~ Psalms 23. (Emphasis mine).

Do you feel the passion for David's song? I do! Even when he saw God as everything, he could look beyond that and see an exceeding abundance of God's goodness. I know we often hear this Psalms read at funerals, but this is precisely the problem we find in the house of worship today, with our imaginations diminishing. We assign certain things to a spiritual box, and Christian tradition tells us, "That is where it belongs, and that is where it will stay." We assign this individual Psalm to death and do not allow it to represent what God can perform, who God is, and do for us now. I submit that Psalms 23 foreshadows God's goodness and our exceeding abundance of blessings as God's children.

Well, I challenge that notion of smallness and confinement. God's Word is a reservoir that we draw upon for our example, empowerment, and exhortation. It is time that we begin to think creatively. We must challenge the congregates' imaginations as apostles, prophets, evangelists, pastors, and teachers. Jesus did. Jesus stretched us in all that he said and did. For instance, do you remember the Beatitudes? "I know that you heard: an eye for an eye and a tooth for a tooth… love they neighbor and hate your enemy,

Markeithia Lavon Silver

but I say unto you, Turn the other cheek... Love your enemies, bless them that curse you, do good to those that hate you and pray for those who despitefully use you and persecute you, that you may be the children of your Father..." ~ Matthew 5:38-45. Wow! This form of teaching was outside the general order of things: Love my enemies; Turn the other cheek; Pray for those that use me. Jesus went above and beyond the call of duty, or so they thought. They never considered the Law of Sowing and Reaping nor thought of the Spirit of Love and how it covers and binds together. They never acknowledged the energy that went into hating their enemy and the havoc it caused to themselves and humanity at large. What you put out will return to you.

For several centuries, the Children of Israel dealt with a person (the outward man) in such a fashion that bred hate, superiority, indifference, and the like. Still, Jesus came and dealt with the heart of the individual. He knew our empathy needed to be in union/in sync with a person's actions to receive the things of the Kingdom. Do you remember Jesus's response to the "keepers of the law" concerning ceremonial hand washing before eating? He told them, in so many words, that tradition was good; however, it was more important to sustain a clean heart, "For out of the abundance of the heart, the mouth speaketh" ~ Luke 6:45. That is right! You manifest in your actions outwardly what is in you! We also consistently perform these operations to mold our hearts and position ourselves "to be begotten children of our Father" ~ I Peter 1:3. To master the art of becoming who we are, we must observe our mind's emotional state. As Jesus pointed out, it is not the action but the thought. It is "not what you say, but how you say it." You heard the term before, "It was not what you said, Johnny; it was the way you said it (the power behind the words)." The force behind the word is our emotions (a psychological concept/ vision of our interpretation of the language we speak to ourselves). They determine the manifested outcome for how those around us

Living Your Legacy Of Greatness

interpret how they should react to us and how we feel and respond within ourselves. *See* Deuteronomy 1:34

Take, for example, Jesus's exhortation of "turning the other cheek." His encouragement transcended the literal interpretation. Specifically, Jesus encouraged us not to turn from the image and likeness of the "Us" spirit no matter how hard life smacked us in the face. A slap on the face stings anyone's skin. Even after the hand has made contact, the memory of its occurrence is ever-present. This event invokes all types of emotions within the victim of injury. Although this may be an unwanted infraction, we are to remain intact. The act of violence against us should not veil our image or our likeness of God. This hostility can be emotional as well as physical. Egregious acts notwithstanding, we must hold fast to our calling in Christ Jesus. From this image and likeness, we can bestow grace upon the culprit inflicting this pain upon us ~ Matthew 5:44.

Nonetheless, metaphorically speaking, we must turn the other cheek and allow them to hit us again without changing *who* we are. Unfortunately, others' words, actions, and circumstances are beyond our control; our socio-economic status, race, ethnicity, where we grew up, parents, or any other socially designated category hurt many of us. We often cannot let it go because the pain is deep and severe. The sting appears too much to bear. In turn, we become hurting people that hurt people in return. We transfer that pain because we forget who we are—we lose sight of God's image and likeness within us. The veil of pain shrouds our true selves.

Therefore, instead of turning the other cheek, we hold on to the pain, define it, and create perceptions that lend themselves to the opposite of what God has in store for us. Unbeknownst to us, this practice may create an anti-Christ spirit. ~ I Peter 1:13-16. Keep in mind what Jesus said at the gravesite of Lazarus. He alluded to the notion of looking beyond the break. Martha told him that her brother "yet stinks." His response was, "If you would only

Markeithia Lavon Silver

believe." If you can reach beyond the break in your life, you will see God's glory in its fullness. If you can see and feel beyond the stench of death, you will see God's glory. "Turn the other cheek," and while you are turning, "forget those things behind you, and press toward the mark of the high calling in Christ" ~ Philippians 3:13-14. Forgive the person and forgive the vision you created because of the relationship produced by those thoughts, passions, and dreams. I must interject here that the Lord has given us the ability to create. We must guard this ability well lest our creations destroy us.

Nevertheless, the Lord's divine will for our lives is amidst the backdrop of our choices, working it for our good ~ Romans 8:28. When things do not work out the way we designed them, we must forgive the vision and adapt to God's divine will. The Lord knows what is best for us. He knows what we do not. His wisdom is far above our own. Still, recall that He wants us to understand in ways we did not previously comprehend.

Moreover, God systematically designs our challenges, tests, and life's twists and turns with a purpose: Conform us to the image of His Son. He incorporates the components that work for our good within every manifestation of desire ~ Romans 8. More importantly, if our vision, amidst God's perfect will for our life, causes us to tarry for its manifestation, we patiently wait. As we await our change, God strengthens us ~ Isaiah 40:31. *He sustains and uplifts us with His Word and promises* ~ Psalms 3:3. We trust that His ways are perfect and that He tailors our blessings just for us. When the vision appears, we are ready to receive and maintain it because He has tailored our trials, perfected us, established us, strengthened and settled us, keeping us from evil ~ *I Chronicles* 4:10, *I Peter* 5:10, and *II Timothy* 3:3, respectively.

Do you recall David speaking to us about the joy within, the vehicle, and the means of getting to our desired destination? In Psalms 37:1-5, David tells us we are not to fret or be envious but

Living Your Legacy Of Greatness

to *"trust in the Lord and do good."* Although these emotional states of mind affect our vision and thought process, I would like to highlight the following verses —4 and 5. He urges us to "delight ourselves also in the Lord, and He shall give thee the desires of thine heart. Commit thy way unto the Lord: also trust in Him, and He shall bring it to pass." Do you see the contingencies here? We must garner joy to bring our trust in God to another level. He shall bring it to pass once you are delighted in the Lord.

Furthermore, we must commit the vision to God and trust the Infinite Power of El-Shaddai to be faithful to the promises He made. You should consecrate your daily activity and work products unto God each day. This gesture brings you to a place of humility and trust in God to bring it to pass. More importantly, sanctifying yourself and your work unto the Lord brings those things under the protection of the Kingdom because they now belong to God. We are not our own but bought with a price, and He does our bidding ~ *I Corinthians* 6:20.

How many times is an idea aborted due to feelings of inadequacy? As you face challenges in manifesting your desires, you become frustrated and fearful and conclude, "I cannot do this." This pattern of thinking must cease to reveal your desires. Bringing your mind to a state of perpetual joy allows you to be free to receive what the Spirit of God has for you. David, dubbed as a man *"after* God's own heart," would dance joyfully before the Lord—positioning himself, in his worship, to receive all that the Most-High had for him. David quotes in *I Chronicles* 29:10-20, humbly saying, "Who am I, and what is my people, that we should be able to offer so willingly...for ALL THINGS come of Thee, AND of THINE OWN have we given thee." Wow! If you read the verses, you will see the praise David renders unto the Lord as he realizes that *all the Lord has blessed him with is God's.* Specifically, God bestows David's blessing upon him with the expectation that David returns the benefit unto the Lord, what is already God's possession. See what joy of the heart will get you when aligned with what the Lord has in store for you. You keep giving it back in joy, and God continues to give it to you. This reciprocal process is phenomenal! Try it and watch the Lord move! It is evident why God loved David! They enjoyed *a heart exchange*, which spilled over into earthly possessions. When we open our hearts, God opens His heart even in our brokenness as we exchange heart secrets.

It Can Be Done If You Trust and Believe

With a joyful heart, a trusting spirit, and a commitment to the vision, God will bring it to pass (will manifest the vision). The foundation and the backdrop of every imagination must be a wellspring of joy and desire for God's will for your life. We require joy as a blanket surrounding ourselves and covering our visions to open the portal of faith. It would be best to feel joy when you think about (it) your vision. Further, you must commit it to the Lord and God's Plan for your life—praising the Lord for entrusting you with the "Us" stuff. If you sense anything contrary to that, you will slow down the arrival of your destiny. There must be a three-chord harmonious oneness between your vision, thoughts, and emotional state of mind (your heart feeling). Bringing these things into balance will ensure your faith-manifested aspirations.

Staying within the vein of David's life, let us glance at the children of Israel's fight against the Philistines. In *I Samuel* 17: 1-58: Do you recall the story? If not, allow me to refresh your memory. David was off attending to his father's sheep. Jesse sent him on an assignment to bring provisions to his brothers fighting in the war. Upon David's arrival, he assesses Israel's position in the war and believes he can contribute. The word was out amongst Israel's children and what they were up against in the war. David exhibits the importance of inventorying our situation and why we

Living Your Legacy Of Greatness

must study our craft, aspirations, or anything we are determined to obtain. David had already decided that he could help destroy the enemy. Please recall the prophecy spoken over Judah that "the house of Judah will [wrap] his hand around his enemy's neck." David was a progeny of Judah.

Before we get to that actual slaying of Goliath by David, let us look at Israel's children's state of mind. Before the battle began, Israel's army was on the mountaintop, symbolizing the perfect alignment to win a war (they felt and knew God's deliverance). They trusted in their God. They were committed to the Lord's way. God was mighty in battle, and they had no reason to suspect anything other than victory. However, between verses 3 and 19, something happened. They had gone from being on the mountaintop to residing in the valley.

What happened?

I will tell you exactly what happened. Something was out of balance: the distorted notion of victory against the enemy, their thoughts, their joy, or all three. First, the enemy whispered to them, "They were small," and they bought into it. Around verse four, the perspective of the battle began to change. Never had they come up against an individual more massive than their standards. This notion of smallness suggests a similar example of how perception rules. The story of the spies that Moses sent to Jericho fell prey to what they envisioned about themselves. *They had mentally lost the fight before it began.* Only Caleb and Joshua returned with the report that they could take the city. The other spies cried, "They are giants; we are grasshoppers in their sight" ~ Numbers 13. This statement is, of course, a paraphrase, but I hope you understand my meaning. Their view of themselves caused them to *feel* small; therefore, they acted small, and if you follow their lead, you will live small, too. As you may very well know, they took the city. I must continue with David and Goliath.

Markeithia Lavon Silver

The word goes out to the land of Israel that the Philistine army was looking for a man to fight. In verses 8 and 9, Goliath declares that Israel was to choose a man to challenge him and "If he can fight with me, and to kill me, then we will be your servants..." As mentioned above, David was an Israelite from the tribe of Judah. Therefore, he also heard the news. This humble thinker contends that David overheard the message and began formulating a vision in his mind. He had a plan. While drafting this vision, David, with joy, commits that vision to the Lord. He also substantiates his idea through experience. In the meantime, from verses eleven through nineteen, the army of the Most-High God was overwhelmed with fear and dismay. They could not see beyond their distress of defeat. Saul offers a reward to the man who will go against Goliath in his anxiety and desperation. He proposes his riches, his daughter to wed, and freedom in the house of whoever will challenge the enemy. However, panic hovered over Israel, and no one came forward except David—the shepherd's boy. They attempted to pass that trepidation onto David, but he would not waver from his vision. He stood steadfast, even amid his eldest brothers. If you know anything about Hebrew tradition, going against the oldest brother is forbidden. However, David was fearless! It is important to note that God enlarged David's image of Him by experience: the lion and bear. Our imagination remains underdeveloped when we do not see God for *who* He is. We must not allow our tests and trials to stunt our growth but enlarge our concept of God's power in all things as David did. *David was fearless in the knowledge of his God!*

Listen to what he tells King Saul and all of Israel in verses 26-28: *"Who is this uncircumcised Philistine, that he should defy the armies of the living God?!"* Can you feel his passion? His brother heard his words, and he was angry with David. He says to David, "Why camest thou down hither? And, with whom hast thou left those few sheep in the wilderness? I know thy pride and the

Living Your Legacy Of Greatness

naughtiness of thine heart; for thou are come down that thou might see the battle." His brother also could not see beyond his fear and anger. He attempted to deflect and transfer his anxiety to David and hide the shame of being afraid in front of his little brother.

Nonetheless, David had a vision and committed that image of victory to God. David goes on to encourage the king and the children of Israel. As you continue to read the passages, you will see that they all lived within the box of unattainability and defeat. They could not see beyond their collective consciousness of fear and terror of the obstacle before them. It was a collective consciousness not of *Our God is great!* But gripped by fear, they could not move forward in battle. If any vision accompanies fear, it will not go forth. It will tarry and possibly destroy it.

Still, David arrives and says to the king in verses 34-37, "Thy servant kept his father's sheep, and there came a lion and a bear…I went out after them and smote them…thy servant slew both the lion and the bear…." Here is where it gets juicy! He tells him, "This uncircumcised Philistine shall be as one of them… [Moreover], the Lord has delivered me out of the paw of the lion and out of the paw of the bear. He will deliver me out of the hand of this Philistine." In other words, with the strength of the Lord, I killed a lion and a bear with my own hands; I can take Goliath with no problem! What joyous passion, what commitment, what determination, what vision! *God had done it for me in the past; indeed, the Lord will do it for me now!*

It is interesting to note that in verse 38, Saul attempts to arm David with his armor (I will give you what I perceive will cause you to win and protect your vision, never considering what he had conjured up in his mind through fear, which did not yield victory). If you recall, in chapter one, I mentioned Paul's admonishment to release those things of the past to grab hold of those things in the future—to the prize of God's high calling in Christ. Sometimes, we are to let go of the old that yields the same old results. If the

Markeithia Lavon Silver

perceptions of yourself and others' expectations of your life render effects of lack, poverty, and the like, change them to what will cause you to be victorious. Saul's armor represented the old way. The previous ways got them in a predicament they were currently experiencing. Notice what David tells Saul about his armor in verse 39b: "I cannot go [into battle or lay hold to my vision] with these; (Whoa!) for *I [did] NOT prove them* (I cannot use these methods that yielded the results of fear of failure. I used the prescribed combination of greatness that I know works). And David put them off him." He refused to accept the notion of smallness, insufficientness, or unattainability. He would not attach a feeling of fear or defeat to his vision. His passion for joy, thoughts of victory, and imagination of handling the situation were in alignment, and he would not allow the fear of the people to turn him around. He expected more than they could see and *knew* the Lord would deliver!

Goliath sees David as small and inconsequential, takes an arrogant stance with David, and dismisses him as a viable threat. David once again utilizes the power of his imagination, his joy of passion, and his thoughts to defeat Goliath. You can see in verse 48 that David, with haste, runs toward Goliath. *He was fearless!* He was going to engage the enemy with vigor and tenacity. When we commit ourselves to our vision and lift it to the Lord in joy, we will also be courageous in attaining it. He utilized the force of his revelation, joy, and commitment to that vision of God as a weapon. As you know, David prevailed and received all Saul promised to the man who would defeat Goliath.

This story, or any story, is not to say that some thought processes are insufficient. However, you can gauge them by how they make you feel. If they encourage and empower you, cultivating your desire into manifestation—keep them. If the thought process does not reassure but brings fear, doubt, despair, or anything contrary to God's promises, get rid of them quickly. Do not allow the seeds of

Living Your Legacy Of Greatness

defeat to ruin your crop! Do not let the seed of doubt take root in your field of victorious living!

As promised, I mentioned bringing something to your attention to bring you joy. In Jesus's exhortation (turn back to it or get a *King James Bible* and look on with me) that we shall do more, something that I never saw before occurs. In all the years, and there have been several, I have read and reread God's word, and I have never noticed this. Is your attention peaked? Great! It is worth waiting for, beloved.

Look at the verse and read slowly: "Verily, verily I say unto you." STOP!

Read the next word. "He." STOP!

Do you see it? If you do not see it, go back to the beginning and look at it again. This announcement is Jesus talking! He refers to us as He—capital H-e, He. At that moment, He is referring to us as our God-selves. Do you see it? "…He that believeth on me, the works that I do shall he also do; and greater works than these shall he do." ~ St. John 14:12. Jesus began the instruction with verily, which means paying close attention to what comes next. Children of God, the "world yet groans for the manifestation of the sons/ daughters of God." Did he not tell us that God reveals the mysteries of His word unto us? In all the sermons I heard preached and in all the Bible studies I sat in, I never overheard any Apostle, Prophet, Evangelist, Pastor, or Teacher talk about the "H" capitalized in this verse. This proclamation says something huge to us! What is it saying?

Although some may argue and even conclude that the interpreter of Jesus's words chose to capitalize the H in He, we know that nothing happens by coincidence or accident with God, particularly concerning the Lord's promises vis-à-vis His covenant and plan for His children. The *King James* version holds this interpretation. Any other versions of the *Bible* do not refer to any form of oneness in God. At that moment, He is speaking not to our flesh but our

Markeithia Lavon Silver

spirits—to the essence of who we are as God's Children, joint heirs with Christ—our highest self, made in the image and likeness of The Most High God. Jesus reminds us of one word that echoes his father, David, "[Did I not tell you] that you are gods." Wow! *Are you able to imagine this*? Can you wrap your imagination around this?! We have come too far to stop at just a mere belief in the Christ-Spirit to accomplish the things of the Kingdom. We must know that we are heirs and joint heirs with Him. While sitting in church, the pastor would say, "I am one with God, and [the earth will manifest] what I say and come to pass!" Each time he preached and proclaimed it, it would empower me to know the Lord as He is and how I should aspire to that is-ness of God on the earth. Jesus tells us that we shall do more significant works according to the power that works in us. Still, we must prepare our minds and hearts for that power to move in its fullness and integrity of Jesus's statement concerning us. When we grasp the ability to be life to this vision that we are one in God, as Jesus is one with God in the Spirit, we will do great exploits, manifesting our authentic selves as sons/ daughters of God. Stay with me now! "They that know their God shall do great exploits!"

Turn for a moment to *I John* 4:17-18: "That we may [posture] boldness…because as he is, so are we in this world. There is no fear in [God's] love." If that does not tell you that you are little Jesus protégés (able to raise the dead, heal the sick, mend the brokenhearted, and set the captives free just as Jesus did), I do not know what does. David displayed this same boldness and fearlessness. He trusted God beyond measure and *expected more every time*, for God referred to him as a man *after* the heart of the Lord. David sought after the heart of God with joyful passion. God blessed him beyond measure, even in the request to bless his son Solomon. Much of what Solomon received was due to his father's relationship with the Lord. Because he expected more, God blessed David's children for generations to come. If you get the chance, read through the prophets, especially Isaiah, and see how God continued to bless David's children because of the relationship he established with God. David always expected more. You, too, receive notification of the reading of God's will; take your blessing and soar, soar, soar! Remember, "He can do exceeding abundantly above all that you may ask or even think!"

What was David's secret? He discovered he did not need to beg the Infinite Power of El-Shaddai God for anything. He just needed to bless the Lord for His goodness and His provision. David would receive and give back freely (*Read* I Chronicles 29:1-16). With that kind of worship, he would increasingly receive what he asked or thought. I love the 34th Psalm, verses 1-3, which says, "I will bless the Lord *at all times*. His praise shall *continually* be in my mouth. My soul shall make her boast in the Lord; the humble shall hear thereof and be glad. O magnify the Lord with me, and let us exalt His name together." (Emphasis mine). You, too, can exalt the Lord's name into the legacy of your greatness according to the Lord's plans for your life. Amen.

I will end this chapter with prose entitled *The Proclamation*:

The Proclamation

As a gardener prepares the soil to receive the seed for growth, we must prepare our minds to welcome change.

We must cultivate the seed of Wisdom with patience, endurance, and anticipation. "We must walk worthy of the vocation by which we are called."

We exist in the womb of the Creator, awaiting birth. The water breaks forth, announcing the coming of our manifested thoughts. We are in sync with Nature to procreate.

Will you engage Nature with vigor and tenacity? Fear is just an illusion at best. Dethrone the enemy's "illusion" with the truth.

Markeithia Lavon Silver

What is this truth, you say? "You are gods and children of the Most High."

It is your birthright to rule!

It is your inheritance to walk in abundance!

This divine status and authority are bequeathed to you by the One who created all!

"The Earth is the Lord's and the fullness thereof...."

Arise!

Arise, child of God, and take your place on the Throne of endless possibilities!

CHAPTER THREE

YOU ARE PART OF THE UNIFIED CONSCIOUSNESS

In the beginning, God created...~ Genesis 1:1.

"And God said, 'Let US make man in our image after our likeness...'" ~ Genesis 1:26 (Emphasis mine).
—The Infinite "Us" Power of The Most High/El-Shaddai/God

"That they all may be ONE as thou, Father art IN me, and I in Thee, that they also may be one IN us...And the glory which Thou gavest Me I [give] them; that they may be ONE, even as We ARE ONE: I in them, and Thou in me that they may be made perfect in one..." ~ John 17: 21-23 (Emphasis mine).
—Jesus

Markeithia Lavon Silver

> *"But without faith, it is impossible to please Him: for he, that cometh to God must first believe that He is AND that He is a rewarder of them that diligently seek Him."* ~ *Hebrews 11:6* (Emphasis Mine).
>
> —*Paul*

The Lord blessed me to know my great-grandparents on both sides of my family. Hattie, my maternal great-grandmother, was about a hundred years old. No one is sure how old she was; the family rumored she could be a hundred-plus years of age. The midwife system delayed birth certificates anywhere from two to ten years during her time. According to her birth record, she was 94 years old. My paternal great-grandparents also lived beyond a hundred years of age. I knew and conversed with my great-grandparents until they passed into glory. Maintaining a God-centered focus on both sides of my family enabled them to survive harsh times. They overcame their dispensation of slavery and Jim Crow laws, enduring mental anguish and hard physical labor while maintaining a rich spiritual life of knowing God as their Savior. The relationships I formed with my great-grandparents were essential in creating my identity. What I believed and valued in life originated with them. Their rearing infused beliefs and values about God, family, gender roles, etc., potentially shaping my future. Accordingly, my mother and father were one with their parents' collective consciousness, as I am one with my parents. These relationships forge a collective consciousness in my family unit that one passes down from generation to generation. Therefore, my family unit's shared consciousness created a self-conscious daughter three times over—a daughter to my mother and father, a granddaughter to their parents, and a great-granddaughter to their parents.

I knowingly observed all three generations' mindsets and how they shaped and impacted my life even today. As an adult, I exhibit

Living Your Legacy Of Greatness

the gentleness of my "Big Gramma." I posture the boldness of my Nana. I maintain the strength and tenacity of my mother. I present my father's silliness and playfulness, the knowledge of the power of prayer, and the joy of cooking from my paternal and maternal Grandmothers. The list is not exhaustive of the things I gleaned from my lineages. As I matured and my consciousness expanded, I chose to shed several things. I decided to shed some tools from my spiritual tool belt like David because I could not prove them. It is prudent to keep what works and let go of what does not as we go along in life. Unfortunately, we tend to hold on to what we are comfortable with, even if it is not working toward our good. The ideas and perceptions yield hurtful, lonely, angry, bitter, and so on.

However, we keep them nevertheless because we are used to them. We go to the extent of coddling, nurturing, and creating offshoots of those ideas and precepts to pass on to the next generation. They are the proverbial clothing inappropriate for Kingdom living. If we desire a different result, we must purpose ourselves to reflect, evaluate, and excavate the root causes of our issues that we do not want. Then, once the reason enters our awareness, we can purposefully change our approach, modify our perspective, and transform our results, letting that unproductive and potentially harmful attire go. When we no longer desire to keep them and see the benefits of throwing them away, we will discard them, never to pick them up again.

I was especially fond of my maternal great-grandmother, Hattie-Mae Fitts. She was one of the sweetest people that ever lived. She was soft-spoken and meek. Recalling her rocking me in her rocking chair and telling stories comes easy. It was a sad day for the entire family when she passed away. However, I knew the Lord blessed her with a long life according to His word. I still reminisce, over four decades later, some of her conversations with me. For instance, one day, when I was about ten, I ran into my grandmother's house to use the bathroom. My great-grandmother,

Markeithia Lavon Silver

affectionately called "Big-Gramma," beckoned me to come to her room.

As I stood in the doorway, she held up a tall blue Tupperware cup and placed her finger on the cup's side, indicating how much water she wanted. She said, "I need to take my medicine, baby; bring me this much water." Removing the cup gently from her hand, I headed for the kitchen. She said softly, "Don't forget to let it run awhile." "Yes, ma'am, I will," I responded. As I awaited the water temperature to reach her desired cold, I stood there watching her rocking in her chair with this glowing, peaceful look. After the water was at the right feel, I held the cup under the faucet and allowed just enough to reach where her finger had instructed. I turned to go back into her room, and she said, in her southern vernacular, "Pass Gramma, her straw baby." I reached for the straw and held the cup for her to sip just enough to take her medication. When she finished, she gazed at me and sweetly said quietly, "If I had a quarter, I would pay you." "You don't need to pay me, Big-Gramma; I will get you water anytime," I replied. She took my little hands and said, "The Lord's gonna' bless you, the Lord's gonna bless you." She pulled me close to kiss me on my forehead, and I smiled, as I always did, and went back to play with my friends. You see, she did this every time I gave her water. About three years later, she went home to glory. I miss her today, but I remember this story as if it occurred yesterday. I will *always* cherish it. Not only does it remind me of her loving self, but it also reminds me that I am the seed of the righteous. More importantly, she blessed me each time she touched and kissed my forehead.

Whenever I feel down, I remind myself what my Big Gramma' said, and my spirit lifts. It never fails. As I write these words, jubilant tears flow down my face. To be sure, the Lord truly has blessed my life and continues to do so. Each time I was in a situation testing my faith, I would cry out to the Lord, reminding Him that I was a righteous seed and that I knew He would not forsake me nor allow

Living Your Legacy Of Greatness

me to beg for bread. I passed this same concept to my children. Although they are the fourth generation from her, they know her by name and the blessing she bestowed upon me, their children, and their children's children.

I suppose you might be wondering why I am telling you this story. I partly recount this story because it is precious to my heart. On the other hand, I wanted to show you, gentle reader, that I am a part of a collective consciousness that stems from the people who raised my parents who reared me. As my great-grandmothers and great-grandfathers nurtured my mother and father, they trained me with the same values and etiquette. They would posture a particular character that engraved certain traits upon my subconscious that governed how I saw the world, even until today. My children feel the effects of what my parents, grandparents, and great-grandparents taught me. Some things change over the years, but much of what they pass on to the next generation creates thought patterns and perceptions of engaging and dealing with life. In turn, those thought patterns develop perceptions that dictate how I/we encounter life. These patterns form a dialogue within our mind, a script dictating our role in this play called Life. As we walk about this road called Life, we converse with ourselves. We glean thought patterns and strategies from previous experiences that cultivate and shape how we approach the world. Whenever faced with a challenge, I remind myself of my great-grandmother's words. Her words create a powerful stance within me, generating an atmosphere of victory by what I know and believe.

Conversely, experiences can also adversely affect my thinking about what others taught me in my tender years. These reference points potentially underscore how I feel about myself and the world. Parents, mentors, pastors, teachers, and persons in authority over children must take their impact on the tender minds of children seriously. What the current generation imparts to the next generation impacts their trajectory in the future. Children regurgitate and reflect on their nurture and nature until God changes them by renewing their minds. If we want them to do better than us, we must adequately prepare them to ascend and not descend.

As we mature, we must understand that we speak to ourselves repeatedly. We must reach the point of understanding that we train ourselves to think about life and all its challenges based upon a narrative created from family values, mores, life experiences, and collective consciousnesses of generations before us. You heard the adage, "Tell a person that they are ugly long enough; they will eventually believe it." It matters not if what someone tells you is the truth or a lie; the more you hear it, the more it will stamp itself upon your psyche, and you will eventually believe what others profess to you, even the narratives you decree to yourself. It will never affect you if you do not buy into what others say about you. However, your mind is forever changed once you invest in what others say about you. I like how Dr. Martin King, Jr. says, "A man cannot ride your back unless it is bent." In other words, if you stand erect, that man cannot ride your back. Once you stand up for yourself, others' words cannot ride you or guide you by their words' yoke. The key is to align your thoughts with what God has said about you and shed the rest!

Do you remember the children of Israel and Goliath? Do you recall what psychological battle David resisted before his fight with Goliath? If not, reread the previous chapter: *Expect to Do More.* As the world revolves, those thought patterns readjust but remain unchanged unless you deliberately change them. Nonetheless, beloved, there is hope! We can trace the root cause of every thought, go back to move forward, and change our perception—changing our lives' outcomes for the betterment of all society. It may seem daunting, but it is well worth the journey!

Most people from the older generations, and some of today, say our children are mere reflections of ourselves. When I was a child, the adults in my grandmother's age group believed that

Living Your Legacy Of Greatness

"Children are to be seen and not heard." I suspect that the value of that was allowing you to listen to the wisdom that adults spoke among the elder folk. Additionally, the adults wanted to protect the children from adult matters, keeping them from growing up too fast. If my grandmother saw a child being unruly, she would say, "If that momma were to do x, y, and z..., that child would not act like that." Her friends would reply, "Mm hum, Myrtle, you are right." In their opinion, children mirrored what went on in the home. Whatever the dominant thought pattern was, that is what the children exhibited. This concept is still salient today. However, my point is that we are an extension of what we come to know as ourselves: the identity we create due to the influences of nature and nurture. Through collective consciousness, we manifest and reflect our experiences, thoughts, and beliefs that stem primarily from our upbringing. Of course, it is more complicated than what I am mentioning here. We all know and can argue the possibility of other influences shaping who we are. Nonetheless, we must embrace the opportunity to reflect upon the Kingdom's dominant thought pattern and live a life of greatness if we dare.

Therefore, I submit that we come from eternity, representing greatness, and should behave as great as we are from eternity. When God spoke from His council of Wisdom, He spoke from a Unified Consciousness (Deuteronomy 6:4) when He said, "Let Us make man in Our image after Our likeness." Accordingly, Beloved, it sounds like we come from that same Consciousness that spoke at the beginning of the world. Guess what? The "Us" Spirit is still saying it. If the "Us" Spirit of God were not declaring these things, we would cease to exist. As I behaved, I was a Silver/Fitts/ Hines, and so on; people knew who I was by how I exhibited and projected myself. Jesus told his disciples in John 13:34-35, "That they love one another, as he has loved them. By this (showing of unconditional love), the world will know that (you dwell in the realm of greatness in alignment with the Father, as I am in alignment with the Father—a united/collective consciousness) you are my disciples that you love one another."

As a child, whenever people saw me playing outside, they knew I was Myrtle's granddaughter by how I responded to them. When I traveled to North Carolina in the summers to stay with my paternal grandmother, Mayolia, her church folk knew I was Mayolia's granddaughter. Being the granddaughter of the Church-mother does get you some privileges, but it constrains how you behave. I knew what perks came with being the granddaughter of a Church-mother because I understood the role required of me as her granddaughter. Moreover, as a child of a great woman, I strove to make her proud, among others. When we realize where we come from, we will begin to behave in a like manner. Furthermore, we will act in a way that is pleasing in His sight. Jesus said: "By this, humanity shall know that you are my disciples."

Oh, boy! The rewards for behaving within the value system of a Church-mother's child would be homemade pineapple/coconut cake, sweet potato pie, collard greens, a pot roast that would water in my mouth, and much more. I *knew* who and to whom I belonged and governed myself accordingly. We do not behave in the spirit of excellence because we do not *know* we are a part of greatness. Once we become conscious of the fact that we are a part of the Greatest Entity on earth and the cosmos, we will begin to live as such. Once we start to live as such, we will unlock the many blessings that the Scripture refers to in *I Corinthians* 2:9, "Eye hath not seen, nor ear heard, neither entered into the heart of man, the things which God hath prepared for them that love Him." Did you hear that? Exceeding abundance is what Paul is interpreting the Scriptures to say. Wow!

I looked forward to the summers I would go to my grandmother's house because I imagined the great cooking I would receive, the beautiful scenery, sitting under the sleeping willow tree in her yard that kept us cool in the summer heat, listening to the crickets at night,

Living Your Legacy Of Greatness

and the phenomenal solitude. I was always excited to learn that I was going to her house. I enjoyed the stillness and the quietness of the night. "That is when the Lord talks to you," she would tell me. My feeling of enjoyment, my vision, and my thoughts of experience from prior visits created a jubilant, memorable time that I shall never forget. I *knew* I was her granddaughter. My parents told me I was her granddaughter. I accepted the notion of belonging to the Silver/Fitts/Hines family by faith. My feelings about being a part of my family had something to do with it; however, I *knew* I belonged because of how they treated me and the bond established from my childhood. Likewise, we *know* we belong to God by our relationship with Him.

As young children often do, I can affectionately recall when my sister and cousins would get upset with one another. Whenever we would get out of line, my 'Nana' would say, "Blood is thicker than mud. No matter how you slice it, you share the same blood running through your veins." This mantra somehow would reconcile our differences. She would also instruct us to hug one another when we were angry, assisting us in looking beyond the situation and seeing the importance of family. It worked. We are grown up and living our own lives, but we are there regardless of the circumstances if we are in trouble. Taught to posture the importance of family and other values that remain until now, we cherish each other. As parents, we teach these same principles to our children. Because of the teachings my grandparents embedded in me, they are a part of my children's lives. I indoctrinate them into the collective consciousness by teaching them; they mentally and emotionally know my grandparents through me.

You can use this same principle to lay hold of the legacy Jesus handed us. Our family, friends, community, and the world know the Christ-Spirit bequeathed to us by the Lord. Jesus instructed the Disciples to "Go forth unto all the land and preach the Kingdom." ~ Matthew 28:19. In his prayer unto the Father, Jesus, just before

Markeithia Lavon Silver

his death, highlighted his oneness with us, as he was one with the Father. In his words, Jesus says, in John 17:21-23, "That they all may be one as Thou, Father art in Me, and I in Thee, that they also may be one in Us...And the glory which Thou gavest Me, I give them; that they may be one, even as We are one: I in them, and Thou in Me that they may be made perfect in one...." Jesus's vision of unification in the Spirit included all of us as one unified consciousness ~ St. John 17. Jesus was the epitome of oneness with the Father. He desired that we be likeminded "all speaking the same thing and *that* there be no divisions among [us], but *that* [we] be perfectly joined together in the same mind and the same judgment" ~ *I Corinthians* 1:10.

In chapter two, I briefly mentioned the social theorist Herbert Mead. Mead contends that the socialization process includes taking on other people's roles to learn their behavior, thereby mimicking what we see, altering and adjusting as we go along, and striving for the best result. I utilized David as an example of this in the 23rd Psalms.

As we take on the other's roles, we create what I refer to as vision building. Mead calls it the *generalized other*. This collective consciousness, according to Mead, exists before you. As you know, God existed before the beginning of the world before our human selves. When you enter the world, this collective consciousness overtakes you, which grooms and shapes your behavior. I must add here that this overtaking is by choice. You might encounter minor influences along the way. However, when you manifest the complete fullness of who you are, there must be complete submission to the unified consciousness of the Kingdom. Without conformity to Kingdom thinking's unified consciousness, you will continue to receive dribbles of your blessings. When you remove the proverbial knots from the waterline, you will receive the fullness and flow of what God has in store for you. Adam exhibited this

Living Your Legacy Of Greatness

God-consciousness in the Garden *before* disobeying God: calling the diverse animals into existence.

According to Herbert Mead, "Human interaction emerges from the vocal gestures which give rise to significant gestures or symbols. Mead was interested in developing linguistic capacity and the unique feature of the human mind to utilize symbols."[13] Symbolic interaction is the social process that occurs within society because of the *internalization of meanings* and language use. Until you internalize the meanings Jesus laid out for us, you merely exist in the Kingdom and do not live or thrive in it. He came that you might live to exceed your concept of life! "The behavior of an individual can be understood [by the performance] of the whole social group of which [they are] a member...."[14] This observance is what Jesus was referring to when he said, "Love one another as I love you that the world might know that you are My Disciples" ~ St. John 13:34. Your behavior projects a model to live. Onlookers understand your behavior in terms of Kingdom behavior, and you are projecting from a place of the Kingdom's values. When you behave contrary to Kingdom principles, you subvert the message of Christ to the observer ~ *II Timothy* 2:14. The world becomes confused when you operate from any other position. Therefore, we must strive to take on the role of the Christ-Spirit to understand who we are as God's Children. In this lies the challenge. Do I continue to live like a pauper or learn to live like a prince or princess? When you choose to live as God's child, your life will transform, and the unveiling of your queen/kingship will manifest.

As mentioned above, Mead asserts that the social (collective consciousness) precedes the individual mind. For social psychology, "the whole (society) is prior to the part (the individual), not the part to the whole; and the part is explained in terms of the whole, not the whole in terms of the part or parts."[15] Individuals adjust among each other "through the communications—by gestures on the lower plane of human evolution and by significant symbols

Markeithia Lavon Silver

(gestures which possess meanings and are hence more than mere substitute stimuli) on the higher planes of human evolution."[16] In other words, when individuals act upon an object, they take the perspective of others towards that object, giving it meaning. For the socialization of Kingdom living to take hold and continue, the leaders must rise and become who God calls them to be. *We are one with God!* The world, even us, is groaning for our true manifestation of our God-ness. We must utilize the symbols that Christ left us to perpetuate the representation of our God-selves. The question becomes, *what are we communicating to others and ourselves?* We must change how we speak and think if we aspire to share greatness on every level. Our thoughts are seeds. The Bible says, "As a wo/man thinks in their heart, so is s/he." We become what we think with passion! Passion invokes belief, and belief invokes be-life, and bam, manifestations of thoughts dictated and focused upon in our mind. Social psychologists refer to this as a self-fulfilling prophecy.

To be sure, you will discover it takes time for some to catch on. Until others grasp these concepts of greatness, you may leave them where they stand. We can find this example in Jesus. Please turn with me to Mark 5:35-41. It is important to note that Jesus notices that some are not on the level to accomplish the deep things of God—for the "deep calls unto the deep" ~ Psalms 42:7. That is not to say that they will never achieve the level of greatness. However, it will take some more time than others. We are to be patient. If we are strong, "we are to bear the infirmity of the weak" ~ Romans 1:1. Notice what happens when Jesus gets the news that a man's daughter is dead. He first says to them in verse 36, "Be not afraid, only believe." Then, in the next verse, he forbids anyone except Peter, James, and John to accompany him.

When you attempt to keep a positive attitude, moving in the direction of change for the better, you do not need any doubters or negative energy around. I can recall my godmother telling me, "I

Living Your Legacy Of Greatness

don't like being in the company of anyone doubtful of what God can do. If you allow them to stay around, they will turn you suspicious of yourself." She often told me, "You cannot tell everyone what God has revealed or will do for you. The deep calls unto the deep. Everyone grows in stages of their faith."

Do not allow your mind to fool you; the energy of your thoughts is exceptionally poignant. For example, if you go to a funeral, you can feel the sadness in the room. Albeit natural, nevertheless, the energy of despair is evident. When Jesus arrived, he observed, "people weeping and wailing loudly." He then asked why they were weeping and making a commotion, "The girl is only sleeping," he said. They began to laugh, doubting his conviction. Their lack of faith went contrary to his statement. Therefore, he put them out because of their unbelief. It is notable how the demeanor of the people changed. They immediately stopped weeping and causing a stir because Jesus's declaration was such that they forgot the sadness. They began the inappropriate behavior of laughing at his surety. Isn't this amazing? You can be on your deathbed, and the ones who love you will start to miss you before you are gone. As soon as you declare the opposite of what they see, they will forget about missing you and begin to ridicule you for your faith in the Infinite Power of God. Do not allow this to happen! Use Jesus as your model. Put them O-U-T!

This story conveys several things to the reader. First, only a few can elevate to where you are in your oneness with the Creator. Jesus allowed only a few to follow him. Second, when you realize the perception of those around you is not in harmony with yours, put them out of your mental and spiritual circle, O-U-T, out! Third, do not allow their venom to poison or deteriorate your faith. My maternal grandfather would say, "Always find yourself around people of equal or greater knowledge than you to facilitate your growth." Even as strong and mighty as Jesus is, he does not want to contend with the negative, energy-consuming thoughts in the

Markeithia Lavon Silver

room's atmosphere. Their perception and negative energy, where the child lay, was like a dark, foggy mist. Even when the sun is shining, if the fog is thick enough, it will delay air flights, cruise ships, and automobile drivers because of the lack of visibility. Fourth, negative and doubtful energy clouds your spiritual judgment—veiling your image and likeness of the Creator. We become fixated on the fog instead of calling upon peace to lift the veil of desolation.

Additionally, you will discover that everyone reacts differently to your situation. Nonetheless, you will need to monitor who comes into your presence. Ask yourself, "Are they supporting my faith or taking away from it?" You will need your energy for healing, deliverance, prosperity, or any promise allotted to God's Children. *Directing your spirit to other matters will only deplete you in the area most needed in your situation*, whatever that might be.

Social Psychologist Herbert Mead asserts a threefold relationship between the symbol, the word associated with the symbol, and the meaning connected to the symbol perpetuating social living. "A gesture by one organism, the resultant of the social act in which the gesture is an early phase, and the response of another organism to the gesture…so that [you] give meaning [to the gesture] in terms of response. Meaning is implicit—if not always explicit."[17] *Not only does connotation affect the organism's responses, but it shapes and creates new replies.* "A gesture on the part of one organism in any given social act calls out a [universal] response on the part of another organism, which is directly related to the action of the first organism and its outcome… The mechanism of meaning is thus present in the social act before the emergence of consciousness or awareness of meaning occurs… Symbolism constitutes objects not constituted before."[18] Wow! As my parents and grandparents told me how to behave, I grew in the meaning of those thought processes as I continued to perform accordingly. Then, I began to act subconsciously, unaware of my actions—it became second

Living Your Legacy Of Greatness

nature to me, unsuspecting of the effects of those actions upon my psyche. I may not understand that your words of ugliness toward me will create in me a sense of unsightliness within the image of myself at this moment; however, when I become a wo/man, I will believe and act upon, from a subconscious position that "I am ugly." This thought process will perpetuate through the people I meet and my life circumstances. On and on until I say to myself, "Enough is enough!" This cycle will continue until I stop speaking these things to myself. Are you at that place where it is enough?

Let us pause for a moment and look at the dualities of your consciousness. Get your journal and entitle this page, *My Dual Consciousness*. Write down some traditions you learned in one column and still contemplate today. In another column, write some of the things people told you about yourself in your childhood that you still hold onto today, maybe even unaware. In the last column, write the thought process you want to believe. You may utilize the affirmations in the back portion of the book, putting your spin on them.

Markeithia Lavon Silver

My Dual Consciousness

Traditions	Things/Definitions About Myself that Others Told as a Young Person	What I Want to Believe
"Spare the rod; spoil the child." However, construed as an instrument to inflict pain on the body to bring about obedience, the "rod" sometimes fostered abuse. However, in some cases, the rod was construed as an instrument of verbal instruction. If you disobeyed your parents, your parent immediately chastised you. Your choice of punishment depended on the mindset of your parents.	You are bad, out of control, and in need of correction. You are not worth a thing.	**I am good as God says I am, and I am *who* He says I am to be! I am called to be a Saint of God! I am beloved of God! I am His treasure!**
Those in authority over you made you repeatedly clean until you got it right.	I cannot do anything right. I am always messing things up.	**I accomplish all that I set out to do in the fullness of Joy.**
Children were to be seen and not heard.	Self-expression is a challenge—no one wants to hear my feelings; what I say does not matter.	**My thoughts align with the Inspiration of God's Spirit, which is full of Wisdom, Love, and Peace. The sound of my voice is easily entreated.**

Deep-diving into your past, for some, may complicate this process. Uncovering some of these hidden thought patterns may conjure up strong emotions. Let us pray:

Abba, Father, Matchless King, an Ever-Present Help in time of trouble, He who calls us friend, we humbly come into Your presence. You called us by name. We are Yours. You promised when we passed through the waters, You would be there; and through the rivers, they would not overtake us: when we walked through the fire, we would not be burned; for You are with us. You instructed us to forget the things of the past. You promised to do a new thing, that You will blot out our transgressions and make a way for us in the wilderness. We trust You in this process, Lord.

We glorify Your holy name. We thank You for the blood sacrifice on Calvary. We know You nailed our infirmities to the cross, that our peace is upon You, and by Your stripes, we are healed. We thank you for the breaker's anointing. We thank You for deliverance. We thank You for healing the inward parts of our hearts and minds. We thank You for victory at the gate of our enemies. Father, we ask that You touch the minds of those reading these words. We ask that You deliver them from all unrighteousness, from their past traumas. Cause them to know that You are on the proverbial boat with them, and there is nothing to fear. We speak peace even now in their homes, jobs, and families. We command peace to be still in the mighty name of Yēšûa (Jesus). Amen, and amen.

If you are having difficulty, I encourage you to talk it through with someone with professional experience to assist you in sifting through your thoughts. If you, gentle reader, are stuck, know that the Infinite Power of El-Shaddai, the Eternal God of the heavens and the earth, the True and Living God, is with you and longs to release you from the terror and fear of your past. You *ARE NOT* alone! He is ever waiting to tenderly touch your heart with the balm of His healing hand, freeing you from the bondage of your past and cleansing your heart space in preparation for greatness. Your history does not define you, and Hope is ever ready to instill Peace in your mind.

Let us continue with what Mead says about imagination. For Mead, taking the role of the other is imagining oneself from the

Markeithia Lavon Silver

other person's perspective. This process allows the self to be the subject simultaneously (the I) with the object (the Me). For Mead, language and symbols are the vehicles one can imagine oneself from another perspective. "Language does not simply symbolize a situation or object which is already there in advance; it makes possible the existence or the appearance of that situation or object, for it is a part of the mechanism whereby [we create] the situation or object... Language simply lifts out of the social process a situation which is logically or implicitly there already."[19] In other words, like attracts in kind. The language will only present itself in a way that already exists in the individual's perceptions—so you act, feel, and are.

In stark contrast to these socially constructed symbols, most of us learn more than abundance from applying Jesus's life to ours; Jesus's blessing of two fish and five loaves of bread to feed five thousand is foreign to us. *He displayed the Kingdom's outlook of plenty, not an earthly view of lack.* We must incorporate this symbol of more than enough into our daily lives. Suppose we internalize this principle more when faced with challenges of lack. In that case, we can immediately supplant the challenge with what Jesus taught us: "My God *shall* supply my need according to *His* riches in Glory" ~ Phil. 4:19.

Moreover, God supplies our needs according to the riches of *His* glory. His blessings sustain you physically. *His* Spirit strengthens your inner god-selves ~ Eph. 3:16. Furthermore, and equally important is the term "shall." This term is absolute and leaves God no room to change His mind. In other words, if there is a need, God *SHALL* meet it! That is wonderful news! We only need to thank Him if a need arises, for we *know* He will fulfill it no matter the situation or circumstance. With prayer and thanksgiving, make our request known!

In addition to taking on the role of the other, Mead asserts, "the 'self' is purely cognitive, and feelings are not involved [in the

Living Your Legacy Of Greatness

developing of the self]."[20] In other words, taking on the knowledge that Jesus left us as examples and ambassadors on the earth has nothing to do with our minds, feelings, or emotions. This statement might seem contrary to what I said about aligning vision, thoughts, and emotional state of mind, but *this* component differs. It is an act of our will to accept Kingdom thinking. However, it is an exercise of our faith to trust the Kingdom's social process *without* our feelings coming into play. Specifically, this acceptance of Kingdom status is where our imaginations should rule. For instance, "Now, faith is the substance of things hoped for the evidence of things not seen" ~ Hebrews 11:1. We are to use our imaginations *and* faith to see beyond this earthly realm, just as Jesus did, regardless of our feelings. Of course, the more joy we can muster along with our faith and thoughts, the more it will strengthen the substratum/faith we present to God for manifestation.

To understand this concept, look at a picture of something that interests you. The impression is not the item itself but a representation *of* the image. The photo appears real because we tell ourselves it is accurate. The substratum (mirrored reflection) is a natural phenomenon because we *believe* it is genuine. More importantly, we *know* it is confirmed by faith. We even dream of owning it. We purposely conjure and structure our thoughts, creating an illustration within our mind and presenting that vision to God. The *Bible* puts it this way, "Calling those things that are not as though they were" ~ Romans 4:7. This, gentle reader, is an example of holding the vision by faith until it materializes in the physical. However, we must strive to create a disciplined thought process, creating the dreams we desire in alignment with His will for our lives for God's glory and honor. As God's Children, we cannot arbitrarily create thoughts and visions yielding undesirable manifestations, unaware of how we arrived there. The arbitrary and capriciousness in creating impulsive visions must stop for the

Markeithia Lavon Silver

benefit of all humanity. The Church must begin to ascent to its rightful place as His own.

"The organized community or social group that gives the individual his unity of self can be called 'the generalized other.' [Typically], the generalized other is the attitude of the whole community."[21] Mead concludes that individuals in this complex cooperative process of activities and institutional functions are *constantly becoming* through the shaping and reshaping of the generalized other [tweaking of vision-building—evolving into who we are as God-Children]. "It is in the form of the *generalized other* that the social process influences the behavior of the individuals involved in it and carrying it on. The community exercises control over the conduct of its members; for it is in this form that the social process enters as a determining factor into the individual's thinking [perpetuating socialization.]."[22]

Jesus's way of thinking should take us over, affecting our processing of life's issues. As Jesus's way of thinking transcends our thought processes, we will eventually think, move, and behave *like* Jesus. If we allow Him and abide in the Seat of Power, Jesus purges us by the Word of our ills and the morass of this world that haunts us ~ St. John 15:3-5. This process begins with our faith evolving to a place of knowing. If we can perceive the greatness of God, displayed by Jesus as our example, we can achieve the birthright of our greatness. If we bind His word upon our hearts, we will live ~ Proverbs 7:1-3.

Moreover, according to Hebrews 11:6, "*But without faith, it is impossible to please Him: for s/he, that cometh to God must first believe that He is and that He is a rewarder of them that diligently seek Him*" is our guidepost. In this process, Mead's reference to the generalized other and its capacity to take us over and mold and shape us into individuals achieving the necessary goal of socialization is synonymous with us being taken over by our capability to the vision-build desired behavior of Kingdom social living. According

Living Your Legacy Of Greatness

to Mead, our emotions do not play a role in accepting the social norms of our community; we accept them as existing rules of our nature that guide us as a lamp elucidates this path we call life. This notion of obtaining them is the same as Paul's notion of accepting God to *be.*

To receive the reward, which is greatness manifested, we must first believe that He *is.* "Is" is indicative of being. When we say, "My mother/father *is* home." We understand my mother/father can be found in *that* building I refer to as home. When John communicated the language of God's being, he told us that we could find Him wherever we needed Him.

Nevertheless, we must conceive *a* God who loves and cares for us to find Him where we need Him to be. I will repeat that. *We will see God wherever we need Him to be! To find Him where we need Him to be, we must conceive a God who loves and cares for us to find Him where we need Him.* Similarly, God told Moses, "I am THAT I AM…tell the children of Israel that I AM sent you." In other words, God is saying, I am whatever you need me to be (*THAT,* I AM). I am a friend (*THAT,* I AM). I am abundance (*THAT,* I AM). I am healing (*THAT,* I AM). You could say that God is whatever you need God to be for eternity. In Isaiah 9:6, God is "*Wonderful, Counsellor, The mighty God, The everlasting Father, The Prince of Peace.*" In Song of Solomon 2:1, He is the "*Rose of Sharon and the Lily of the Valleys.*" If we cannot conceive a God in our mind's eye (imagination), this representation of who God is means zilch.

In part, our undeveloped imaginations are to blame, and we *fear* our greatness. Not because we shall do remarkable things but because we do not know what we will do with our power, which frightens us. The other part is that we do not believe that He *Is.* We have fallen so far away from God's presence that we create Him in *our* image instead of vice versa. Since the Fall, we have heaped on carnality to the point that we cannot enter or lay hold on the

Markeithia Lavon Silver

legacy of greatness left to us by Christ. The acceptance of who God is begins Kingdom socialization. We must accept it without contemplation or forethought and without feeling. We must choose as an act of our will and exercise our faith that the Lord *is*! He is a rewarder to those who diligently seek Him! ~ Hebrews 11.

My philosophical friends would disagree because one must utilize the *principle of sufficient reason* to conclude that God exists. Well, the socialization process does not work that way. A social fact does not need proof that it exists—it merely does, especially when it can be measured and defined by the function of the whole. Further, as social theorist Herbert Mead puts it, "The whole (society) is prior to the part (the individual), not the part to the whole; and the part is explained in terms of the whole, not the whole in terms of the part [or parts]."[23] In other words, you are the part, and God is the whole. God explains and sets the tone of Kingdom social living, *not you.* He sets the standards. Then, those standards take hold of you, and you follow suit. Simultaneously, those standards mold you into your greatness.

I mentioned in chapter one that we need Jesus to utilize as a mirror to emulate. Jesus was the express image of God, and He mirrored what we might change in our lives and reflected what *was* to come. This concept is a paradox. However, we become stuck on our deficiencies, not our potential greatness. The hope is that Jesus lets us know that we are *one with him, as he is one with the Father*, and the actuality of greatness is only a choice away. This notion of greatness brings the fullness of triumphant joy. Jesus desired that our joy be complete. Specifically, he tells us in John 15:11 and 16:24, "These things (symbols, signs to live by) I spoke unto you, that my joy might remain in you (live as I lived to reach your entitlement of sonship), *and* that your joy might be full…Hitherto you asked nothing in my name: ask and ye shall receive, that your joy might be full (I will give you what you ask for that you will see

Living Your Legacy Of Greatness

who and what you are to my Father and me, and what He created you to be—great)!"

This jubilee that Jesus was talking about is the process of fulfillment within the believer's life, spawning from the knowledge and understanding of knowing *who* you are. This place is where you are unrestricted in receiving Love from the Father. There is no fear, lack, or brokenness in this posture of greatness. Expressly, "There is no fear in (God's) Love. But perfect Love casts out fear..." ~ I John 4:18. Living from this realm of Love, you are nurtured spiritually, emotionally, and physically. This perfected Love is the underpinning of your being. This Love enables you to stand tall as "more than a conqueror above all circumstances" ~ Romans 8:37. In this place of Sonship (son/daughters of God—His most holy treasure), you can view the sea billows as cleansing waves, as the very Love of God saturates you in His grace. Your spectacles change, and you are now equipped to sing sweetly within your spirit, *"I can see clearly now... All the dark clouds that had me blind...It's going to be a bright, bright, bright sunshiny day."* Why? You now know *who* you are and what God created you to be. Great!

This declaration is not to say that trials will not come. In fact, according to Romans 8:28, "Trials come to make you strong." God designed trials and tribulations to invoke a sense of creative power within you. God devised trials as tools to burn the impurities off your soul, and when you overcome the tribulation, when you master the test, when you are converted, strengthen your brothers and sisters ~ Luke 22:32. These tests allow you to train your mind on what you desire. If you will, the contrast, knowing what you want enables you to focus and envision what you want precisely. This explanation is just a fraction of why they work for your good. You would not know what you truly desire if tests and trials did not come. The proof of this is in *I Corinthians* 10:13, which states, "God is faithful, who *will not* suffer (allow) you to be tempted (tested) above that ye are able (power over)."

Markeithia Lavon Silver

In other words, God attends to you so that He will not allow you to be tested above that which you do not maintain power over, not just any power but explosive power *(Dunamis)*. It is worth noting that God winks at our ability to subdue and master our minds in His conversation with Cain before the first murder. God says to Cain, "If thou doest well, shalt thou not be accepted? And if thou doest not well, sin lieth at the door. And unto thee *shall be* his desire, and thou shalt rule over him. ~ Genesis 4:7. I love the *Berean Study Bible's* interpretation, which says, "If you do what is right, will you not be accepted? But if you refuse to do what is right, sin is crouching at your door; it desires you, but you must master it." Here, God lets us know that we must master, overcome, and subdue our thoughts so we may lay hold to our dominion. My pastor always says, "Dominate your thoughts, dominate your mind." If we master our thoughts, we will be like Peter in converting his position from inadequacy to a posture of greatness. When we are converted, strengthen our sisters and brothers. ~ Luke 22:32. Jesus rose from the grave with all power in His hands over the enemy. He passed that power over to us. ~ Matthew 28:18-20. *See also* Colossians 2:15.

We retain the capability to eradicate a thought from the mind! We hold the ability to resurrect ourselves in Christ Jesus! We possess the power to choose what path we shall take! We also retain the skill to fix our mind on an object and obtain it! If we conceive what we desire, perceive what we want, and align our thoughts with God's thoughts, we can accomplish it!

The word *able* in Greek comes from *dunamis,* which means power. This power stems from on High and is a part of our make-up as God's Children. The sooner we come to *know* our oneness, the sooner we can exhibit the power of that oneness for the better of humanity. Also, Romans 5:3 and James 1:3, respectively, state that "Tribulation worketh patience and patience, experience, and experience, hope, and hope maketh not ashamed; because the love

Living Your Legacy Of Greatness

of God is shed abroad in our hearts by the Holy Ghost which is given unto us." As mentioned, we engage in the experience that teaches us and provides a distinction. These differences we receive versus what we desire trigger our creative ability to envision a different outcome that changes our position. With this knowledge and understanding, we develop hope that removes condemnation or shame. Because of this abiding hope, "there is, therefore, now, no condemnation to them which are in Christ (that trusts in Him), who walk not after the flesh but after the Spirit." Posturing this mindset positions us as overcomers ~ Romans 8:1.

LIVE IN YOUR SPACE, CHILD OF GOD, AND POSTURE GREATNESS BECAUSE THAT IS WHO YOU ARE!

I will end this chapter with an old familiar refrain—a hymn by C. Austin Miles that speaks of the joy of oneness with God and another prose entitled *A Place Like No Other.*

"I come to the garden alone, while the dew is still on the roses; And the voice I hear, falling on my ear, the Son of God discloses. And He walks with Me, and He talks with Me, and He tells Me I am His own. And the Joy We share as We tarry there, None other has ever known."

A Place Like No Other

What do you see?

Are you able to see what I see?

I see a bench in a garden filled with beautiful flowers. As I walk along, the fragrance speaks to my weary soul and lifts me to a place of rejuvenation. If you listen carefully, you will hear the birds singing a melody of joy.

What do you see?

I see a crystal-clear waterfall gently falling from above into the earth of my soul, satisfying my every desire. This place of peace

Markeithia Lavon Silver

and harmony draws me—to God's bosom. Are you drawn to this place? As I stand beneath the waterfall, it tenderly touches my soul; I feel the rays of the Sun softly touching my face, and the calm breeze whisks through my hair.

This Waterfall is where I live (in my mind) today. Will you join me?

CHAPTER FOUR

LIVING WITH THE MIND OF GOD

"Let <u>This Mind</u> be in you, which was <u>also</u> in Christ Jesus."
~ Philippians 2:5.

—Paul

"Let every man be fully persuaded <u>in his/her mind</u>."
~ Romans 14:5c.

—Paul

"The whole creation groaneth and travaileth in pain together until now. And not only they but [we] ourselves also...[are] waiting for the adoption..." ~ Romans 8:18-23.

—Paul

Ask yourself, "Do I possess all God desires for me?" You might respond, "In the spirit realm, I do." Why, then, have those desires not revealed themselves? What is the cause of your manifested desires on hold? What spiritual strongholds quench the fulfillment of what your imagination proclaims?

Do you believe in your vision?

Markeithia Lavon Silver

Did you decree and declare your vision according to Kingdom rules? Are you excited at the mention of your dreams coming to pass?

Did you cultivate the vision with the thoughts necessary to enrich the soil of your mind?

Did you weed out the tares that attempt to choke, delay, and destroy your vision?

Did you accurately assess your sync-ability factor?

Line up your thoughts (feelings and beliefs) with your image and watch the All-knowing El-Shaddai God move on your behalf. Become excited about your idea and your blessing, and then thank God for His benefits towards you as Jesus did at Lazarus's gravesite. God heard you. Now, watch the Holy Spirit remove the grave clothes off what you thought was dead and manifest your desire for greatness!

We must take on the proverbial role of the Christ-Spirit if we want to do great exploits. The Mind that was in Jesus must be in us. We must receive *"this* Mind." We must *reflect* this mind. We must embrace this Mind and think it is not robbery to become Christ's expressed image in the earth. Paul encourages us to be like-minded and *in agreement with* the Mind of Christ. He is specific in what "mind" to take on. He does not admonish us to take on his mind or any of the Disciples' minds but take on the Christ-Spirit's Mind. The Mind of Christ opposes and counteracts the mind indoctrinated by Adam and Eve in the Garden that fateful day. Eve took on the mind of another birthed by a lie (the enemy), which ignited another kind within her soul, causing her *and* her husband's spiritual death. Jesus blotted out the handwriting of ordinances against us, which was contrary to us, and took it out of the way, nailing it to his cross. He spoiled principalities and powers; he made a shew of them openly, triumphing over them. He stole back the keys to the Kingdom and handed them to us. We are complete in Christ

~ Colossians 2:10-15, St. Matthew 16:19, and Revelation 1:18, respectively. *We are the mirrored reflection of Christ* and should manifest in kind. A mirrored image effortlessly reflects the figure precisely as it projects.

Let us look, at minimum, at what we can accomplish with a mind of oneness with the Father in Christ. With the Mind of Christ, we can take a little, bless it, and create more than enough. Do you know the story? Jesus took two fish and five loaves of bread and fed five thousand people. Preceding that, He turned water into wine. With the Mind of Christ, you can call those things that are not as though they were. Just as Jesus called forth new life in Lazarus, we too can call forth those things that are not and as though they were.

This Mind of Abundance, also found in the Old Testament, is a testament to the Almighty Power of God. For example, in *I Chronicles* 29, David asked God to bless his son, Solomon. He speaks about God's glory and His many blessings during his request. In verse 19, David asks God to give Solomon a perfect heart to follow His commandments. Then, God anointed Solomon as king over Israel, and he resides on the throne instead of his father, David. While David was still alive, verse 23 says that Solomon prospered.

Furthermore, when you get to verse 25, you find that "the Lord magnified Solomon exceedingly in the sight of all Israel and bestowed upon him such royal majesty as had not been seen on any king before him in Israel." God blessed him beyond David's request. I submit that taking on the Mind of Christ will afford you the same opportunities. Afterward, *God will place you on display for the entire world to see that humanity might know you serve a mighty, powerful, and victorious God.* The wonderful thing about these blessings is that they occur long before Solomon's prayer request for wisdom. This evidence of God's blessings toward those who walk righteously before Him, in and of itself, is a testimony of God's greatness. Let us continue.

Markeithia Lavon Silver

In verse 18, David requests that God keep the notion of His greatness in the people's imagination and prepare their hearts to receive His concept of abundance. David knew that abundance and honor flowed from God, not humanity. Beloved, God created provision as a by-product of our oneness with the "Us" spirit; God is just waiting for us to take hold of what He prepared for us from the beginning. To embrace our greatness, we must *know* it is there and trust God to perform His word. We can achieve and live within our long-awaited destiny of greatness if we conceive and perceive God's magnanimity and blessings.

How can we do this? What do we need to do to claim our birthright? God is calling for our growth. First, you must choose to answer and accept the call. The Infinite Power of El-Shaddai/ God calls for the Holy Spirit's increase inside us. The "Us" Spirit is calling us to become greater! Accepting that growth does not come without due diligence on our behalf. We must turn our hearts and minds toward God, seek His face, and acknowledge and repent of our transgressions towards God and His Covenant. Recall the exercise in chapter one: *Things I am Telling Myself*? You took the time to unearth the things you believe about yourself. Well, acknowledging your sins is similar. You must admit where you are for deliverance to be at hand. If you are angry and unable to forgive, tell God about it. Addicted to food, tell Him. When you are hurting and do not know what to do, go to Him and bear your bleeding heart to the One who can heal and guide you. Frustrated by the way your life has unfolded, confess it to him. Release yourself from the things that would so easily beset you and run this race with patience ~ Hebrews 12: 1-2. Second, there is training involved and appropriate maintenance that will keep us there. We must strengthen our prayer life and intimacy with God and foster stillness, knowing He is God.

Living Your Legacy Of Greatness

He is calling for the growth of the Power of Truth on Earth. "God has called us unto liberty," my sisters and brothers ~ Galatians 5:13. Will you accept the call?

"[Did] I not tell you that you are gods?" "According to your faith be it unto you." "Let every man be persuaded in her/his mind." Everything that we desire to do begins in our mind, with imagery and thought. The imagination houses the ability to conceive the infinite Power of God's blessings and His enduring grace and mercy. Is your mind persuaded to move to greatness? Will you accept the call to greatness? Enlarge your mind to encompass your destiny of greatness!

Jesus exhibits this Power at the gravesite of Lazarus. Ask yourself, 'Did Jesus display faith, or was *his stance one of assurance posturing knowledge of the Father's abilities*?' I submit to you that it is the latter. He prayed to glorify the Father, saying, "Father, I thank Thee that Thou hast heard me. [Moreover], I knew that Thou hearest me *always*...." After Jesus prayed, He raised Lazarus. (Emphasis mine). With the Mind of the Christ-Spirit within us, we can speak with the same assurance and authority Jesus spoke in healing the sick, raising the dead, and setting the captives free. Jesus said, in John 5:19-20, "*The Son can do nothing of himself, but what He seeth the Father do*: for what things soever He doeth, these also doeth the Son. For the Father loveth the Son, *and showeth Him all things that Himself doeth*: and He will show Him greater works than these that ye may marvel." (Emphasis mine). The word *seek* in Greek is *blepo*. *Strong's Concordance* defines *blepo* as looking at (literally or figuratively), beholding, looking on or looking to, perceiving, seeing, sight, and taking heed. *Thayer's* definition identifies this word as a discerning feature of the bodily eye, to be possessed of sight, having the power to see, to gaze upon, to perceive by the senses, to discover by use, to know by experience, and metaphorically to see with the mind's eye having the power of understanding, discerning mentally, observe,

Markeithia Lavon Silver

perceive, discover, to consider, to weigh carefully, and examine. What a powerful, privileged position! When we are in the presence of God, seeking His face and placing our ears to His heart, we will receive our marching orders by *seeing* them in all of these categories mentioned.

Do you *see* it?! Jesus can do nothing of himself except what he *sees* the Father do! Jesus saw in the Spirit what the Father had done/is doing/will do with his spiritual eyes. "All power [had been] given unto him in heaven and earth" ~ Matthew 28:18. But, Jesus restrained from using his absolute power on earth that he might teach us a life of dependence and faith, a life which was to become ours in Christ. Throughout his ministry, Jesus did nothing apart from the Father. He *knew* it was offensive to God to act with personal and worldly knowledge independent of God's wisdom and instruction because he was the Son. God's will and Jesus's will are one—they worked *as* One. He taught us how operating from this seat of Power of Oneness in the Spirit wielded great power. Therefore, we *see* in our spiritual minds the things of God. Our imaginative mind, housed within our creativity given to us by God, is where everything happens. Good God from Zion! Can you imagine?! We will get there because God called the end from the beginning! ~ Isaiah 46:10.

Does this pattern of learning plus oneness sound familiar? Of course, it does! Jesus says the same thing about us. He tells us that the Holy Spirit will come and teach us, witness to us, and lead us into *all* truth. More importantly, the Holy Spirit will not speak of Himself but what He hears from the Father. Then, living with the Mind of the Christ-Spirit causes us to do great works that the world might marvel at and say, "Great is our God!" Jesus, by example, showed us how to posture greatness and live a life of oneness dependent upon God's wisdom, knowledge, skill, and understanding! I would be remiss if I did not mention that our pursuit of God affects our display of power. Unless and until we

Living Your Legacy Of Greatness

unearth fallow ground, let go of the past, and trust God, we will hinder our ability to possess the land the Lord thy God has prepared for us! We must prepare our hearts, transform our minds, and allow God to conform us to the image of His Son so that we might be the firstborn of many brethren. ~Romans 12:2, 8:29 respectively.

What does it mean to posture your greatness? The *Bible* tells us, "As Jesus *is*, so are we in this world" ~ I John 4:17. (Emphasis mine). If Jesus held a particular stance on God, we also enjoy the same capability. To posture is not an arrogant position. In fact, posturing in Christ draws from the strength of humility, pulls from the stability of God's strength, and recognizes that we can do nothing outside Him. To posture is the ability to discern within the Power necessary to sustain us, perform through us, and live in us as we travel this road called life. When you can posture as Jesus did, you will perfect your faith into a realm of knowing. *Knowing* is beyond our notion of faith. It is faith perfected.

Jesus stood at the gravesite, *knowing* he could not raise Lazarus alone. He needed the Power of Life to flow through him. To harness that power, one must be humble: "not of myself or anything I shall do, lest any wo/man should boast" ~ Ephesians 2:9. As Jesus said, "The Son can do nothing of himself, but what he sees the Father do: for what things soever He does, this also does the Son do." If this does not encourage you to immerse yourself into the reflective image of doing what you see the Father do, I do not know what will! Thus, from the space of humility, one can be confident that the Infinite Power of El-Shaddai/God of the Universe has your back. Why? We are a mirror image and likeness of the "Us" Spirit!

Conversely, when one operates from a space of pride, the Power will elude those individuals, rendering them impotent results ~ Proverbs 3:34, *See also* James 4:6. A proud heart not plugged into the Source of all Power will cause that individual to stumble and fall ~ Jeremiah 50:32. When you posture greatness, you possess the knowledge that you are a conduit by which the Power flows and not you, lest you should boast. Standing from this place and space of confidence solidifies your stance against adversity. "Greater is the Power within me than the power in worldly affairs" ~ I John 4:4. This Power strengthens you in times of weakness ~ *II Corinthians* 12:10. Specifically, the knowledge gained from these experiences enlarges your faith to a position of knowing. Ascending to a place of knowing erects a standard. Notably, that standard of knowing houses confidence, which embeds itself within an individual's psyche, creating an atmosphere of abundance. In this place, you can recall ALL the things God has done, reinforcing what God will do—now, in the present, and in the future ~ Psalms 116.

Furthermore, this confidence brings an all-abiding Peace. Even when uneducated, you stand boldly like my paternal grandmother and say, "Tell the Lord about it, and Him will fix it (excusing the vernacular)!" My paternal grandmother worked in the cotton fields and had an eighth-grade education, but she trusted the Lord in all she did. Whenever I faced a challenge, she often told me, *"Don't you worry, suga' Granma's gonna be prayin' for you, and God's gonna work it out for you. When you get home, I want you to go into your closet, drop to your knees, and tell the Lord bout' it. Him will fix it for you!"* Tears would sometimes flow as her anointing broke the yokes that were holding me down. Her words empowered me over the phone seven-hundred-and-fifty plus miles from me. She encouraged me to "keep on keeping on, holding on to God's unchanging hand." The Lord never allowed her words to fall to the ground; God worked it out each time!

My grandmother was steadfast in her stance. She *knew* God cared. Her experiences and relationship with Him solidified that. She believed God was capable of anything! God came through every time, reassuring her to continue trusting Him. She possessed a spiritual discipline that assured her of God's Providence, Provision, and Protection. He never failed her! This show of confidence is what Jesus did for the folk standing around as Lazarus came forth—His attitude of knowing produced an atmosphere worthy of revealing God's glory. We, too, can reach a level of apprehending and comprehending this level of confidence, but we must do our due diligence. After we acquire a spiritually disciplined mind, lose the garments of this world, and lay hold of the "Us" Spirit within, we will walk confidently in Christ's victory. Just as the wind blows away the chaff, leaving only the wheat, so too will the Word of God burn away anything contrary to His Law: His faithfulness, His grace and mercies, His love and kindness, and His provision and protection. His comfort and wisdom shall shine forth as a new day, rendering a more abundant lifestyle and spiritual prosperity.

We must discipline ourselves, train our minds in the power of God's word that we might walk in our space of greatness, posturing who we are as God's Children that the world might revere the Most-High God ~ John 5:20.

The pastor once said, "There will come a time when we do not need faith." How will that happen, I would ask myself. When shall it happen? Why will it happen? By reading Jesus's words at the gravesite, I understood that we will still need faith as a foundational springboard into the realm of knowing. The experiences will teach us to operate within the Power of God's Anointing. This faith (knowing) will perfect our faith—a beyond-great faith! I know this sounds radical, but keep reading. Just as there are levels of glory, there are confidence levels in God. Our trust in the veracity of God's word and promises matters! Jesus spoke about them and consistently operated from this highest level of assurance—the Christ-Spirit. There is a level of anointing in God, which opens blinded eyes, unstops deaf ears, and sets captives free by speaking the word. Turn with me to *II Kings* 5 if you do not believe me. This passage is a story about Naaman, who was a leper. The maid of Naaman's wife tells Naaman of a prophet who can cure him of his disease. Desiring the prophet to cure him, Naaman goes to his king in Syria and requests a letter that he might take to the king of Israel.

Markeithia Lavon Silver

Upon his arrival, the idea of a leper entering his country frightens Israel's king. When the prophet Elisha heard that the king was troubled by the visit, he tells him, in verse 8, "Wherefore have thou rent thy clothes? Let him come now to me, and he shall know that Israel has a prophet." Naaman set out on his journey to meet the Prophet of God. He arrived at Elisha's door, and in verse 10, "Elisha sends a messenger unto him saying, 'Go and wash in Jordan seven times, and thy flesh shall come again to thee, and thou shall be clean.'" Here is where it gets good, right down to the crevices of your soul. In verse 11, Naaman gets angry and walks away. He said, "I thought He will surely come out to me, and stand, and call on the name of the Lord, and strike his hand over the place, and recover the leper." Elisha performed no "laying on of hands," no anointing of oil, and he did not even go and lay eyes on the man. He just spoke, and it was! If you notice, the *Bible* capitalized the "h" again in he. This enhancement in the first letter of a word speaks to the God-ness in Elisha. I submit that the same God-ness that Jesus referred to when he said, "*He* that believes in Him," is the same "*He*" mentioned here.

Beloved, God has a place beyond the general representation of faith. This perfected faith operates in knowing God will back your play when aligned and in sync with Him. Chapter eight will discuss this concept: *The Process of Discerning and Creating God's Will (Reality) for Your Life*. Again, just as there are levels of learning and glory, there are levels of faith/and trust. I am sure you observe this stratification in your life. There are some you trust more than others. Right? Of course, you do. Likewise, Jesus mentions them when he encounters them: a measure of faith (which we are all given), little faith, great faith, and in the Mind of Christ— a knowing.

Similarly, the works of the prophet Elijah highlight a place in God that exhibits knowing God's character and ability to anticipate God's thoughts toward a matter. For instance, Israeli

Living Your Legacy Of Greatness

King Ahab disobeyed the Lord. During his rule over Israel, he was egregious by taking Jezebel as his wife and promoting idolatry. Additionally, Ahab built an altar to worship Baal, an idol god. Elijah, a representative of God, walking in his God-ness, attempts to straighten Ahab out, but to no avail. Elijah then warned Ahab of a drought. In *I Kings* 17:1, he said, "As the Lord God of Israel lives, before whom I stand, *there shall be neither dew nor rain these years, but according to my word.*"

Good God from Zion! You do not learn until James 5:17 that Elijah prayed beforehand that this would be the outcome. He knew God heard him, had his back, and would honor his request. Why? Elijah was a prophet of God and very astute in the laws and promises of God. Elijah's ability to decree that there would be no rain found its nexus in the Scriptures and promises of God. In *Deuteronomy* 11, Moses instructs Israel to love the Lord and keep His charge, statutes, judgments, and Commandments. ~ Verse 1. Moses reminds them of God's instructions and the many miracles He performed in Egypt. He encourages them to keep all God's commandments that (1) they may be strong, (2) that they may possess the land that they set their eyes upon to possess, (3) that He will prolong their days in the land God swore unto their fathers, and (4) that they will be able to partake of the riches of the land flowing with milk and honey. If they adhere to all that God required of them, "to harken diligently unto God's commandments, to love the LORD your God, and to serve Him with all of their hearts and soul," God will give them *rain in their land* in its due season, the first rain and the latter rain:

> [So], thou mayest gather in thy corn, and thy wine, and thine oil. And I will send grass in thy fields for thy cattle, that thou mayest eat and be full. ***Take heed to yourselves, that your heart be not deceived, and ye turn aside and serve other gods, and worship them; And then the LORD'S***

Markeithia Lavon Silver

wrath be kindled against you, and he shut up the heaven, that there be no rain, and that the land yield, not her fruit; and *lest* ye perish quickly from off the good land which the LORD giveth you. Therefore, shall ye lay up these my words in your heart and your soul, and bind them for a sign upon your hand, that they may be as frontlets between your eyes. ~ Deu 11:14-18.

Do you *see* it? The prophet Elijah called the judgment of God upon Israel because they turned away from His commandments and waxed cold in their hearts towards Him, resulting in the worshiping of idol gods. When Elijah "stood" before Ahab and pronounced judgment that there shall be dew nor rain, God honored his decree. The word stand in Hebrew is *âmad*. It means literally and figuratively to abide behind, appoint, dwell, be employed, stand by, stand firm, and other words that denote a prophet's (Elijah) position in God. Elijah performed his duties under what today we call the *law of agency*. This phrase is a legal term. It governs the relationship between the principal and an agent. The Principal authorizes the agent to speak on their behalf. In other words, if God (the Principal) calls you (the agent) to the office of a prophet, He authorizes you to speak on His behalf according to His word. Where prophets get into trouble is saying *their* word and not the word of the Lord ~ Deuteronomy 18:18-22, Job 38:2, Jeremiah 14:13-22, Psalms 81:8-13. The principal is not obligated to stand by, stand with, or affirm the agent's word if the *agent goes outside the scope of their authority*. Thus, the agent is liable for any infraction from words spoken outside the principal's authority. The same holds true for God and His prophets. *See* Jeremiah 23:16, 30-40.

In contrast, when we live with the mind of Christ and remain in the Vine, we shall ask anything according to the Father's will,

Living Your Legacy Of Greatness

and He will answer. He hovers over His will, ready to perform it! ~ Jeremiah 1:12.

Likewise, another fitting example of the prophet calling forth the judgment of God is in *II Kings* 1, where the Moabites rebel against Israel. King Ahaziah is stricken with a disease after falling through a lattice in his upper chamber. Ahaziah sends his messengers to seek guidance from the idol god, Beelzebub, whether he shall deliver him from his infirmity. God sends Elijah to meet these couriers and tells them their king shall not recover but die. It is important to note that Ahaziah's disregard for His presence in Israel offended God. In other words, in verses 3 and 6, He said, "How dare you disregard, disrespect, or overlook the True and Living God of Israel and seek instruction and guidance from an idol god! For that, you shall surely die!" ~ *II Kings* 1: 6. Ahaziah sends a captain and an additional fifty men, totaling one hundred men, to track the prophet Elijah down in his indignation. Elijah was on the top of the hill (representing his place in God. From a strategic position, the high ground is the best place to observe your enemy—therefore, we must both watch and pray consistently). In the name of their king, they commanded Elijah to come down (They were demanding that Elijah change his seek—his relationship with God)—forget about God, and obey his king (the carnal mind: flesh). Elijah responded, *"If I be a man of God,* then let fire come down from heaven and consume thee and thy fifty" ~ *II Kings* 1:10. (Emphasis mine). In his rebellion and refusal to submit to the True and Living God of his fathers, Abraham, Isaac, Jacob, and later his father, David (a man after God's heart), Ahaziah sent out another captain and fifty men after *one man*. The fire consumed them all! Then, the king sent another captain with an additional fifty men. However, this captain was humble and wise. "He sought Elijah that his life and the life of his fifty servants would be precious in his sight" ~ *II Kings* 1:14. The Lord told Elijah not to fear the men and go with them unto the king and prophesy. Elijah conveyed the heart and

Markeithia Lavon Silver

mind of God concerning the king's egregious actions in verse 16. *Verse 17* says, "[Ahaziah] died *according to the Word of the Lord, which Elijah had spoken" ~ II Kings* 1:17. This result is powerful to the believer! *Your place, power in God, and the words you speak are impacted and fortified by the backing of the Power of God! When you are in your place, you are in the mind of God, and what you say according to His will is extraordinary, even to shutting up heaven's rain and calling fire down in the glory and honor of God in His holy place!*

Jesus showed the same confidence and assurance at the gravesite of Lazarus. They both committed their vision to the Lord; they knew God would honor their request. When Elijah said, "Before whom I stand," he was, in essence, telling Ahab, "God has my back!" Similarly, when he stated, "If I be a man of God..." he essentially was saying, if I am *in* God, and God is *in* me, without hindrance or inhibition, if His word resides *in* me and governs my life, if I walk *in* the prophetic as an intercessor of God, if my relationship with God shows forth His glory, and seeks to turn the hearts and minds of His people back to Him, then, let so and so occur. We must strive to posture this same confidence in knowing, seek to hear the heart and mind of God, and fortify our relationship with a consistent prayer life. "If any man speaks, let him speak as the oracles of God; *if any man minister, let him do it as of the ability, which God giveth: that God in all things may be glorified through Jesus Christ,* to whom be praise and dominion forever and ever." Amen. ~ I Peter 4:11. Our life or the life of another depends upon it!

Living Your Legacy Of Greatness

When You Know You Are Covered, You Are Fearless!

When we can say and believe like David, *"The Lord is my light and my salvation, whom shall I fear? The Lord is the strength of my life; of whom shall I be afraid? When the wicked, even mine enemies and my foes, came upon me to eat of my flesh, they stumbled and fell. Though a host should encamp against me, my heart shall not fear though war should rise against me; in this will I be confident."* ~ Psalms 27. We will be fearless in the sight of our enemies. What confidence is David referring to in this declaration? He is His Light and His Salvation! No one else can hold that spot but God, so he relinquishes his fear and holds fast to the assurance of his vision of greatness coming to pass. Elijah also knew God covered him, and as we know from the Scriptures, it did not rain for three years, and fire came down and consumed the captains and one hundred men. Similarly, God restored Naaman to his natural state through the command of Elisha.

Allow me to bring back to your remembrance the story of Peter faltering while walking on water. Let us look at Peter's thought process after Jesus placed him back into the boat. As the Scriptures unveil the growth of Peter, we discover Peter did not stay weakened. Later, Jesus speaks to Peter about the process leading him to greatness. Jesus first warns Peter of satan's "desire to overtake him, that he might sift him as wheat." If you know anything about culinary arts, you know that a sifter is a metal apparatus filled with holes that thin flour by raking the arm back and forth over the flour. Once the baker thins the flour by sifting, s/he uses it for baking. Specifically, the baker sifts the ruff and ridged flour to achieve the right texture, producing soft, viable flour necessary for baking. The sifter separates the flour through many holes until it is of the right quality and consistency. Can you imagine having your life separated in many different directions? First, you try to focus on one situation. Then, another one, which is just as important, pops

Markeithia Lavon Silver

up. Finally, you address another issue, and another, until your mind goes in all kinds of directions. You will lose your mind if you allow the circumstances of life to weigh you down. Jesus tells him that after he experiences this sifting process, "[He] prayed for [him], that [his] faith [will not] fail: and when thou art converted (from an individual of impotence to a person of strength, a person that cannot perceive what God can do to a person that knows, beyond a shadow of any doubt, what He will do, from a person that focuses on his conditions to a person who looks beyond his surroundings and walks on water), strengthen thy brethren" ~ Luke 22:31-32.

The commission to fortify his brothers and sisters does not come until he completes the process (a person of inferiority to excellence in God). Once Peter completes his metamorphosis, he receives the Mind of Christ to assist others in getting there. When he has gone from thinking with little faith to thinking with the Mind of Christ, he will be "meat for the Master's use." Peter, of course, could not see what Jesus saw regarding his faith. Peter declared he was ready to go with Jesus to prison and even death. Jesus knew Peter's intentions were good, yet Peter had not discovered who he was and, thus, could not accompany Jesus on his journey. Peter needed to shed some things to realize his power in God. The Scriptures inform us that Peter arrives *in* God *in* the place Jesus foretold in Luke 22. Specifically, Peter heals people with the shadow of his body as he passes. He was now able to fulfill the words spoken to him by Jesus: "Feed my sheep" ~ John 21:17. That is amazing, right?

Can you imagine doing this? You can do it, too, if you trust God, align your thoughts with His, and believe!

Please turn with me to Revelation 3:22 and 4:1. Jesus speaks to the church and ends by saying, "He that hath an ear, let him hear what the Spirit saith unto the churches." In the next chapter, in the first verse, John says, "Behold, a door was opened in heaven…I heard, 'Come up hither, and I will show thee things, which must

Living Your Legacy Of Greatness

come to pass..."" Beloved, the Lord is calling us up to greatness! How do we see, create, and perform the things of God? We must come up higher. We must go through the process of being tried. We train our minds to recall God's blessings, prepare our hearts to embrace greatness as our nature, instruct our tongue to speak what Jesus spoke that we might live, and live exceedingly and abundantly in our space of Kingdom distinction. We can do it if we only believe it!

Jesus teaches that we must discipline ourselves by the Word of God. "Faith cometh by hearing, and hearing by the Word of God" ~ Romans 10:17. As you hear and internalize the Bread of Life/ Word of God, your faith increases. Imagine this: I come to you by the calling of my name. I am Faith, and the call is the Word of God. When faith hears the Word of God, it supplants doubt, fear, and despair. Faith appears as a standard against all adversity and trials ~ Isaiah 59:19. It rises and does not tarry, lifting a standard during a storm ~ *Id.*

"Let patience [complete] its perfect work" ~ James 1:4. This unique trying of your patience will give you the experience you need to increase your faith, preparing and propelling you to a place wanting nothing. *The more God allows you to be tested, the more you can grow in the experience of what God can and will do. The more you are tried, the more those trials, by the grace and mercies of God, conform you into the image of His Son* that you might be the firstborn of many brethren ~ Romans 8:29. It is incumbent upon us to continue to perfection in Christ ~ Hebrews 6:1. This season requires us not to rest upon our laurels but allow the Holy Ghost's teaching to take us higher. God is calling us to more extraordinary heights in Him than the glory we possess! The world and even ourselves are awaiting the fullness of our sonship in Christ Jesus! Sons and Daughters of Zion, now, God's beloved treasure, is the time! Do you want to go higher?

Markeithia Lavon Silver

The Hebrew tradition's shepherd's staff is an example of operating in the fullness of the experience gained by trials and tribulations. Within the tribe of Levites (the priests), the shepherds utilized the staff to carve the name of God and the things the Lord had done to bless and deliver them. The *Midrash* explains that every time God rescued the children of Israel, they wrote it down. Every time God blessed them, the shepherd marked the occurrence within the grain of the staff. If God healed, they engraved it on the staff. If He blessed, delivered, or set free, they marked the staff of the righteousness of His right hand upon them. The Tribe of Judah passed this staff down through the lineage from generation to generation. Simultaneously, the staff's engravings reminded them of God's strong hand of deliverance when they faced a storm. His mercy, kindness, and provision reminded them of His sovereignty and Providence. This posture is catapulting them to trust what He would and could do while keeping their continued focus on God ~ Read Psalms 116:7, where David reminds himself of his peace and strength by resting in God's Sovereignty.

Likewise, this occurred at the bank of the Red Sea. Moses had a staff with all that God had accomplished up to the moment of the Red Sea. The staff etched his encounter with God on the mountain to the various diseases unleashed in Egypt to save Israel's firstborn. God reminds him of what was in his hands and *what the Lord had already done*. He held the faith of the past experiences to part the Red Sea in his hand ~ Exodus 14:15. If you read the text, you will see the Lord, first, asks him, "Why are you crying unto Me? [You] speak unto the Children of Israel and tell them to go forward." Then, the Lord tells Moses to "lift the rod in his hand (which reminded him of what God had already done) and then stretch out his hand over the sea and divide it. In essence, God told Moses, "You do it!" Good God from Zion! This act displayed by Moss is the perfecting of your faith! God will push us out when we attempt to hide and say, *"Trust Me!"* In other words, "After all I showed you and

Living Your Legacy Of Greatness

performed on your behalf, you are now in a place to operate in the Power I have given you!" *You do it!*

Try it! When God answers a prayer, please write it down. When He blesses you with abundance, put pen to paper and record His works and faithfulness toward you. If He makes a way of escape, do not forget to write it. Keep a journal of what God does for you. If the *Living You Legacy of Greatness Journal* accompanies this volume, use it to keep your God's accomplishments. When you feel anxious, reread what your past experiences reveal, and you will bless your soul. First, remember to honor Him, bless the Lord's name, stretch your hand over what you desire, and watch God move on your behalf. Befittingly, we will entitle this portion of the journal *The Rod in My Hand!*

The Rod in My Hand!

The Experience	God's Response
Breast Cancer	Complete Healing! He kept my mind in perfect peace, provided me with a great support system, sustained me financially, kept a roof over my head, clothes on my back, food on my table, and protected my family. DELIVERED!
Homelessness	Never was forsaken, provided shelter for my family and me, and touched the hearts of strangers to bless me financially. DELIVERED!
Wanted to Complete my Education	God made provisions for me to succeed in my education: scholarships, grants, and mentors. God took me from Undergrad to Master's and then to Doctorate. DONE!
I wanted to author a book that would bless the children of God.	DONE! DONE, and DONE!

To encourage and reframe the responses to life's obstacles is a song I thoroughly enjoy, entitled *I Am Healed*. I like how Donald Lawrence and his choir sing this chorus, *"May have some scars...But I am healed. Circumstances... I am still healed. Disappointments...I am healed. Oh, oh, oh, I am healed! I am healed! With His stripes, I am healed!"* The point here is to utilize these moments of experience, which creates a sense of knowing God will do just what He promised. We enjoy the experience, but the knowledge also relinquishes the pain and anguish that may come with it. When we forget the past things, we forget the impressions they attempt to leave upon the mind that blur your objectivity—past, present, and future. Looking around, we see that we are getting by—that the Lord has been gracious toward us. This exhibit of God nestling alongside us whenever we beckon Him underscores what David referred to when he encouraged himself. If you get the chance, read *Psalms 116*. David sings of his Love for God. He is in a place of despair, but in the 7th verse, he reminds himself to "Return unto thy rest, oh my soul, for the Lord has dealt bountifully with thee." If you begin noting all that God has done and the prayers that He answers, God will elevate you, moment by moment, to a place of knowing. It takes discipline, in any case. Nevertheless, if you train yourself to scribe everything, you will be a blessing to yourself and others.

It is not an overnight process. This book comes from things I wrote over several years, from my childhood until now. I am claiming my inheritance! Are you?

"Being confident (this means we can count on it, trust that it will happen) of this very thing, that He that has begun a good work in you will perform it...." ~ Philippians 3:1. Moreover, Jesus informs us, in *Luke* 18:30, we shall receive "manifold more in this present time and in the world to come...." Lay hold to your legacy of greatness and get ready to accept your abundance!

I am ending this chapter with a chorus line from a contemporary gospel by Fred Hammond and spiritual prose entitled *Longing:*

"We are blessed in the city, we are blessed in the field, we are blessed when we come and when we go. We cast down every stronghold. Sickness and poverty must cease, for the devil is defeated. We are BLESSED!"

Longing

My soul thirsts and longs to remember who I am. Where can I travel, and to whom can I speak to bring me to a renewal place?

I must go...

I must press onward...

I must remember...

Do you know who I am?

Do you know who you are?

God filled the world with so many clues. I need to examine them all. My life requires it.

I must not fear turning over the rock or what might crawl out.

It is a glorious mystery awaiting my hand of engagement.

The Universe desires to join me in the holy union of spiritual matrimony.

We are One, you see!

We are One.

I must remember…

The glory of His goodness is in all I hear, see, smell, taste, and touch. I shall not fear, for all is good. To dread goodness is to fear the One who created me. Should I fear the Hands that love me beyond measure? Should I cringe at the breath breathed in me by the "Us" Spirit?

As I ponder the question deep within my soul, I see Creation Shining as the Bright Morning Star.

The Kingdom *is* within me!

CHAPTER FIVE

TRANSFORMATION: A NECESSARY PROCESS OF GROWTH

"...Be ye transformed by the renewing of your mind, that you may prove what is that good, and acceptable, and perfect will of God." ~ Romans 12:2b (Emphasis mine).

—Paul

"Brethren, I count not myself to have apprehended: but this one thing I do, forgetting those things which are behind, and reaching forth unto those things which are before. I press toward the mark for the prize of the high calling of God in Christ Jesus...let us, therefore...be thus minded." ~ Philippians 3:13-15 (Emphasis mine).

—Paul

"To wear the things of this world as a loose garment."

—St. Francis of Assisi

Markeithia Lavon Silver

I recall 1989, beginning in the police academy as a new Boston Police recruit. I was excited to become an officer of the law in six months. I had never been in the military and did not necessarily understand the forthcoming dynamics during my training. However, I was a part of the Naval NJROTC in high school. I understood some of the languages I would encounter during my educational training (i.e., yes, sir/ma'am). I did not know that my trainer's job was *transforming me* from a civilian perspective into a law enforcement mentality or approach.

To become a police officer in the city where I resided, the senior officers would train and discipline me in that field. The role of law enforcement was unlike any other job I had encountered. By that, I mean the language of corporate America was the extent of my employment knowledge. Similarly, the employer required a professional demeanor, but working in corporate America did not include protecting a life, running after criminals, or being concerned for the constitutional rights of others. I was accustomed to customer service, but not how I was about to learn. In any new employment undertaking, you can expect further training in the manner associated with that profession. Every employer has parlance entailing specific rules, exclusive language governing their employees, and policies regulating application and response to procedures. I was in for a new experience that would remove the glasses of "Jane Citizen" and replace them with the spectacles of the overseer of "Jane Citizen." The Lord was enlarging my territory to accommodate my new responsibility.

"For unto whomsoever much is given, of her/him shall be much required" ~ Luke 12:48. The more obligations you take on, the more responsible you need to become. As we enter each level of glory, we must shed the prior mindset to lay hold of the new. Keeping yourself attached to the past will prevent or stymie your ability to enter your future. You must proverbially die at one level to be reborn in the next realm. To be sure, this conversion is no

Living Your Legacy Of Greatness

easy task by any means. Letting go can be one of the hardest things to do. However, if you desire to live as God's child, you must "suffer it to be so" ~ Matthew 3:15. Sometimes, it might appear that you are walking alone. Remember that you are not alone or forsaken in this instance. Correspondingly, God will prune your relationships and bring new ones into your life that will assist you in maintaining and growing at your new level. Therefore, you must continue to be open to change. If you are not flexible and amicable, you might miss your blessing of growth and your appointment with destiny. More importantly, you must be humble and teachable. The Word puts it like this, "now I say, that the heir, as long as s/he is a child,[1] differs nothing from a servant, though s/he be lord of all; but is under tutors and governors until the time appointed of the father." ~ Galatians 4:1-2. Good God from Zion! As you grow in stature in knowing *who* you are, you shall endure people in authority, teachers, and mentors until you come to the complete understanding of your status, awaiting your precise appointment by the Father. Are you humble? Do you occupy a teachable spirit? Are you a student of learning? Are you *bendable* in the Spirit? If the answer to these questions is yes, prepare for a great shift in your life!

The inevitability of change is necessary for growth in anything you embark upon, not just the things of God. Salvation is free, but to move effectively in the Holy Spirit takes work. It takes

---

[1] The Hebrew word for child in this Scripture is *nēpios. Strong's and Thayer's Concordence* define *nēpios* as an infant child or baby. It is a child that is untaught, unskilled, and immature Christian in the faith. There are different levels of Sonship each displaying different levels of congitive abilities: 1) Nēpios, (2) Paidion (3) Teknon (4) Huios, and (5) Teleios. Each stage of development highlights spiritual growth and maturity. Therefore, at each stage of development there are benchmarks that identify your advancing to the next level. I would encourge you, gentle reader, to do your own research on the topic of cognitive growth in the spirit so as to test where you are and what you need to do to grow accordingly.

discipline. It takes the sacrifice of the old to receive the new. It takes *knowing* that God is faithful. It takes you to allow God to stretch your imagination *and* your faith. It takes *knowing* that "The Lord orders the steps of a righteous wo/man." It takes *knowing* that you *go through it* to *grow through it.* God has walked out your steps and set provision before you, for He calls the end from the beginning. However, it takes you *to know* that it is there and joyful about your faith manifested before it came. Are you ready? Ask Him to endow you with knowledge, wisdom, understanding, and skill for the glory and honor of the Kingdom. Ask Him to cause you to *see, know, and understand* your authority in the Kingdom. He will do it! ~ Exodus 31: 3 *See also* Daniel 1:17, *I Corinthians* 12:18, James 3.

Appropriately, every new job requires a level of discipline. Employees expect to learn new office culture, policies, and procedures that govern their positions. If the employee lacks the expectation of change, the employee becomes stagnant, risking termination of their job. With that said, let me take you through some of my disciplining experiences. First, my academy class purchased a uniform. The Academy provided a list of things we had to buy to specifications. Next, the recruits *looked* identical. Although never stated in any literature, law enforcement officer training is undergirded by the notion "that [we] all speak the same thing, and that there be no divisions among [us]; but that [we] be perfectly joined together in the same mind and the same judgment. ~ *I Corinthians* 1:10. Finally, we embarked upon training that would cause us to *act* alike—to some degree. Behold, it is good and pleasant for brethren to dwell together in unity! ~ Psalms 133:1. I would venture to say these precepts make the "blue wall" strong and often impenetrable among law enforcement agencies across the country, even abroad. Piercing the veil is no easy feat. I look forward to the day when the Bride of Christ is unified in the spirit, perfectly joined together in the *same mind* and *judgment.* This leg

Living Your Legacy Of Greatness

of the race is the responsibility of the intercessors. May the pouring out of God's Spirit cause us to *see* what is incumbent upon us as believers in this hour. Amen. Okay, let us continue.

On the first day, the senior officers taught us how to stand at attention, para-military cadence while marching, and turn when necessary. I was familiar with this. As mentioned earlier, I participated in the NJROTC program in high school. We would endure the wintry weather, exercise, and intense academic training for several months. No matter the situation, or inclemency of the weather, we had to be on time. Being tardy was unacceptable. Being on time, we would learn, depended on taking over another shift and keeping the city protected. For example, if assigned to work from 7:30 am-4:00 pm, you need to be there to relieve the shift before you, which would end at 7:30 am. This schedule ensures proper coverage of the city in perpetuity. If you were late, that would mean the town went uncovered, potentially placing the citizens you swore to protect in danger.

After an inspection on the first day, our senior officers told us how to "properly" wear our recruit uniform; we filled out paperwork that entailed whom to call in an emergency and register our motor vehicle. After being given most of the rules and regulations governing our appointment, we were dismissed and expected to return bright and early the next day in sweat clothes. Did I mention that my academy class began in the winter? I smile each time I recall our line formations. We were in filing ranks of two, and the line started with the tallest person ending with the shortest. Two other women and I were always at the back of the line. We would run to a field about a mile away every morning and begin a series of calisthenics. Once we completed the exercises, we would run back to the academy. Upon returning to the academy, I and another recruit were *always* last. In a stern voice, one of the trainers would ask us, "Are you the last recruit?" He met us at the entrance each day.

Markeithia Lavon Silver

"Sir, yes, sir!" We responded. Each time, he would catch us and order us to do squat thrusts. If you know anything about squat thrusts, you know they are strength builders for the entire body: shoulders, stomach, and legs. We would need to count each time we completed one, "One, Sir. Two, Sir!" etc. When finished, we requested dismissal. I smile and laugh each time I think about it. We were last each time because we *were* last in the ranking file. I am grateful to my trainer for this body-building experience. It prepared me to sustain myself on the city streets, where crime could sometimes be rampant. Further, I *know* from that experience that I can push my body to its optimal level and survive.

Another experience I enjoyed was the awareness of clearing a building. During the latter months of the academy, our captain and other trainers took us to an abandoned building to learn how to search a building to determine if the suspect had left. However, the skits we encountered were not actual but virtual examples of authentic experiences. These experiences gave us a basis for knowing what to expect on the streets. We also practiced car stops, which the Academy considered the highest level of danger. When an officer enters a situation not knowing what dangers may be present, it creates increased stress. When making a motor vehicle stop, the officer communicates the location, plate, and vehicle description to the dispatcher; in case the "car-stop" escalates to danger, fellow officers will know where to respond. If the officer felt suspicious of the driver and occupants, it also warranted a description of them. Other training experiences included the firing range, operating a cruiser, fighting techniques, and a shooting assimilator.

The academy trained us to react in real situations to ensure officers' safety. The senior officers drilled these tactics into our minds through repetitive training. Accordingly, the officer reverts to their training when encountering life-threatening conditions, which became their instinct, not the officer's previous responses. Therefore, the senior officers repeat the police training for maximum

Living Your Legacy Of Greatness

effect. Whenever the Academy approves a contemporary training style, the officers return to the academy and learn the new proven technique. Law enforcement always seeks to better their jobs to provide a safe environment for their citizens. It may not appear to the citizenry that way due to the many violent acts portrayed on the news involving officers and persons of color. My academy taught the best possible scenarios for affecting an arrest. Likewise, I suspect other academies train and discipline in like manner. The conflict arises when individual experiences supersede training. This supplanting of personal proficiency with training occurs when the officer does not allow a complete emergence into the culture of policing, does not follow the rules, and, when placed in a stressful situation, converts to what they are most comfortable with—personal experience versus training. If it is not training that guides, severe problems arise—people die needlessly. Likewise, I cannot tell you the number of times I observed a person who says they are Holy Ghost-filled, speaking in tongues, and yet ready to annihilate someone over a simple matter. Well, to them, the situation pushed them beyond the Holy Ghost they stood for and converted to their flesh.

At the beginning of the chapter, Paul inspires us to transform from sinner to disciple by renewing our mind (a reprogramming and maturing in our thinking, behavior, and character by the Word of God) to *prove* God's good, acceptable, and perfect will. As you allow God to alter and reset your thought process, you can detect, or rightly divide, as Scripture says, God's will for your life. Is this not wonderful? Similarly, this sounds like David's experience spoken previously. If you recall, David used the same concept of evidencing his abilities when confronting Goliath. You will use your expertise to guide you while simultaneously learning new things to incorporate into your life. As you go from glory to glory, you will assist others in reaching their actuality of greatness. Your faith stance allows others to build their own ~ Luke 13:19.

Markeithia Lavon Silver

The word "transform" in Greek is *metamorphoō*. We derive the biological term and explanation *for* the change of form or structure in an individual or species after hatching or birth. In biology, striking changes of form or structure due to hormones and other factors alter and differentiate the physical changes in growth and alterations of an organism's physiology, biochemistry, and behavior. In other words, metamorphosis encompasses a change in size and shape and a transformation in the molecular structure within the brain, causing behavior modifications.[24] The etymology of the word metamorphosis derives its origin in three Greek words: (1) the prefix **"meta-"** comes from a Greek word meaning "beyond" or "change." (2) the root **"morph"** comes from a Greek word meaning "shape." (3) the suffix **"-osis"** comes from the Greek word meaning "state or process." Therefore, we see, etymologically, the biological term *metamorphosis* and the Greek term used by the Apostle Paul in Romans 12:2, which involves the consistent *process* of changing appearance, character, behavior, and shape. Therefore, transformation is continual. We *continuously* grow in the breadth, length, depth, and height of God's word. ~ Ephesians 3:16-21.

Additionally, Apostle Paul lets us know that once our minds are renewed and matured in the Word of God, this renewed mind makes available an opportunity to "prove what is good, acceptable, and the perfect will of God." By implication, this exhortation denotes a change in spiritual position once metamorphosis initiates. If you do not *transform* your mind, you are not permitted to "prove" what is good, acceptable, and the perfect will of God. As you reach beyond your current state, like a caterpillar pushing its head out of a tiny hole, sending the blood flow to its wings and becoming a butterfly, you manifest into a son/daughter by renewing your mind. "But as many as received him, to them gave [the] power to *become* the sons of God, *even* to them that believe on his name" ~ St. John 1:12. The

Living Your Legacy Of Greatness

operative word in this powerful verse is *become*, which denotes a transformation process into the image of His Son ~ Romans 8:29.

I would be remiss, however, if I did not caution you to be aware of the ability to transform in the direction of either side of the spectrum of change. I will draw your attention to Adam and Eve's experience in the Garden. Before Adam and Eve's disobedience, their physical, spiritual, and soul eyes are aligned with God's purpose for their lives. They were naked and not ashamed. The enemy, described by Moses as more subtle than any other beast of the field, convinced Eve by imbuing her with the pride of life, the lust of the flesh, and the lust of the eyes to disobey God's instruction (or formula for death) and eat of the Tree of the Knowledge of Good and Evil. Adam and Eve chose autonomy over the relationship with God. They elected to distrust the veracity of God's instructions, lulling them into a web of deceit and, ultimately, death. This option altered their spiritual bodies into a body of flesh, constantly warring with each other ~ Galatians 5:17, James 4:1. Apostle Paul refers to this fleshly nature as an infirmity. When you accept Christ as your personal Savior, you make the conscious choice no longer to yield your members (body) to unrighteousness but to righteousness (behold, all things become new) ~ Romans 6:19, I Peter 2:11. The word flesh in Greek is *sarx*. As you can imagine, *sarx* refers to the *flesh* covering the bones *and* humanity's nature. According to *Thayer's* definition, it "denotes mere human nature, the earthly nature of [humanity] *apart from divine influence, and therefore prone to sin and opposed to God.*" (Emphasis mine). Therefore, Christ's blood sacrifice changes your sinful nature. The Spirit of God leads you, and the carnal mind no longer holds you in bondage to the fleshly nature obtained in the Garden by disobedience ~ Romans 8:12-17.

This type of development is reminiscent of the transformation I experienced as a recruit officer in the police academy. The senior officers taught us how to load and unload a weapon at the firing range.

Markeithia Lavon Silver

We also learned how to take apart and clean our department-issued equipment. We practiced shooting from various distances, using many types of targets to eliminate "tunnel-vision" and techniques that allowed us to manage a situation if ever hurt. Moreover, the senior officers trained the recruits to protect themselves until help arrived. Operating a cruiser also entailed a specific discipline. The training involved driving at varying speeds, turning corners without knocking over any cones, and backing up the colossal wagon. Accordingly, the goal was to accomplish our tasks without knocking over any cones because the cones represented people and objects. The objective was to successfully execute the capture of any criminal that might be fleeing in a car safely—without hurting or damaging any person or property. Similarly, drills properly affecting an arrest are designed to apprehend the subject without incident.

One of the funniest things I remember about the driving course is bringing a pillow to prop behind my back. I am short for the average woman, and attempting to break would send me forward. This minor setback caused me trouble controlling the car's steering speed. However, I completed my driving course with excellence at the end of the exercise. Of course, taking the driving course is a requirement, and each recruit must pass it to complete the academy. Driving at high rates of speed can be fun, but it is dangerous. Without proper instruction, you could hurt not only yourself but others. The preparation was to ensure the minimum amount of damage to property or injuries to people, at least to a high degree.

The fighting techniques were instrumental in increasing our stamina if we needed to wait until assistance arrived. The senior officers trained us to fight our opponent for three minutes until help arrived. Typically, your assistance is instantaneous, but just in case, the Academy instructed you to hold your own. The police department I worked for strategically placed officers geographically to reach their fellow officers in distress within three minutes.

Living Your Legacy Of Greatness

Self-defense is essential in law enforcement. The most practical training sessions are officers protecting themselves against the shooting assimilator and clearing a building. The shooting assimilator has a computer program that creates scenarios for the officer. The training officer assigns a weapon wirelessly attached to the computer. The machine awaits your response when a suspect attempts to break or has broken the law. Sometimes, a suspect may shoot, injure, and even kill you because you did not un-holster your weapon quickly enough to respond to the threat. Conversely, there are times when you might unholster quickly and injure a private citizen. Therefore, an officer's good judgment when utilizing deadly force is vital to being effective on the street.

In addition to all of this, you must learn the legal aspects of your employment. Accordingly, the recruit officers spend most of the day in the classroom. In a classroom setting, the recruits learned Constitutional Law, Criminal Law, Juvenile Law, and Domestic Law, including sexual assault and rape, Motor vehicle Law, and report writing. After six months of academy training and education, the recruits graduate as police officers. The police department issued badges and equipment, including a service weapon, baton, handcuffs, and pepper spray. Some departments now issue stun guns, limiting the use of deadly force affecting an arrest. During academy training, the senior officers taught the recruits to utilize each piece of equipment effectively. Ultimately, the Academy transformed the recruits from regular citizens to overseers and protectors of the law.

Likewise, training occurs in the spiritual realm. The shift from Jane Citizen to the overseer of Jane Citizen is crucial in law enforcement. The graduate becomes an intermediary between the law and the citizenry. The law is no longer something abstract or outside of the layperson's understanding but an integral part of the psyche of the trained officer. Specifically, the officer *internalizes* the law to guide the officer in protecting the law. The trained

Markeithia Lavon Silver

officer responds through their training in reacting to peacekeeping situations. The feelings and emotions of the officer are no longer a factor in upholding the law. The Academy designed the training to assist you in compartmentalizing your emotions and feelings on sensitive subjects. Repetitive measures facilitate your ability to be a good officer and peacekeeper of the law. The Academy transformed the officer from a layperson perspective into a disciplined law officer. At least, that is the intention. The recruits began as Jane and Joe Citizens and graduated (*becoming*) protectors of the law. Issues arise when an officer does not rely upon their training. This outcome may stem from many factors. However, complications manifested because the recruits did not immerse themselves during training, and that which was comfortable to them (their nature) responded to the situation. Thus, continuous training is necessary to replace an individual's nature to reduce unwanted outcomes. In other words, a recruit must conform to the discipleship of law enforcement to be effective.

The word disciple in Greek means disciplined one. You find Jesus hand-picking his disciples, telling each of them, "Come and I will make you *become* fishermen of wo/men" ~ Mark 1:17. You cannot *become anything* without change; you cannot *become* disciplined without training. Moreover, the art of becoming is an *art of continual practice.* I went into the Academy with the mind of a regular citizen. I came out as a protector and intermediary of the law. If I had continued to hold on to the mindset of the "normal" citizen, I would not have been an effective officer. My training prepared me for what might happen. If the scenarios I practiced did occur, I would *know* how to respond because of my training. I internalized my training, providing an intuitive response in any situation. The activity *became* my nature.

I am still a citizen, but I am more than that. I maintained a dual consciousness. I now possessed something to offer myself as an officer *and* something to give to the city where I worked. Similarly,

Living Your Legacy Of Greatness

after salvation, you become more than a citizen of the Kingdom. You bear something to present to yourself, humanity, and the Lord. You evolved into a fully-fledged God-child—living, moving, and having your being *in* God.

One might say while reading this, "I am not strong enough to do what you mentioned. I am weak and vulnerable. I try; however, I miss the mark. My mind keeps telling me that I cannot do it." You are not alone and can stop your mind from telling you these things! Uncover where these feelings of inadequacy originate and defeat them with the affirmation of your oneness with the "Us" Spirit. Immerse yourself in God's word and respond as Jesus did when tempted: "It is written…! You *must* embrace the power of the Holy Ghost and conform to the image of His son, Jesus Christ ~ Romans 8:29. Our weaknesses resulting from the Fall are supplanted with the Power of God through Christ to walk in our authority as heirs and joint heirs of Christ ~ *I Corinthians* 15:35-49; *II Corinthians* 12:9; 13:4, 9; and Romans 8:17.

Let us explore the notion of weakness and vulnerability and how they may affect our moving away from a feeling of inadequacy. Ask yourself these questions:

1. What is—or is there—the difference between weakness and vulnerability?
2. What might we learn from our weaknesses or vulnerabilities?

Weakness is *lacking* the strength of will or stability of character, yielding easily to temptation.

Vulnerability is being capable of receiving an injury or possibly being wounded [In other words, you are open to being hurt].

Markeithia Lavon Silver

From these definitions, we gather that weakness and vulnerability easily represent a coin with two sides. In the flipping of the coin (changing from one state to another), from weakness to strength, vulnerability to security, respectively, the turning resembles a place and space between the change. Specifically, when one strives to change, vulnerability is a temporary place. When you do not turn from weakness to strength, vulnerability can mutate into another form of weakness, fortifying the present weak state of mind.

We learn life's lessons in this space of vulnerability (references next time). Here, we rely on self-examining our mental position or perspective. Thus, in transitioning from weakness to strength, we experience vulnerability (a place of unfamiliar territory where we are subject to injury), a position outside our comfort zone, where we must discover, uncover, and rediscover our strength. However, during these moments of vulnerability, we must recognize that God is an ever-present help, our Shield and Buckler ~ Psalms 46:1. He will hide and cover you in the Secret Place ~ Psalms 91. Tell yourself, "Although it hurts, I will trust You, Lord!"

"Trials come [to take you outside of your comfort zone] to make you strong. Moreover, your trials are the fire that comes to purge you—working it for your good [giving you the spiritual breadth, depth, length, and height perspective of any matter]" ~ See I Peter 1:7, 4:1-2, &12, and Romans 8:28. This grasping of insight allows you to see a situation from all sides, even afar off.

We are familiar with our weaknesses. Yet, converting them to strengths will always require a position of vulnerability. The challenge becomes not allowing you to slip back into a place of familiarity, realizing that the pain of change yields more significant results than the pain of remaining the same, yet choosing the former to transform because it is necessary for growth.

Trials then become the vehicle by which one transitions from one state to another. When we submit to a constant evolution into

Living Your Legacy Of Greatness

our true selves, this state of elevation is a perpetual process with a growth spurt at each encounter. We must strive to be gentle with others *and* ourselves during the process. Transition and transformation are two different processes. Transition is a process or period of changing from one state or condition to another. Transition explains the spaces between one state or condition and another. Whereas transformation, as described in the Apostle Paul's exhortation, is a thorough or dramatic change in form or appearance. Metamorphosis often describes this form, appearance, character, behavior, and shape change. ~ Romans 12:1-2.

We all experience change and transformation if we are committed to growth. That transition period can appear daunting if we do not understand what is occurring. When we look at nature, for example, we comprehend to a certain degree that transition occurs in most, if not all, things. When springtime is upon us, we see the signs that spring is coming. It may be cold outside, even freezing, but the trees are budding, and some birds that flew south for the winter are soaring in the morning skies. The signs tell us that spring is on its way. It is in transition. We know almost with an assurance that spring is coming! Thus, we must be patient. Likewise, when transitioning, we must be patient, for He knows His thoughts towards us to bring us to an expected end ~ Jeremiah 29:11. This anticipated end springs forth in its perfection because God's timing is perfect. He is never late and does not slack concerning His promises toward us ~ *II Peter* 3:9. More importantly, He is our portion and satisfies our soul when we wait on Him. ~ Lamentations 3:22-26.

In Daniel 2:2-22, we understand that wisdom and might belong to God. He and He alone change the times and the seasons. He removes kings and sets up kings. He gives wisdom to the wise and knowledge to them that know understanding. He and He alone reveal the deep and secret things. Finally, He knows what is in the darkness, and the light dwells with Him. Therefore, God *sees* what is in the transition before it arises. When we are patient and pay attention to the changing seasons in our lives, we become aware that God's timing is perfect and accomplishes exactly what it sets out to do. The *Bible* says, "Let Patience have her perfect work, that you may be perfect and entire, wanting nothing. ~ James 1:4. We are to learn from our past experiences that we might have hope through patience and comfort of the Scriptures." ~ Romans 15:4 Thus, awaiting God's timing accomplishes a few things: (1) it enlarges and deepens our faith. (2) Forces us to wait for our change and trust Him through our situation ~ Job 14:14, Lamentations 3:22-26. (3) It ensures that He and He alone get the glory, honor, and praise for deliverance, healing, sustainability, and the like. ~ Psalms 65:1. (4) It causes us to understand that our time is in His hands and not ourselves lest any man should boast ~ Psalms 31:5, Ephesians 2:9. Finally, (5) Awaiting on God's timing undergirds our humility. ~ *I* Peter 5:6. We must be gentle with ourselves and others during transitioning and transformation.

Therefore, *the need for grace is essential* to our growth and that of others. What is this thing called grace? Let us also explore the definition and function of grace.

Amazing Grace

Vine's Expository Dictionary defines Grace **as (1) Unmerited [underserved] favor and (2) Power to endure.** Grace in Hebrew is *chên,* meaning to be gracious. From a subjective view, it shows kindness and favor. Objectively, it is an aura of beauty, favor, graciousness, pleasantness, preciousness, and well-favorability.[25] The word derives from the Hebrew word *chânan,* which means to properly bend or stoop in kindness to an inferior, favor, and bestow pity, compassion, or mercy upon another. In the Book of Wisdom/ Proverbs attributed to King Solomon, the king primarily uses the

Living Your Legacy Of Greatness

word to describe the interactions between our fellow humans as gracious acts toward someone in need.[26] Outside of our human interactions, *chânan* is used by the Agent of grace, our Heavenly Father. In Greek, the word *charis* means graciousness, especially the divine influence upon the heart and its reflection in the giver's or receiver's life.[27] *Thayer's Concordance* says grace is that which causes joy, pleasure, sweetness, charm, loveliness, goodwill, lovingkindness, favor, or kind act done without expectation of return—the absolutely free expression of the lovingkindness of God to humanity finding its only motive in the bounty and benevolence of the Giver; unearned and unmerited favor.[28]

I submit that Grace extends from the "Us" Spirit that affects humanity; forgiving the repentant sinner brings joy, pleasure, sweetness, and loveliness to the soul of the recipient of God's grace. The beneficiary of His grace emits a thankful heart to Him for His unmerited favor of justification by faith through Jesus Christ. In other words, He does not give us what we deserve in judging our sins but forgives us. We are transformed from a sinful nature to a divine nature by the Holy Spirit, which guides us in seeking the righteousness of God through the renewing of our minds in Christ Jesus. Grace also means disposition, attitude toward another, and goodwill. This thing called grace *renews and replenishes the believer and safeguards the preservation of the individual's relationship with God.*

Therefore, as members of the Kingdom, grace flows in and through the members of our human race and has a two-fold function: it flows *from* the River that flows in *and* through us. Accordingly, we must enlarge it through our God-selves and not our human selves when extending grace unto others. When we impart grace through our human selves, we become frustrated in our efforts, even when bestowing grace on ourselves. Conversely, when we spread grace through our God-selves, we can endure *with* grace [power to endure]. Remember, you may reach a place

Markeithia Lavon Silver

of depletion if not monitored through daily communion with the Father. We must return to the Source of our strength to receive a refilling from the Infinite Power of God's grace ~ *See* St. John 15. Accordingly, we cannot present grace without first *receiving* grace within us. When we choose not to receive a refilling, we will inevitability operate from a realm of frustration, which can manifest into anger and resentment. In turn, this place of emptiness can manifest, if not addressed, separation from El-Shaddai, the Source of All things, which brings Life. Separation from the "Us" Spirit will bring detriment to us spiritually. No one wants to live in a place of spiritual bankruptcy in perpetuity. Therefore, we must bestow grace upon others and ourselves throughout the growth process and ensure our refreshing from the River that flows from heaven and never runs dry ~ St. John 4:14, 6:35, & 7:38.

We cannot extend grace apart from the Creator (the "Us" Spirit). More importantly, imparting grace through our human selves brings arbitrary and capricious judgment and disapproval. Nevertheless, offering forgiveness through our God-selves is tempered with Agapé (feasting love), a "love that covers a multitude of sins" ~ Proverbs 10:12, I Peter 4:8. In doing so, this grace will cause the recipient to change, even ourselves. Recognizing the bestowing of undeserved favor causes one to appreciate the grace, triggering an I must change attitude to meet the Grace I am receiving ~ St. Luke 15:11-32.

"We can come boldly to the Throne of Grace [fountain of unmerited favor] to obtain grace [to drink the essence of Power and Endurance] in this our time of need" ~ Hebrews 4:16.

May you always believe and know that God is awaiting your presence at the fountain of grace that you might endure during your time of need. Here, love and mercy for the journey extend to you and through you from the righteous hand of the Father as God's Children in Jesus Christ's name. Amen.

Living Your Legacy Of Greatness

My Testimony

Because of the many trials I experienced as a child, I endured many places of vulnerability. As a young adult, I observed hurtful situations in my family life. I vowed never to be in some of the same conditions I experienced as a child. As a result, I was an emotional wreck and did not know it. My relationships were rigid. I had trouble trusting and my past complicated friendships. I knew many people; however, I was close to no one. Perceived as a loner, I read a lot, walked alone, and learned to enjoy solitude. However, the same state I was trying to avoid was pulling me in. Why? It was a reference point because I had not chosen to change or eliminate it. My anxiousness displayed and rooted in fear of these experiences overtook me.

In contrast, my tenacious attitude also comes primarily from this. Determined that those experiences would never happen to me, I fought to ensure they did not. However, what I tried to avoid would always seem to find me. I knew how Job felt when he said, "For the thing, which I greatly feared is come upon me, and that which I was afraid of has come unto me" ~ Job 3:25. I was running from the fear of the experiences of my past. Therefore, I feared the exact outcome I observed regarding love and relationships as a child. However, "fear hath torment." This emotional status meant I had not allowed God's healing love to cleanse and purge that space of emotional hurt. My attacks of mental resistance were an attack *against me*.

Nonetheless, I learned it was in defense of that wound that expanded my fear. Until much later, I never considered exposing the emotional damage, accepting the vulnerability, understanding the positive aspects, and turning it into strength, never to be tormented again. Scripture tells us that we must forgive—that includes ourselves and others. Please read the *Parable of the Unforgiving Servant* in St. Matthew 18:21-35. Jesus tells the story

Markeithia Lavon Silver

of an unforgiving servant who asked his master for forgiveness. He received grace and compassion from his master. However, when the opportunity arose for him to forgive another, the unforgiving servant withheld his earthly grace and compassion. In the same manner, the master forgave him. He should have forgiven likewise, but he did not. When the master heard about it, he was wroth, says the Scriptures. ~ Matthew 18:34. The master threw the wicked servant over to the tormentors until he paid all he owed. When you harbor unforgiveness of yourself or others, you develop, repeat, and etch your self-narrative repeatedly in your mind. Inevitably, your constant repeating of the same hurt creates grooves and reference points for each new encounter with others. Therefore, when responding to a situation, you react based upon your past hurt and not the present situation, tormenting your spirit and piling on more pain—making a mountain from a molehill—because unforgiveness reigns in your life. This process can lead to physical sickness and mental health issues if unchecked.

Thus, holding on to past hurt placed me in a state of vulnerability, desiring the flip (change) to God's strength level. After all these years, I recognize that I wavered between weakness and vulnerability, never making complete turns to power over my circumstances. I was weak because the tools to change were not in my possession, or so I thought. Consequently, I allowed my mind to fall into the illusion of more pain; I remained vulnerable; I repeatedly allowed myself to internalize the injuries from unsuccessful relationships and indulge in feelings of unworthiness and inadequacy. I nurtured them to expand and grow further in my inner self. My refusal to forgive *me* and the visions I created regarding the object of my affections kept me in bondage. I learned I could not control others' actions and thoughts, no matter how insecure they made me feel. I realized I had given my power and control over to the perception of "how someone else felt about me." This mindset was a trick of

Living Your Legacy Of Greatness

the enemy—a spirit of hindrance that kept me from laying hold of my sonship. That was too much power for anyone to hold over me!

My worship and praise belonged to God, not the problems (idol gods in high places) whirling around in my heart-spirit. When the epiphany came, I discovered I possess control over my emotions, thoughts, and focus. With this knowledge, I can acquire security in the Holy Ghost. He sustains and gives life abundantly for the asking, and the choice to let go will lead me out of this wilderness of pain. I am Zion's daughter, and the Holy Ghost endows me to walk in Victory! As a daughter of the King, I enjoy the power to decree and declare rules and announcements. I own the Power in Christ to speak a prophetic advantage over my and others' lives.

I began to decree and affirm, "I joyfully enter the corridors of my mind's past, eliminating any knowledge, thought patterns, or behavior that may hinder me from laying hold to my destiny of greatness." My life changed as I began to repeat these words and other affirming thoughts (see affirmations in the journal or back of the book). I was at peace. I was no longer in the hands of the proverbial tormentor. I forgave myself. God's word encouraged me. I was willing to trust and allow others in, never fearing pain or despair. *I was free!* The illusion of people hurting me and never trusting others was now a thing of the past. If I felt my old thinking pattern draw me into thinking contrary to God's word, I reminded myself that this person was not the person who hurt me. I accepted my place in the now and lived in the present moment. This change did not occur overnight. It was a process because I needed God to build me up for such a time as this. Just as it took time to become an officer of the law, God would take time to restore and prepare me for greatness in Him.

Peace of mind, oh gentle reader, is the effect of certainty (a place of knowing), allowing patience its perfect work in your life, which renders the cultivating of faith, increasing it to confidence. Without faith in your life, doubt will seek out fear to procreate.

Markeithia Lavon Silver

Metaphorically speaking, the object of your faith is hope for the manifestation of a thing. Faith is the substratum you present to the Infinite "Us" Power to represent your thoughts. You see, the mold of the idea is your faith within the mind, bringing it into fruition by repetitive focus. The mold (repetitive focus) and faith (belief) are designed in the imagination. Our faith's working requires us to await its manifestation externally, what we conceive and perceive internally. Therefore, let *patience* have its perfect work. When we invoke the realization of our dreams and desires, we must *be purposeful* about what we focus on, the intensity of our thoughts, and how we create our concepts. We must procure a disciplined plan of action. That action can only manifest by a vibrant prayer life! ~ *See* Proverbs 15:29 and James 5:16. Let us pray:

Father, You are our Strong Tower, an ever-present help in times of trouble. You assure us of hearing us when we pray, and we bless You for being such an awesome, loving, and gracious God. Now, God, we ask that You forgive us for holding on to our past. Forgive us for not forgiving ourselves and others. We ask that You deliver us from the proverbial tormentors and perfect Your love in us now. Teach us, oh Lord, the way of Thy statutes, and we will keep them until the end. Give us understanding, and we shall keep Thy law; we shall observe them with our whole heart. We need Your grace so that we may have peace and joy. You promised a Covenant of Peace, and we now receive it in Jesus's mighty name. Cause us to forget those things behind us that we may press toward the things before us toward the high calling in Christ Jesus. Amen

If you recall, I asked you to compile a list of things you tell yourself repeatedly. Let us look at that list. As I mentioned, I once desired to write. However, my imagination envisioned something

Living Your Legacy Of Greatness

else. Due to spelling challenges, I thought my life did not adequately prepare me to write. MY WRITING OVERFLOWED once I reconciled my desire with my thoughts and vision. This book is a testament to that. I joyfully thank God's (the "Us" Spirit) command of the Universe to provide technology and spell-check. I laugh on the inside as I write these words. Why, you might ask? I am confident and assured that I can now write according to God's will for my life. He endowed me with knowledge, understanding, wisdom, and skill over thirty-five years, and this is just the beginning!

Have I arrived? No, I still face challenges that I must contend with often. Nonetheless, I keep moving forward! Therefore, I ask again, are your thoughts and desires in alignment? Fuel them with joy! Go forth and design well! If they are not, fortify your will with your religious practices, whatever they may be. It is important to remember that prayer brings about awareness. Intimacy with God is necessary for uncovering your thought's root cause. A joyful heart opens the windows of heaven to pour out unhindered blessings and surrender to the will of the Lord for your life. This practice will put you in a position of refocusing and a certainty that He can and will deliver.

If you concentrate on what you do not retain, you will continue *NOT* to lay hold on your destiny. Because what you focus/be-life (belief) upon will expand, manifesting in kind. Why do your thoughts grow into a demonstration of your ideas? The repetitive, persevering interaction with your mind's beliefs and the emotional focus causes them to grow. The proverbial nutrients interact with the spiritual thought seed, evoking and invoking growth. However, when you are proactive in unearthing those reference points, you can bring them to the forefront and change how you think about them, creating new reference points, new soil, and, thus, exceptional results. When you utilize religious practices: prayer, meditation, and a heart full of thanksgiving unto the Lord for what

Markeithia Lavon Silver

you do gain, more will come. *"Seek you first the Kingdom of God, and ALL things shall be added unto you."* Matthew 6:33. There is a method to the madness. *If your center of attention is on things, you then supplant those objects in your worship of God, the Infinite One creating an idol god* ~ Psalms 106.

The *Bible, Torah,* and the *Qur'an* all speak about how the Lord is a jealous God. You, in turn, bring evil (negativity) unto yourself and your situation. The good is the promises of God and "Whatsoever things are true, honest, just, pure, lovely, of good report if there be any virtue, and if there be any praise, think on these things" ~ Philippians 4:8. This verse implies the constant motions of Universal Laws at work. The Laws of Belief, Correspondence, and Attraction manifest your focused thoughts.

Moreover, if you busy your mind with Harmony in the oneness of God, perfect health emerges, mind, body, and spirit within and without, and goodwill toward humanity. Remarkable things happen when you are in your rightful place. You will not need to chase after material wealth, ministry, a husband, a wife, starting a business, or anything you can conjure up. If you *pursue God first,* the other things will overtake you!

Evil, therefore, is anything contrary to the Word of God concerning His creation, promises, and mercies. To call forth is to conceive, perceive, and believe in the mind or thought process. This development of thought is faith in action. This thought process creates an atmosphere for God to move in your life and situation. In contrast, if you busy your mind with worry and not in remembrance of the One worthy of worship, you, in turn, make an idol god out of your situation, replacing God with your situation in worship. No-thing has a right to be worshipped except the Lord— not even our problems. We are to bring our issues to God with praise and thanksgiving ~ Philippians 4:6.

Every thought or vision created within is the cause, and the consequences or circumstances are the results. Therefore, change

Living Your Legacy Of Greatness

your ideas and concepts to change your outcomes or occurrences. Undoubtedly, "the Lord does not change the condition of a nation (or person) until they change the condition within themselves (their soul/mind)" ~ *Surah* 13:11. We can reframe our reference points by making our conscious mind aware of them and take responsibility for our choices. You can only accomplish this by spending intimate time with God, reading His Word, and decreeing the Kingdom's promises over your life.

Did you ever experience walking into a department store with a sale going on, but you did not know it before your arrival? You stroll down the aisle, noticing the picture frames are just what you were looking for to put those old pictures on the wall. Before that, they sat in a box looking bland as ever. Now, you purchase those new frames encasing your precious photos, and a feeling of settleness comes over you. They look different; the fresh look makes you feel accomplished. This example is the similitude of reframing: to purposefully look at all of life's situations and create a frame that is pleasing to you, according to what God already spoke concerning you—you are loved, God accepts you as the beloved, you are great! You are a King's child and joint heir with Christ who rose with *ALL POWER* in His hands and sits on the Father's right hand. We stand under the *Blood Covenant* of Jesus's sacrifice and share in the Power of God through Christ! Can you *feel* that? *See* that? Can you *imagine* that? Do you *know* that you can operate in that power? Can you? Begin with creating a spiritual reference point that includes Christ as the Door. First, we must unearth the ones not serving us well.

By reference points, I mean those experiences embedded in our minds that govern our perceptions: childhood experiences, past relationships, what your teacher said, what your mother or father said concerning you, abuses you endured, and the like. Change these, and your perceptions will change your thoughts and actions.

Markeithia Lavon Silver

Whoever is guided by God's laws: His precepts, His promises, He shall direct in the path of righteousness, and they will not falter.

You may ask, how can one think of lack when the Lord promises to give you what you need? Therefore, it is evil to presume a lack in opposition to the promises of the Everlasting Infinite Power of El-Shaddai—Jehovah Jireh, my provider. God cannot and will not lie ~ Numbers 23:19, I Samuel 15:29, Hebrews 3:12. If He established it, He shall bring it to pass. ~ Genesis 41:32. Thus, I submit that not receiving and conceiving His promises is a form of evil. Who are we to reject the blessings of God? Are we greater than He is? "The evil one threatens you with poverty— (this is only in the minds, but we believe it and posture inadequacy affecting our circumstances)" ~ *Surah* 2:268-271. Meanwhile, the Lord bestows upon you His grace and promises you forgiveness from Him and bounty. His wisdom is indeed a benefit and of tremendous good when granted to an individual ~ James 1:5. Faith allows us to conceive and perceive the promises of the One who knows all things, taste it before it materializes, and be it within our minds.

How can one consider unforgiveness as an option when His mercy is everlasting? Once God forgives us, we must also forgive ourselves, or we will place ourselves in a position of calling the evil of unnecessary punishment, not befitting of one who has already found pardon by the Ultimate Judge. The sentence we impose upon ourselves does not stem from the heavenly realm but from within the mind—a trick of the enemy, an illusion of our thoughts, who dupes us into believing that the Righteous Judge, God, never forgives. This thought process brings about oppression and depression, lending itself to hopelessness—contrary to what the Lord offers by His grace and mercy. God told the Prophet Jeremiah to tell the Children of Israel that "He knew the plans He had for them...Plans to prosper them, give them hope, and a future" ~ Jeremiah 29. God knows the plans for our lives, and, once in motion, by the Lord's command, nothing can divert, cancel, or change it ~ Phil. 1:6.

Living Your Legacy Of Greatness

Moreover, to call forth the good is to stand without a doubt that the Lord is ever merciful and gracious toward us. We thrive when we seek His face, praise Him for His mercy toward us, and walk in the peace of His forgiveness and abundance!

More importantly, if we are in remembrance of the One who sustains all life, there is the faithfulness of the Infinite Power of El-Shaddai remembering us in our coming in and going out ~ Deuteronomy 28. If we are operating under the Most-High God's commands, following the Wisdom of that guidance puts us in a position where He will meet all our needs. When we are aware that we are in error, we must straight away correct our situation and ask forgiveness, knowing, without doubt, the Cleansing Power of God will purge us, forgive us, and restore us to our rightful place ~ *I John* 1:9. There is no lack of Provision in the Infinite One El-Shaddai. The Holy Spirit is the best facilitator of our affairs. Stay focused, my friends, on your goal of dominion and excellence! Therefore, I conclude that anything thought or act contrary to this (God's Word) is evil ~ Hebrews 3:12.

As we grow in godly wisdom, knowledge, and understanding, we can shed the things of this world "as a loose garment." Likewise, as we mature and begin working, we learn the delayed gratification scheme. Individually, as we mature in our learning, we set goals for our lives, saving money to gift ourselves with what makes us happy. I mentioned earlier that one of the most significant rewards I gave myself was releasing all the negativity building up inside me. Fortunately, the concept of delayed gratification is not applicable here. The only labor we engage in is being available for ourselves to enjoy all of life's sacred pleasures.

My sense of spiritual detachment would end in reading *Morning B.R.E.W.: A Divine Power Drink for your Soul* by Rev. Dr. Kirk Byron Jones, M.Div., Ph.D. This book would become another lifeline in my full recovery. Dr. Jones admonishes us to "Be still. Receive God's love. Embrace personhood, and Welcome today," as it is now. This combination of devotional activities enables the person to abide in the stillness of God's love. This book was instrumental in assisting me in finding my way back to my place of rest. Being still enabled me to analyze and silence the turbulent storms raging in my life. Also, it allowed me to explore every parameter of my patience. Next, receiving God's love was the cornerstone of my peace. I was fortified by feeling God's love and envisioning and accepting it. Embracing my personhood allowed me to trust my strengths *and* my weaknesses. These three concepts prepared me for the last step, welcoming the day. You harvest enormous power when applying these concepts to your life. You cannot just say the words; you must *lean into* them, allowing the full manifestation of God's love to cover you like a warm blanket on a cool night. He envelopes us as a means of serenity, security, and stability so that we will not panic in life's situations; instead, we choose to rest in Him as the Sustainer and Provider of all we need ~ Psalms 23.

Moreover, when we spend time with Him, we bask in the lather of His Love, and everything is right with the world. He comforts us. He urges us on. He hides us when the enemy is afoot and pushes us out for ministry in perfect timing.

Dr. Jones's insight regarding this spiritual drink is like riding on a gentle, soft, proverbial cloud. Depending on this symbolic blanket of God's unyielding grace and mercy gives you a sensation of safety and security. This sense of protection reminded me of my children when they were younger. They often fell asleep on the car ride home. Upon arrival, I would tenderly move them to their beds. I would gently pick them up and rest them on my shoulders. They rested their heads upon me loosely and limply, feeling loved, safe, and secure. On many occasions, they would never wake up. They trusted "Mommy" would take care of them. My morning B.R.E.W. experience was much like this. As I return daily to the Creator's loving arms embellished in His presence, there is a sense of blessed serenity. *I am safe in His arms. God hides me in His Pavilion, where my troubles cannot find me.* A river wells inside me that purges the grudge of life's disappointments and replenishes my spirit to a place of renewal.

A church hymn says, *"I come to the Garden alone, while the dew is still on the roses...And He walks with me, and He talks with me, and He tells me I am His own. And the joy we share, as we tarry there, None other has ever known."* Therefore, we must dare surrender our thoughts, desires, and worship unto the One who created us so that God can cleanse, restore, and empower us to engage in life with purposeful intent.

Motives of the Heart

I would be remiss not to mention the conversion of the heart in the restoration process with specificity. Accordingly, we must examine our motives emanating from our hearts for a few reasons. Reflecting upon our heart motives is challenging, especially amid worldly pressure to succeed, perform at an optimum level, or compete to be the best. Societal cultures often produce unhealthy competition and a false sense of pride that hardly ever creates sustained inner peace and joy. *For some, once the glory of rising to the top diminishes, emptiness follows, and a constant seeking to fill that void ensues.* Consequently, we are unsatisfied with what we achieved in the past, and the door opens for ulterior motives to flood our hearts. Then, we search to experience that feeling of accomplishment again by any means necessary, which governs our every move. On the other hand, a conquest may not be the driving force but a vision like marrying at a certain age. I recall making a vow to myself that I would marry at eighteen. Raised in the church, I thought it a noble and righteous vision. However,

Markeithia Lavon Silver

I never considered God's plan and timing for my life. My motive dominated my relationships, resulting in short-term interactions. If I thought dating over ten months warranted the question, "What are your intentions?" I asked. Most young men felt the inquiry was too deep for their taste. I was determined to marry, never considering anything else. This mindset resulted in broken relationships and pain. Nevertheless, by His grace and mercy, deliverance was on my horizon!

As Christ's followers, we forget the most important commission—we are here to serve ~ Matthew 23:12. Thus, understanding how to keep our motives true, honest, just, pure, lovely, [of] good report, virtuous, and praiseworthy is essential in the transformation process ~ Philippians 4:8. I believe David is one of the most significant examples of trusting and seeking God. Whether we are motivated by vainglory, lust, vision, or the like, David humbly shows us how to ask God for assistance in heart matters. David passionately requests God purge him with hyssop and create in him a clean heart ~ Psalms 51. David's candid account of his sin shows us that the effort to obtain and maintain a pure heart is a constant struggle. Crying out to God, letting go of the pain, and activating our faith allows us to partake in God's healing bread ~ Matthew 15:22-29.

God is forever with us, beloved! I love the theme song of *Touched by an Angel,* which captures a glimpse of God's faithfulness, love, tenderness, long-suffering, and attentiveness towards us. The song says, "When you walk down the road, heavily burdened, heavy load, *I will rise and walk with you.* I will walk with you till the sun does not shine…walk with you *every time.* I tell you, I will walk with you!" (Emphasis mine). God promises to lift a standard through every storm ~ Isaiah 59:19. He will be there through the waters, the rivers when the tempest is raging, and the fires that will not burn or kindle upon you ~ Isaiah 43:2. Remind yourself of this hope each day! ~ Psalms 42:11.

Living Your Legacy Of Greatness

More importantly, the *Bible* instructs us to ask the Lord for assistance and cast our cares upon Him ~ *I Peter* 5:7. *See also* Matthew 11:28-30. We seek the Lord to transform our thoughts and visions and seek deliverance and freedom from pain and anguish ~ *I Chronicles* 4:10. However, we must also evaluate whether His righteousness guides our motivations. If not, then, as King Solomon says, "Let us hear the conclusion of the whole matter: Fear God and keep His commandments: for this is the whole duty of man. For God shall bring every work into judgment, with every secret thing, whether good or evil...for to accomplish anything outside the whole duty of humanity is 'all vanity'" ~ Ecclesiastes 12: 8-14. The enemy's devices do not fool us or influence the body unless we give him room ~ *II Corinthians* 2:11 and Galatians 5: 19-21. The fall of Adam infiltrated and damaged our body of righteousness, resulting in knowing good and evil outside God's wisdom. Not only did this day's entrance of disobedience usher in deceit and death, but Adam also embarked upon the first exhibit of idolatry— *he chose his relationship with Eve over his fear, reverence, and relationship with God!*

Consequently, sin is familiar to us ~ *I Corinthians* 10:13. Through the blood sacrifice of Christ, God enables us to walk after the Spirit and not the flesh, overcoming temptation. If we falter, we need only confess our sins. God is just to forgive and cleanse us from all unrighteousness ~ *I John* 1:9. More importantly, we must remind ourselves that no trouble, mistake, or past is too big for God to fix. We are never outside of His tender reach of redemption and restoration. For "it is God which worketh in you both to will and to do of his good pleasure" ~ Philippians 2:13. Nonetheless, keeping the act and consequences of our choices continuing in our awareness keeps us grounded, humble, and in a constant understanding of our needing God and His righteousness ~ Psalms 51:3.

Markeithia Lavon Silver

Likewise, Apostle Paul admonishes reviewing our motives before praying and asking for something from God. He concludes that even if we make a request, we ask wrongly. Why? We "have not because we 'ask not,' and that we ask amiss to consume our selfish desires upon our lusts" ~ James 4:2-3. We constantly renew our minds after receiving Christ as Lord and Savior ~ Romans 12:1-2. Accordingly, He draws us and gives us the power that works in us to *become* the sons of God—in conformity to the image and likeness of His son ~ St. John 6:44, Ephesians 3:20, Romans 8:29, St. John 1:12, respectively. Therefore, yielding our will to God allows us to obtain and maintain righteous and pure intentions. We are *new creatures in Christ*, and each day, His power will enable us to lay down the old self as God renews our new self in the conformity of His son Christ Jesus, that we might be firstborn among many brethren—for we are heirs and joint-heirs with Christ ~ Romans 8:17. If we live our legacy by Kingdom's standards, we are encouraged to shore up our motives, led by God's word, and surrender all to His plan from the beginning for our lives—greatness.

I do not want to end this chapter without circling back and mentioning the importance of the Law of Correspondence and how it plays an integral part in manifesting the legacy of greatness God intended from the beginning. The enemy is subtle—he is the father of lies and a murderer from the beginning. ~ St John 8:44. If he can get you to receive a seed of another kind to thwart God's good work in your life, he will do it! As sons and daughters of God, we must be vigilant and sober concerning what we allow to germinate in our mind soil. When God breathed into Adam, he became a living soul housed by a body and guided by the strength of God's Spirit—the Kingdom, as Jesus put it! The Hebrew word for soul is *nephesh*. The soul is the seat of our appetites. The soul houses our emotions, passions, activities of our will, and character.[29] Once a thought/ seed is sewn into our soul-mind soil, we gravitate to the objects of

Living Your Legacy Of Greatness

our focus. This definition, in short, is the Law of Attraction. Social Science determined and unveiled that the Law of Correspondence and Attraction guides our social interaction through socialization. Our minds expand, and contract based on the various symbols we create and assign as sacred or profane. The enemy knew this proprietary information before the Fall and his expulsion from heaven. He knew that if he could convince Eve to think differently about the Tree of Knowledge of Good and Evil as an object of her affection, her attraction to it would trigger Correspondence, and she would disobey God.

Accordingly, our belief system cultivates and nourishes our thoughts, causing germination and growth. Additionally, nutritional ingredients like the pride of life, the lust of the eye, and flesh correspond with the soul's appetite and nourish our thought seeds growing unwanted tares. Therefore, we must allow Philippians 4:8 to guide nourishing the righteous seed within us. Understanding these Universal Laws and how they affect our lives is imperative in studying to show ourselves approved to divide the Word of Truth rightfully. ~ *II Timothy* 2:15.

When you consider these things, your view of the events unfolding in the Garden changes your outlook. Your viewpoint leaves you suspecting that these laws have been in effect since the beginning. When you read Genesis 3, you find that Eve conversed with the serpent on whether or not she should eat of the Tree of Knowledge of Good and Evil. However, you now discern that deception was not the only thing at play. More importantly, he wickedly sought to invoke and evoke the Laws of Correspondence, Attraction, Belief, Sowing and Reaping, and judgment resulting from gendering with another kind. The enemy was after her mind soil that he might alter her kind from within and bring death. He sought to gender the seeds of pride, covetousness, and lust, enlarging her seat of passion and desire and bringing death to her kind (humanity). ~ Colossians 1:19-21.

Markeithia Lavon Silver

In order to understand what she was contending with, you must start at the beginning. God lays the foundation for understanding this upheaval in Genesis 1. As you read the Scriptures, you understand that God speaks through Moses, regarding creation as an allegory *and* textual interpretation. God reveals insights and mysteries to Moses concerning the creation of the earth and its ability to produce seed after its kind, the beasts of the field, and Adam. No two seeds were alike, and each seed reproduces after its kind. Scientifically, every seed has within it the necessary ingredients to produce its kind. Change the molecular structure of a seed, and you have another kind, even if it *looks* similar. The enemy understood a seed's marvelous, wonderful, and intricate function ~ Psalms 139:14. We discover in Jesus's ministry that the Kingdom is within and is likened to a sower that sows seeds. ~ Mark 1:15, 4:26-29, Luke 17:20-21. Therefore, the accuser of the brethren is after the *Kingdom* in you!

First, God informs Moses that there were no others over heaven and earth in the beginning save God. However, God is described as the "Us Spirit" in Genesis 1:26 when they consider making man in Their image and after Their likeness. In the previous verses, before God creates anything, He is observed in the spirit by Moses to be moving upon the face of the waters. Then, He spoke, "Let there be Light." He divided the light from the darkness and saw that the light was good. Here, light and darkness are representations of illumination and ignorance. When something illuminates, it brings light, which reveals and uncovers the dark places—what is light educates our ignorance. In other words, Moses uses the word light as a metaphor for revelation, a bearer of deliverance, as in Psalms 37:1, justice, righteousness, guidance or instruction, and the glory of God, as in the light that emanated from Moses' face in Exodus 34:29-35. God created the Light, the earth, the firmament, the grass, water, and the seas, each yielding its seed after its kind.

Living Your Legacy Of Greatness

Next, one must consider that when God was creating the earth, Lucifer (the light bearer who led the sons of God into worship) was present and understood the workings and laws of heaven, unlike Job, whom God questioned to explain whether he knew the foundations of heaven and how they were laid. *See* Ezekiel *28* and Job 38-40. Lucifer also knew that it was against the laws of God to gender one kind of seed (beast of the field, herb, or even certain types of clothing) with another. *See* Leviticus 19:19. Moreover, he comprehended the results of violating this law. In Genesis 1:12, Moses unveils for us the reproductive process of the seed and its laws. The verse says, "And the earth brought forth grass, and herb yielding seed *after his kind*, and the tree yielding fruit, whose seed was in itself, *after his kind*: and God saw that it was good. This description of how a seed reproduces after its kind reveals the Law of Correspondence at work in the seed. Each seed yielded its seed of itself, not of another. This point is critical as an apple seed cannot produce a pear or an orange but will produce an apple. If you gender an apple seed with another seed, you produce *another* kind. Lucifer, prior to the Fall, is aware of this concept and its repercussions. The Hebrew word for yielding in verse 12 is *zâra'*, pronounced zaw-rah. It means to sew, figuratively to disseminate, plant, conceive seed, plant, or yield.[30] In other words, yielding, a verb, is an act of sewing the ground or field or of planting a seed that has the potential to disperse and manifest into other areas, literally or figuratively. Here, one must understand that your mind is allegorically earth, and your thoughts are seeds planted in your earthen vessel and manifest after its kind. *See* Proverbs 23:7. Each seed or thought has everything necessary to reproduce after its kind.

After God created the beast of the earth after his kind, the cattle after their kind, and everything that creeps upon the earth after its kind, He created Adam after the image and likeness of the "Us" Spirit. We are God-kind and possess a spiritual body.

Markeithia Lavon Silver

Finally, this logical progression takes us to the Fall. It gives us a clearer understanding of what Eve was contending with the enemy, his wickedness, and the Laws of Correspondence, Attraction, Belief, Sowing, and Reaping in conjunction with the function of the soul housing a seed. Therefore, when we arrive at Genesis 3, we see the enemy taking advantage of Eve's ignorance of what will result in her disobedience due to laws of the gendering of another kind and the law of sowing and reaping yielding after its kind—the Law of Correspondence.

Reading this information, one might ask why this material is essential. Adam and Eve transformed into another during that exchange with the enemy. Reviewing this information should illuminate the subtlety of the enemy. It hopefully will allow you to appreciate the blood sacrifice of Christ while understanding that a legacy awaits your response. More critically, grasping that *the enemy is after the Kingdom within you and aims to bring death* at all costs. However, he cannot do it without your permission. The accuser of the brethren needs a host body and cannot enter without your giving him a place. ~ John 14:30 & Ephesians 4:27. His wicked nourishment prohibits the transformation process. If you allow him, he will steal, obfuscate, and choke the righteous seed within you. ~ Matthew13:18-23 & Mark 4:16-20.

Finally, I tenderly remind you, oh gentle reader, that Hebrews 6:1 petitions us to maturity, stating, "Therefore leaving the principles of the doctrine of Christ, let us go on to perfection; not laying again the foundation of repentance from dead works, and of faith toward God." Although it is God's desire for us to develop and mature in quantity and quality, there are occasions when we stagnate in our growth due to carnality. We must surrender these things and allow the Holy Spirit to unearth them so we may walk in our legacy of greatness.

I will end this chapter with the refrain from a song by Judson Van DeVenter, *I Surrender All,* and prose entitled *Surrender.*

"All to Jesus I surrender; all to Him I freely give; I will ever love and trust Him, in His presence daily live…I Surrender All. I Surrender All; All to Thee, my blessed Savior, I surrender all…."

Surrender

Will you choose to surrender more deeply to freedom—freedom from the concepts and ideas of this world? Will you allow the Joy and Peace that Love brings when it reigns completely in your heart?

Will you overlook the many prisons of hatred, pain, broken hearts, inadequacy, and not being good enough and choose to be encapsulated by the freedom of love, peace, and joy?

Will you run from the terror that aims to take you hostage, prohibiting your growth, chasing after that which will loosen the chains of despair: perfected Love?

It is morning! Joy will follow. Resist anything that will clip your wings of freedom, Peace, and Joy. Do not allow the knife of hatred, jealousy, fear, abandonment, rejection, or any pain to pierce your heart, causing the Life bequeathed to you by Christ to leave you slowly. Surrender your all to the freedom of Peace, Love, and Joy.

CHAPTER SIX

BE AWARE OF WHO YOU ARE

"They that KNOW their God shall be strong and do great exploits!" ~ Daniel 11:32

—Daniel

"Have I not told you, you are gods, but you shall die like men..." ~ Psalms 82:6.

—David

"... Behold, the Kingdom of God is within you." ~ St. Luke 17:21

—Jesus

"We are accepted in the Beloved..." ~ Ephesians 1:6.

—Paul

"...And this is the CONFIDENCE that we have IN HIM if we ask anything according to His will, He HEARETH us." ~ 1 John 5:14

—John

Markeithia Lavon Silver

While a police officer working overtime on the day shift, I received a radio call directing me to a particular address. The dispatcher indicated that the call involved the sighting of a small child wandering around without supervision. Near the home was an elementary school, and children hurried along to make it in before the tardy bell rang. Familiar with the area and the routine of school children walking to school, I did not suspect anything serious. Nonetheless, I rushed to the location in case a potential danger ensued. As I approached the area, I observed a small child about two years of age looking around as if she had lost who was with her. Immediately, I exited my cruiser and ran over to her. It was a miracle that I spotted her as she was tiny compared to the cars driving by as children disembarked to attend school.

I asked her name and where her parents were. She responded, "Mommy." I said, "Where is your mommy?" She kept repeating, "Mommy." I asked, "What is your mommy's name?" She again responded, "Mommy." Of course, I took her back to the station house and eventually found her parents. This incident troubled me as a mom. My daughter knew her name, my name, phone number, job, and where she resided. At first, I thought it was a language barrier because she was Latina. However, when one of my peers spoke with her in her native language, she did not know her parents' names or where she lived. Eventually, the babysitter contacted the family, and we connected with them several hours later.

The child could identify her mom and dad if they were before her. However, she did not know who she was and could not convey that information successfully to onlookers. Do you, gentle reader, *know* who you are? Can you articulate to another person that the Kingdom resides within you, as Jesus said in St. Luke 17:21? More importantly, can you conceive such a status and walk in your god isness by faith? *Lord, God, enlighten the eyes of our understanding according to Your Word in Ephesians 1:15-23, so that we may have eyes to see and ears to hear in Jesus's name. Amen.*

Living Your Legacy Of Greatness

How do we come to know who we are? Faith and persuasion—"Faith comes by hearing and hearing by the Word of God" ~ Romans 10:17. More importantly, "Let every man be *FULLY* persuaded in her/his OWN mind" ~ Romans 14:5. In other words, faith shows up when you are speaking and persuaded by the content of God's spoken word. You must listen to God's Word and say what you hear with the mind's persuasion, and faith will follow. Rearrange the word listen, and you will get the secret of listening—S I L E N T. God speaks and operates in the stillness of silence. *"Be still and know that I am God!"* ~ Psalms 46:10. I know that you heard, and some of you adopted (graphed into your lives and in your minds), a season of busyness is productivity. However, God said, "BE STILL." You will come to KNOW the I AM God and the amazing you God created in this holy stillness. Good God from Zion! Are you ready to *KNOW* the "Us" Spirit that formed, shaped, and breathed into you? Are you prepared to meet you?

Gen. 1:26 says, "And, God said, 'Let *US* make man in *OUR* image *AND* after *OUR* likeness." With the "Us" Spirit's breath, we praise El-Shaddai and speak the Power of God's word. In Christ, we live, move, and acquire our being! In His infinite wisdom, Abba, Father *gave* us His Spirit! His Kingdom *is* within us! We are again granted privileges upon reconciliation into the Kingdom in this image and likeness through Christ.

Pay close attention to *Webster's Collegiate Dictionary's* definition of image and likeness:

Image: an optical [of or relating to sight—physical, mental, and spiritual] representation formed by a mirror [outward—physical and inner—spiritual]; an optically created duplicate; a personification of something specific <you are the image of joy>. [More specific, Beloved of God, you are in the image of God!]; a [mere] representation; to make the likeness of; to reflect; I *LIKE THIS ONE*—To transmit (*a*

Markeithia Lavon Silver

replica of the content of a storage device to another storage device). In other words, we are the mirrored reflection of God, and He transferred a replica of information *(The Kingdom)* into our being when He breathed into our nostrils. We possess the capability of *knowing* what God knows! What a mighty God we serve!

Likeness: Resemblance to another.

I John 4:13-17 declares, "Hereby *KNOW* we (that is the Children of God) dwell *IN* Him, and He *IN* us, Because, He has *GIVEN US HIS SPIRIT*…because, *as He IS, so are WE in THIS world*…." At your leisure, look into the mirror and watch your movements. With every gesture you make, the image can make the same motion effortlessly. Right? Likewise, when we recognize *who* we are, we will do exactly what Jesus did in the Father and as we will do in Christ. ~ St John 5:17-20. We are a chosen generation (set aside and distinguished), a royal priesthood (Kings, Queens, Priest, and Prophets of God), a holy nation (God's Kingdom), a peculiar people (Preserved by God); that ye should shew forth the praises of him who hath called you out of darkness into his marvelous light. We are the exact opposite of the seed of the enemy! Marinate and digest that into your soil mind and walk in your legacy of greatness, gentle reader!

When we believe these things to be accurate, we can develop a valid argument supporting our belief and philosophy regarding our walk as sons and daughters of God.

Premise 1: God made me In the Mirror Image of the "Us" Spirit—a reflection of who *HE IS*. As a son and daughter, I can do everything He does.

Premise 2: God made me After the Duplication and Likeness of the "Us" Spirit—God filled me with the same "spiritual stuff"

Living Your Legacy Of Greatness

as the "Us" spirit. The Infinite Power of El-Shaddai, God of the Cosmos, resides inside me! He gave me His Spirit!

Premise 3: The "Us" Spirit breathed into me and made me a living soul! The "Us" Spirit placed a content replica in me! Because God breathed *HIS* Spirit into me, the exact scope and essence of God reside in me. Moreover, God's Spirit is eternal and dwells in me continually.

Therefore, it necessarily follows from premises 1, 2, and 3 that if I reflect God, and He gave me His Spirit, God *must reside in me, and I must enjoy* Holy Vision *at my spiritual fingertips. I possess* Creative Abilities, Godly Wisdom, Understanding, Knowledge, *and* Skill. *I potentially possess all of what God knows. I continuously walk in the ability to unlock/stir up wisdom, knowledge, and skill in every area. I can constantly reach the heart of humanity in the Christ spirit. I walk in the ability to preach good tidings to the meek, bind up the broken-hearted, proclaim liberty to the captives, power to heal the sick, raise the dead, and set the captives free!*

IF THE FORMER IS TRUE, I MUST CONCLUDE THE LATTER!

(Right here, you need to get up out of your seat, or wherever you are, and begin to praise God for your status and entitlements in the Kingdom) Good God, from Zion! Glory! Hallelujah!

I come already with an AMEN inside of me. "He has clothed me with the garments of salvation; He has covered me with the robe of Righteousness…For as the earth brings forth, her bud…The Lord God will *cause righteousness and praise to spring forth before all nations!*" ~Isaiah 61:1-11. (Emphasis mine). Sons and daughters of Zion, God released a prophetic anointing that causes us to *see, know, and understand* His will. This anointing of greatness shores up the remnant in the righteousness of God. This impartation births a fresh wind and anointing upon you, your family, and your ministry. As the King's children in Christ, you can create decrees and pronouncements, hear the people's petitions, and take their struggles to the gate ~ Isaiah 28:6. I, therefore, "the prisoner of the Lord, beseech you that ye walk worthy of the vocation wherewith you are called, with all lowliness and meekness, with longsuffering, forbearing one another in love; endeavoring to keep the unity of the Spirit in the bond of peace" ~ Ephesians 4:1-3.

The world groans, and not just the world; we await the manifestation of God's daughters/sons—the princesses and princes of the Kingdom of God. The world, and we, are waiting for us to lay hold to our inheritance of sonship!

GET READY! GET READY, DAUGHTERS AND SONS OF GOD! *God is awaiting your choice to embrace your legacy!* WHAT ARE YOU WAITING FOR, BELOVED? DO NOT LET FEAR STOP YOU FROM PUSHING FORWARD INTO YOUR DESTINY! THE KEEPER OF RECORDS CALLED YOUR NAME REGARDING THE WILL AND TESTAMENT OF GOD! Press on in His presence! He will not disappoint!

RISE AND TAKE YOUR RIGHTFUL PLACE IN THE KINGDOM!

The choice is yours. Will you approach the Throne of Grace and receive your induction, release, and anointing into greatness beyond your wildest dreams? This transformation is not about material prosperity. However, wealth is a by-product, a fringe benefit of your godly status that will hunt you and overtake you simply because you seek the pleasure of God and His Kingdom. Specifically, it is about ownership, entitlement, and abundance.

Moreover, it is about worshiping the Most High God, El-Shaddai, for His goodness and tender mercies. An all-encompassing legacy of greatness bequeathed to the children of God in their obedience

Living Your Legacy Of Greatness

to His call. Encapsulated within this legacy comes the fullness of joy and pleasures at His right hand. Likewise, it brings healing and a manifested restoration of God's children back unto His bosom (a familiar source of protection, security, stability, and affection—Psalms 91. *See also* Psalms 23).

Will you strive to KNOW HIM, TRUST what *HE* says, STAND ON HIS PROMISES? Will you do it for yourself *and* the world? Did you ever ask yourself, "What is precluding the Children of God from operating in the fullness of their "legacy of greatness?" The time is now and is far spent—we must self-evaluate our position, enabling us to move from glory to glory. *PUSH! BREATHE AND PUSH!* You must take on Jacob's attitude, which held onto the Angel of God until He blessed him. Do not let go. Hold on and push! Travail, cry out, if necessary, but push! If your circumstance wants to disqualify you from receiving your blessing, do not let it, Push! Your mind wants to keep you boxed into the notion of lack; do not let it—push! Do you remember the woman with the issue of blood? Her focus was to touch Jesus! *Get your focus on and push!* See it on the other side and advance one day, week, month, and year at a time! I cannot let it go…push! Puuuush! Do not consider the smallness of your step; keep moving!

I dare you! They that know their God shall be strong and do great exploits! Move from where you are to a higher place, exceedingly abundantly above all that you could ask or even think, and then jump! *I promise you* the bridge will be there. God will not disappoint. Once on the Bridge, you will be well on your way to grasping what God bequeathed to us before the world's foundation.

Hear what Ernest Holmes says in *Thoughts Are Things* regarding Dominion:

There is a God-Power at the center of everyone's being. *This Power knows neither lack, limitation nor fear, sickness, disquiet, nor imperfection*…because you are an individual

Markeithia Lavon Silver

[with free will to choose your greatness], *you can build a wall of negative thoughts between yourself and this perfection.* This wall, which keeps you from your greater good, is *cemented together by fear and unbelief, mixed in the mortar of negative experience.* (Emphasis mine).

What do you think about that? If we can relinquish our fears and doubts, we can lay hold of who we are in God! Take the step, my friend. *Take the step!*

As in building a house, you must first begin with the foundation, counting the cost—your thought focus and vision-building affect your outcome ~ Luke 14:28. However, we are oblivious to the harvest of our seeds of thought. *We plant arbitrarily and capriciously into our mind's earthen vessel, never considering the effects.* Next, you must concern yourself with the support beams, the outer walls, and the covering, which is the roof. The Father seeks a place to dwell fully – to "worship in spirit and truth" inside us—He seeks communion and oneness in Him ~ John 4:24. He desires to tell us secrets about Himself and His creation. He longs for our eyes to be open to the things in the spirit ~ Ephesians 1. God wants to clothe us in a garment of salvation and cover us in a robe of righteousness ~ Isaiah 61: 1-11. However, we must prepare a place for Him to dwell unhindered. The sanctuary of worship is our house (our body, mind, spirit), where the Father wishes to commune with us and use our members for His glory. *I release a prophetic space of newness in God. I decree and declare by the authority vested in me, through Jesus Christ, that you will create a special place for you and God to meet daily.* God desires to light the candle inside of you, dispelling the darkness. "For thou wilt light my candle: The Lord, my God, will enlighten my darkness" ~ Psalms 18:28.

Accordingly, there must be a purposeful plan to attain this communion with the "Us" Spirit and Infinite Power of El-Shaddai.

Living Your Legacy Of Greatness

Commitment matters, gentle reader, and what we oblige to should be entered with reverence and forethought. "There is no success without commitment...When we organize how we think, feel, and behave, we [potentially dominate our outcome]... Likewise, our approach to life's circumstances [according to our belief system] matters. When we are aware of what they [our experiences and thoughts manifested] are, and we perceive and keep them in line with our belief system, we develop a successful strategy," says Al-Ghazzali. [31]

The foundation and application for receiving the fullness of abundance begin with four significant challenges. First, you must purposefully remove fear and doubt from your perspective. The fruit of fear and doubt are not profitable for the greatness God designed for you. You must lay the axe at the root and hewn it down in Jesus's name ~ Matthew 3:10. You acquire this sense of fearlessness by communion with God. The *Bible* reveals in the book of *I John*, "There is no fear in God's love." Fear prohibits one from completely being one with God. The word fear comes from the Greek word *phobas*. This rendition is where we get our word phobia or fear of something. This meaning would suggest that *fear of* something or phobia denotes mental failure or the inability to overcome something mentally. So, one interpretation of "there is no fear in God's love" might read as thus, "there is no failure or inability to overcome while standing, embraced by, clothed or covered by, blanketed by, in the presence of, or overshadowed by God's love." Fear fuels the perception of feeling naked and vulnerable. Adam felt vulnerable (bare) and fearful (afraid) after disobeying God's command not to eat the *Tree of Knowledge of Good and Evil*. Reread the passage on vulnerability and weakness from earlier. This time, ask God for wisdom and understanding. Giving into this feeling of nakedness and unprotectedness stunts our ability to grow, keeps us from God

Markeithia Lavon Silver

(recall, Adam hid because he was naked), and prevents us from being who God created us to be. Thus, the first application for receiving the fullness of Life abundantly begins with communion with God and removing fear –submitting your vulnerability to God.

Second, laying the foundation to receive God's love must accompany the practice or art of disciplined thought. According to the Bible, we call upon this power, placing our imagination under subjection ~ *II Corinthian* 10:5. Anything that rises against the knowledge of God (oneness in Him) you cast down, uproot it from your thought process. Additionally, the *Bible* speaks of renewing the mind. Paul said, "Let *this* mind (the Mind of Power, the Mind of the "Us" Spirit) that was in Christ be also in you. Also, *be transformed* by renewing your mind" ~ Romans 12:2, Philippians 2:5-11. (Emphasis mine). Transformation is a moment-by-moment, day-by-day process. The *Bible* says, once again, "Faith comes by hearing." One must be willing to expand and stretch the mind. Renewing the mind entails the openness to receive innovative ideas, challenges, and obstacles of change that may present themselves. Indeed, letting go of the old is challenging, but with the power of the mind's intent to change, you can do it! *By the Authority of the Kingdom in Christ Jesus, I decree and declare that your supernatural ability to let go of the past and lay hold of God's destiny for your life begins now! Amen.*

In *Disciplines of the Spirit*, Howard Thurman says, "Discipline of the [mind and] body is part of the wisdom of the body, one of the abiding characteristics of life." He goes on to illustrate that this discipline is consistent with nature. Thurman observed a plumbing crew digging a hole to fix a pipe. Thurman says, "I saw that a large section of the sewer pipe had been exposed: around it and encircling it was a thick network of roots that had found their way inside the pipe by penetrating the joints in many places. The tree was more than four hundred yards away. This [distance] did not matter to the roots. They were on the hunt—for life." Therefore, if you are on

158

Living Your Legacy Of Greatness

the quest for God's heart (the wellspring of life), you will, by any means necessary, find the Source that sustains you and unearth the god-reflection within you. The more you search, the more aware you become of the Life residing in you—the Sustainable nature you yearn for and seek. ~ Psalms 27:8.

Third, one must engage the mind with thoughts that facilitate growth to receive the maximum abundance of Life. Christ was the personification of oneness with God. Scripture refers to Him as the "'Word' made flesh" ~1 John 1. He was the express image of God's person. ~ Hebrews 1:3. We, too, can become the "Word made flesh" because He (Jesus) says as much to us. "Greater works shall you do," and "As Jesus *is*, so are we in this earth." ~ St. John 14:12 and I John 4:17, respectively. However, it will take a willingness to submit your spirit to discipline (a disciple) of the mind. *I decree and declare by the Authority of the Kingdom in Christ Jesus a disciplined nature that allows you to read God's Word with understanding and insight, shoring up your mental stance in Christ, fusing your oneness in the Lord. Amen.* It is not good enough for a trainer to tell the trainee that s/he must complete several sets of ten to achieve the goal of toning. The trainee must apply the trainer's instructions to their life. This metaphor is what I believe Paul meant by the statement, "Faith without works is dead." There must be an application of the Word (Law) or new knowledge upon the mind for transformation. The more trained the mind, the closer one becomes filled with God's Spirit—greatness.

"Faith comes by hearing." This statement denotes a constant reiteration of what you hear and speak to yourself. "I heard it," without repeatedly reiterating to yourself, will not get you beyond faith to a place of knowing. It is in this place of awareness that constant miracles happen. This realm is beyond faith—a perfected faith, a posture walking in the Truth of God's Word. Faith is necessary to please God, according to Hebrews 11:6. Correspondingly, just as the school system's established rank determines your educational prowess, there are levels of faith: little faith, great faith, and perfected faith. This knowledge controls the outcome of the fullness of your abundance. This stance permits you to call those things as though they were not; it allows you to intervene and stand in the gap for others at the gate of spiritual warfare, laying the axe at the root and hewn down unprofitable fruit.

However, you cannot reach the next level by going to it; you must die to it. In other words, you must give up and let go of who you are today, in your faith, discerning, and emotional mind. Accordingly, you can enter God's next level of assurance once you reach a place and space of knowing. To achieve this new level, you must sacrifice the old self, relinquish who you were, and embrace who you are becoming. Then, the next level of birthing in faith occurs. There is labor pain, cervix expansion, and baby delivery, like in any natural birth. One must be ready to endure releasing or shedding the old and reveal the perfected you. Incidentally, sustaining the process is entirely up to the individual aspiring to grow to the next level. *If there is no pressing to move forward, holding on to the past may delay your birthing process.*

Similarly, the former class will prepare and elevate you to the next grade level when going from grade to grade. If you do not pass the final exams, you may need to stay back and repeat the step. The previous self, however, is foundational in moving forward. The past self serves as a springboard that maintains the continuity of your trajectory toward greatness. To sustain your new level, you must be open to change—drawing upon the previous state, nonetheless open to expanding and creating new ideas as God releases new revelatory wisdom and understanding ~ Revelation 4:1.

Proverbs 23:7 states, "For as s/he thinks in her/his heart, so is s/he." Romans 14:5 declares, "Let every wo/man be fully persuaded in her/his mind." Each person convinced thoroughly in their thinking

Living Your Legacy Of Greatness

must believe that they are free of the old self before a change can occur. Often, after repenting to the Lord of our pride, arrogance, slackness, failure to commune with God, and giving in to the flesh, we cannot forgive ourselves even if God forgives us. Holding on to past issues, whatever they may be, the full manifestation of your god-ness, the word wrapped in the flesh, can or will not reveal its fullness until the past knots are removed or transformed. I mentioned that I believe this position of unforgiveness of self to be wicked after God forgives us. It is contrary to God's word. *The lake of forgetfulness is where my sins lay* ~ Micah 7:19. *Who am I to drudge them up? You are going against God, unaware. Do not let the accuser fool you!* Thus, the wavering, or double-mindedness, will hinder receiving God's abundance for you and others. ~ James 1:8. It is incumbent upon the believer, who is in a place of knowing, to bless others so that they may rest upon the knowledge of another until they reach a place of understanding. ~ Romans 15:1.

Jesus displays this ability in Matthew 9:28-29, where the blind man rests in Jesus's knowing. Jesus asks, "Do you *believe* I can do this?" When the blind man answers in the affirmative, Jesus says, "According to your faith, be *it* unto you." "It" represents many things. Correspondingly, it (prosperity, growth, spiritual, and material wealth) manifests according to your faith level.

To be sure, when you reflect upon this place of awareness, this manifestation of faith occurred many times in your lives at different intervals. For example, you desire your own home or car and say, "*This* will be mine." Proclaiming this desire was, often, without asking in the Lord's name. Let us be honest; we desire it long before going to God about having it. In line with the Universal Law of Belief, the power of intention within the mind manifests your desire. This comment is not to exclude the Christ-Spirit because Jesus included us. He says we are one in Him as He is one in the Father. Thus, whatsoever we ask God, He hears us. In *1 John* 5:14, John says, "This is the confidence we [posture] approaching God:

Markeithia Lavon Silver

that if we ask or think *anything according to His will,* He hears us." Why? He knows our thoughts afar off ~ Psalms 139:2.

Furthermore, if we know that He hears us—whatsoever we ask or think—we know that we shall attain what we ask of Him. It is the will of the Lord for us to bless and be a blessing in return. In his encounter with Lazarus's death, Jesus epitomizes this display of knowing (perfected faith) ~ John11: 4.

Consequently, we waiver and do not live in our space of divine consciousness because of fear. God promises to give us our heart's desires, but we allow fear and doubt to creep in and hinder our blessings. We need to change our protocol—*God must come first.* Before acquiring or starting a project, we must seek Him first and wait patiently for instructions. Let us turn from this fragmented spiritual thinking and embrace Kingdom thinking, knowing He hears us *ALWAYS* and cares. God is in the business of blessing. "The Lord will give grace and glory: No good thing shall He withhold from them that walk uprightly" ~ Psalms 84:11. *I decree and declare a prophetic advantage over God's people that we will purpose in our hearts to seek God first, no longer wavering in instability but walking circumspectly, revealing what is good and acceptable in the Lord in Christ Jesus's name; That we will protect the righteous seed, the Kingdom within us to the glory and honor of God n Jesus's name. Amen.*

Finally, one must be willing to excavate the mind to determine where the babies of fear reside. Psychology refers to them as reference points. These reference points write the script or narrative of our lives that we repeat and perform daily. Thus, the helm (internal script) of the boat (our lives) is steering (controlling) the entire ship (life of the individual). One must continuously choose to receive the Love of God. Receiving the Father's Love may be a painful experience for some because of your past encounters with pseudo-love. Although you may encounter blocks initially, you must remind yourself that the love you received in the past that caused pain and anguish is

162

Living Your Legacy Of Greatness

not the Love God wants to bestow upon you. Each time you reject the old notion of love and receive the righteous Love of the Father, you reframe your thoughts on love, changing your perception, thus changing your circumstances and the people you attract into your life.

As we move from little faith to great faith to a place of divine consciousness, we arrive at the position Jesus declared, "We will do greater works." (*See* John 17). We come to understand, "As Jesus is the Light, so are we in this earth!" (Read *I John* 4 in its entirety) (*See also I John* 1:5-7 and *I John* 3:22-24). If we dwell from this seat of power, no-thing (obstacle or circumstance) can deceive us, overtake us, or thwart God's plan and purpose for our lives. Nothing can persuade us to think differently from the Lord; no situation can move us because God's word plants us by the Rivers of Living Water; no circumstance can remove us from the Vine, and *WE WALK IN VICTORY, ALWAYS ABIDING IN LOVE*. The challenge becomes changing our lives' reference points, allowing the fullness of God's love to fill us. In turn, we become one in God's love, opening the door to abundance—a place of perfected faith and divine awareness. Letting go of the old self, "Working out our salvation," and killing the flesh daily (the tares old ways of thinking and doing) (Philippians 2:12) will create an atmosphere of abundance.

Confronting these reference points may be challenging. Nevertheless, we must engage these reference points to supplant them with Kingdom thinking. You will discover these reference points ranging from childhood tragedies, a sexual assault, an abusive husband or wife, an abusive parent, a word or phrase spoken over you by someone you trusted and respected, and good and bad relationships. I must add here that not all reference points are

Markeithia Lavon Silver

negative. Some are positive. To be sure, some people purposefully intended to create a positive precept and image within you. You must ask yourself, "Does this reference point help or hinder my growth?" It is my genuine opinion; if it is not assisting you on the trajectory of greatness, let it go!

One of the hardest things encountered with retirement from the police department was letting go of the job's daily routine. After 20 years of service, one becomes accustomed to monitoring and protecting the citizenry. In addition to this second-nature behavior, you fear, to some degree, losing status. However, once you decide to let it all go, making room for the joy the Most High has in store, you will see you can obtain it all. Like David, as discussed in the preceding chapters, he realized that it all was God's creation and that we were stewarding over God's possessions.

Moreover, he did not need to beg, borrow, or steal what he desired. All David's spiritual development required was blessing the Lord's name and thanking the One who sustains and gives life. Try it and see what happens!

I challenge you, gentle reader, to look within yourself and take responsibility for manifesting your thoughts and actions according to Kingdom intelligence. At first, it was no easy feat to look within me and accept that I did not cultivate pleasant, confident views regarding "me." I had to admit I was also out of physical shape, not to mention I was spiritually a wreck. I allowed the many trials and tribulations to shake my faith. As I grew spiritually, I became conscious of how my thoughts negatively affected my body. I let God's healing within my mind, body, and spirit for complete restoration to occur. I realized factors in my breast cancer manifestation consisted of several things: being overweight, unhealthy negative thoughts that were swirling around inside my inner self, the stress of everyday life, and a sense of spiritual separation from the One who sustained me. This acknowledgment of my feelings is not to say I believe I intentionally caused my

Living Your Legacy Of Greatness

sickness. However, I imagine these realities contributed to it. Likewise, scientists have proven that stress and other factors place an individual at risk for diseases. Additionally, my lack of knowledge concerning how I felt about myself, failed relationships, and the like began deteriorating me unawares ~ Hosea 4:6.

I made it through several storms and felt weary, wounded, and worn. Life was administering traumatic blows, which I felt were unwarranted. Tests and trials became a part of my everyday life. I became depressed and began to neglect my health. More importantly, I could not find complete solace in my religious studies. My storms consumed me, and I constantly focused on their twists and turns. My problems had replaced my worship experience with the Father. I created an idol god of my dilemmas. I was feeding them sustenance with my thoughts of despair and ruin. I needed to cease giving them worship that I might live ~ *I Corinthians* 8:4, Hebrews 12:27-29. Instead of having a mind of gratitude and appreciation, I responded to the storms in my life, just like Peter. I, too, exhibited "little faith" and found myself sinking in the sea of my troubles.

Similarly, after Jesus granted him permission to step out of the boat and walk above his circumstances, he allowed himself to focus on the cares of life and began to sink. I never considered my mental, physical, and spiritual state at the crux of my many dilemmas. Accordingly, when I started tracing back my illness's root cause, I discovered that my thought focus, visions, and emotional energy behind those thoughts opened the door to disease in my physical body. Jesus says, "*As* you believe, be it unto you." ~ Matthew 9:29. *As* the operative word here precedes the manifested "unto you." I recognized that I had constructed a wall, mortared together by fear, doubt, anger, regret, and resentment, to name a few. This barrier prohibited me from fully receiving the Loving Grace of the Creator. Unable to receive His enabling Power, I propelled myself into darkness and gloom.

Markeithia Lavon Silver

Once I allowed myself to hear what I was speaking to myself about "me," deliverance was at hand. Like Adam, I was telling myself that I was naked. Accordingly, I recognized that my life, constructed as it was, was a mirror reflecting my thoughts and actions. The revelation from this knowledge allowed me to determine that my feelings (good, bad, or indifferent) and actions resulting from those thoughts could change them. All I needed was to do it, a will to "rise, take up my bed, and walk." As I un-dammed the wall of fear, doubt, anger, regret, and resentment, I felt a cleansing begin. It was INVIGORATING when I allowed myself to release the reference points of childhood, past experiences, how my family did things, old thought patterns, and life's disappointments. The mind of Christ had given me the nudge I needed. I felt lifted from a state of doom and gloom to a perpetual Joy realm enveloped by the Love and Inspiration of the Creator. This change would reveal a different outcome as I allowed the influx of God's Spirit to flow through me freely and richly.

As soon as I became conscious of who I was and whom I believed in, I could draw off that unspeakable Joy of the Lord, which became my Strength. ~ Isaiah 49:5. I returned to my place of rest; thus, I observed and received the Eternal's Loving grace. I postured in mind, spirit, and body that "God loved me with an everlasting love, and underneath was His everlasting arms." "God accepted me in the beloved." I no longer needed to fight for God's attention; I knew the Creator loved me, and God's Mind was *in* me. This God-power enabled me to grab the Throne of Grace firmly, changing my thought processes and behavior. Thus, reflecting positive thoughts and demeanor manifested complete and total healing in my life. I began to love and care about myself, and my peace returned. My endurance strengthened; I wanted to lose weight; the Power of God restored my love for life. More importantly, I wanted to "live and not die and declare the [good] works of the Lord!"

Living Your Legacy Of Greatness

I believe life's circumstances allowed me to empathize with how David felt when speaking of death's "pains, grabbing hold of him" ~ Psalms 116. He remembered all God had done for him when he came to himself. He recalled that God never left him, nor did he forsake him. He, in turn, commanded his Spirit to *"Return unto thy rest, oh my soul, the Lord has dealt bountifully with thee...."* He asked, "What shall I render for all of His benefits towards me...." I had experienced a place of darkness, loneliness, and fear. Nevertheless, like David, I can say, "*I Love the Lord* because He heard my cry; He inclined His ear unto me!"

When renewing your mind, God's Love lifts you out of the miry clay through your faith and places you on a rock to stay; the experience is memorable.

Appropriately, renewing the mind, letting go of the old, and grabbing hold of the new, like any other life challenge, requires discipline. I am not writing this implying that it is an effortless process. I am saying that where there is consistent affirming of who you are in the Creator, there is a poise demonstrated by you so that you will conclude, "I shall acquire what I say!" It is according to your faith. Faith is the key that unlocks the door to perpetual grandeur. The *Bible* puts it this way in Hebrews 11, "For without faith, it is impossible to please Him. For s/he that comes to God must first believe that He Is and that He Is a rewarder of them diligently seeking Him." Once you make up your mind and posture within that, you are "As Jesus is," and nothing will be impossible to obtain. The only requisite is a repenting heart and faith in Jesus as the Savior of your soul. Jesus urged us to believe what we pray. He did not speak this jubilant exultation idly. He intended us to *do* "greater works!"

Similarly, the Apostle Paul encourages us to "be strong in the Lord and the Power of His might" ~ Ephesians 6:10. When we operate within this Power, we are mighty. If we trust Him, Jesus assures us of divine peace within our hearts and minds.

Markeithia Lavon Silver

Besides, Jesus said, "My peace give I unto you, not as the world gives you, give I unto you." The peace that Jesus is referring to is an all-abiding peace. Like no other, this peace is at the center of your being, where you access it at will. When tossed and turned in the dark and dreary, stormy seas, and the waves are raging high in your life, this abiding peace will keep you anchored, assured that Joy will break forth like the dawning of a new day. You only need to believe and *know* that it will!

One might say, "I developed breast cancer. I did not ask for this breast cancer, or why would a loving God allow something of this magnitude to happen to a kind and loving person like me?" My response would be, "How you treat your neighbor is not in question here. The question is, in what manner do you treat yourself."

As I began to self-examine my emotional state, pulling the blinders off, I realized I was angry about life. To be sure, I was functional. I went to work daily, parented my children, kept my home, and did everything most people do to maintain life. Nonetheless, I was angry because I was a single parent. I was angry because I had not gotten married. I was angry because of the unsuccessful relationships I had experienced. I was angry that I had recently reacquainted with my father, and he had passed. I was furious that the woman I *knew* loved me, my "Nana," was no longer living. Anyone who knows me knows that I am a giver. I would give you the shirt off my back if you asked me for it. I *felt* no one offered comfort in all my giving, and I was angry.

I allowed these things to occur based on my perceived inner image. A large part of me felt that was the way to live life. Just because I had gone to the altar, accepted Christ's Spirit into my life, and believed in the remission of my sins, it said nothing of my anger inside. I was an emotional wreck. Learning to release all that junk would be the greatest gift I would ever give myself. I recall times that I would pray, asking the Lord to allow me to slip into heaven, in my rest, when I would close my eyes to fall asleep. Never once

Living Your Legacy Of Greatness

did I consider that all the stress and strain, the anger and frustration, the lack of exercise, and the absence of peace would manifest cancer in my body, but it did. I cannot blame a loving God for the revealed outcome of my choices. I asked for and focused upon doom within my consciousness. The seeds of hopelessness germinated, grew, and harvested my selections. It speaks to His glorious gift of choice. I chose to live the way I was living. If I wanted different results, I had to change how I thought and envisioned my life. The writing of this book is a testament to the many changes that occurred in my life. Now, I write to encourage you, the reader.

Your experience may be different. You may eat the right foods, exercise daily, and feel great about yourself. Your encounter with cancer or other illnesses may result from the environment. Whatever the cause, I prompt you to take responsibility for discovering why you developed this disease. Do not waste valuable time angry with yourself, others, or God. Use the energy to change whatever caused it. In your journey of discovery, you may be able to assist and enlighten someone else. For instance, through my own experiences, I found that I could help others in treatment and inspire them to keep a positive attitude, no matter how they feel. Keeping an optimistic attitude of full recovery proved to be an asset to several people's lives, and they appreciated me. However, if I had not gone through this experience, how would I have strengthened my sister or brother? Being able to help someone else has its gratification, even amid a storm. I give God *all* the glory!

I discovered I had created my thoughts (seeds) as I uncovered myself. I realized that my first line of defense against my attacking thoughts was against me. This pattern is analogous to a disease that attacks the body from the inside. It (the body) appears alien to itself and destroys itself. This invasion of my thoughts upon my body is what I was doing until the Spirit arrested me. When we think contrary to Kingdom thinking, we become aliens to our spiritual selves. In turn, we destroy our spirit from within the mind. This

Markeithia Lavon Silver

result is precisely what the enemy seeks for you—death. Then, we wonder why we are unhappy, depressed, or suicidal. When we believe something true, the Universe is under divine order to deliver. Al-Ghazzali writes, in *Knowing the Self*, "It is the state of the heart, the place of our intentions that holds us accountable [to our thoughts]. Our beliefs are the guiding principles that give meaning and direction to our life. They filter our perceptions of the world. When we freely believe something is true, a command is delivered to our spiritual heart (mind) telling us how to represent what we come to believe as true." As a manifestation of God's vision, filled with the power to create what we envision, humanity must be mindful of the focus and energy they place upon their thoughts, which underlie the expression of our images. Let us pray:

Father, You are an ever-present help in times of trouble. We rest in the assurance that You hear us when we pray. Abba, Father, we ask that You empower us, who are reading this prayer and trusting in our hearts, to take control of our thoughts and visions concerning ourselves and others. We want to glorify You in our thoughts and actions. Teach us, oh Lord, the way of Thy statutes, and we shall keep them until the end. Give us understanding, and we shall keep Thy law. Yes, we shall observe them with our whole hearts. Make us go in the path of Thy Commandments, for in them we delight. Cause us to stand erect in this season as we focus upon Your righteousness and whatsoever things are true, whatsoever things are honest, whatsoever things are just, whatsoever things are pure, whatsoever things are lovely, whatsoever things are of good report; if there be any virtue, and if there be any praise, we will think on these things. Thank You for hearing us when we pray. In Jesus's name. Amen.

Feel free to personalize this short prayer by exchanging us and we for me.

Remember, gentle reader, disobedience ate away God's glorious body, enveloping them, making Adam and Eve naked, unclothed, and ashamed. However, there is hope. Our loving Father performed the first sacrifice and clothed them with skins protecting them until He revealed His redemptive plan through His son, Jesus Christ, the express image of His person. We now walk in that victory if we dare! ~ Hebrews 1:1-2, St. Luke 10:19, and Revelation 2:26.

I will end this chapter with prose entitled *My Place*.

My Place

I hear Sweet, Melodic harmonies from heaven softly raining and resting upon the garden of my mind. This calm drizzle soothes my innermost being.

My garden is arrayed with beautiful flowers whispering a scent of uniqueness. The tulips, daffodils, and roses all delight in the melody sung by the gentle Wind. They respond with a score directed by the Light.

I, too, like the hummingbird, seek to express my destiny's sweet, pure calling. I am one with the "Us" Spirit God. In sacred silence, I receive a cup of loving grace.

Nearby, I see the Oasis of Restoration. This sanctuary is where I dwell. My Refuge is always accessible to me. I look within, and it is there that I bathe and receive my soul's massaging grace. Whenever weary, I travel to My Place of rest and dive into its waters' tender, serene warmth. Here, all I do is drink; all I do is drink...

CHAPTER SEVEN

NO-THING TO FEAR

"For God hath not given us the spirit of fear; but of power, love, and a sound mind." ~ II Timothy 1:7

—Paul

So shall My word be that goes forth out of My mouth: IT shall NOT return unto Me void, but it shall accomplish that which I please, AND it shall prosper IN THE THING whereto I sent it." ~ Isaiah 55:11

—The Most High/El-Shaddai

"Out of the abundance of the heart, the mouth speaketh." ~ Luke 6:45

—Jesus

"Let not your heart be troubled, neither let it be afraid." ~ John 14:1, 27

—Jesus

Markeithia Lavon Silver

> *"Call those things that are not as though they were...who against hope believed in hope...being not weak in faith... Staggered not at the promise of God...it was imputed to him for righteousness" ~ Romans 4:17-22.*

—Paul

What is this "thing" called fear?

First, fear is a frequency. When you operate in this fear frequency, you risk hindering your spiritual growth and delaying aspiring to your most fabulous self. Fear, moreover, results from the state of fallen Adam. However, from a place of redemption, "There is no fear in love, but perfect love casteth out fear: because fear hath torment. He that feareth is not made perfect in love" ~ *I John 4:18.* Of equal importance, "God hath not given us the spirit of fear; but of power, love, and a sound mind." ~ *II Timothy 1:7*

Oxford Dictionary defines frequency as the rate at which a vibration occurs that constitutes a wave, either in a material (as in sound waves) or in an electromagnetic field (as in radio waves and light), usually measured per second.

Fear, in Greek, is the word *Phobos,* a subjective term. This viewpoint means that fear, dread, or terror is felt only from the participant's perspective. An impressionistic view is the opposite of an objective evaluation of facts or feelings. When subjectively viewing your truth, your feelings, tastes, past experiences, or opinions influence you. This definition is not to say you do not *feel* fear. It is to say you are biased in your assessment. Fear is that character "as a roaring lion" that seeks to devour you and the greatness seed inside. Objectivity, when considering fear, is free of feelings when representing or considering the circumstances and facts at hand. Fear, as the Bible says, carries with it a component of torture. ~ *I John* 4:18. Thus, when you are affected by the vibration of fear, you are simultaneously being tormented, which I submit

Living Your Legacy Of Greatness

occurred with Adam in the Garden after Eve's disobedience, persuading Adam to disobey God. ~ Genesis 3.

Similarly, other lines of frequencies, i.e., love, courage, anger, hatred, despair, hopelessness, and the like, edify or destroy your inner self. The most significant and potent frequency is (Agapé) love. Daily, one should strive to live in a love-frequency space and place. Why? This space and area of love are where miracles happen. The consistency of love opens doors, healing occurs, and you can connect with others on a deeper level. Additionally, operating within the love structure enhances your ability to understand others; it heightens your discerning ability, and, most notably, this experience breeds clarity of thought.

Consider this analogy: thoughts are waves traveling at different speeds, like a transistor radio. Only people nearby can hear you when you transmit over a weak signal. If you emit a strong beacon, people listen to you across hundreds of miles, even states, in signals designed for syndicated radio. Similarly, operating on any channel other than love retards your growth and ability to connect on deep levels with your fellow humans. It is imperative to understand that when I say "*be* heard," I am not referring to an audible voice. I highlight the underrated ability to see and hear the heart via its vibrations. Parents do this all the time. Husbands and wives do it, too, when they attune their inner ear to their loved one's heart. You may experience this for yourself. For instance, you call someone you know, and as soon as the person picks up the telephone and says hello, you *know* something is wrong. You are in tune with their vibrational channel and deduce that something is awry.

Similarly, you may come into the presence of someone you love and immediately discern that something is wrong. Your husband or wife comes through the door, and how s/he breathes tells you something is wrong. It is more than just reading body language or facial continence. It hears with and through the frequency of love.

I dare say this is how Jesus healed the sick and raised the dead. Therefore, he said we are to "love one another as he has loved us." Just think about it for a moment. Jesus's love transcended generational curses, death, and the collective consciousness of ignorance within the Sadducees' and Pharisees' minds. The world shall know that we are followers of Jesus by the love we maintain in our hearts. We are first to love ourselves and then, infused with passion, love our neighbor as ourselves. That means to love without inhibition and esteem another higher than ourselves.

With this kind of love in our hearts, there would be no war, poverty, or lack; everything would be at our fingertips.

Wait a minute; this sounds familiar.

Of course, this occurrence is precisely how it was in the Garden before the Fall or, better yet, before Adam changed frequencies. Nonetheless, Jesus came to show us a way back to that space and place of pure love and connection to our Source of all things amazing—the "Us" Spirit. Ask yourself, "Do you *want* to be free from the babies of fear and doubt?"

If the answer is yes, we must first evolve into a space and place of unification with God, followed by unified humanity. In this harmonious place, we will discover, uncover, and recover our legacy of greatness bequeathed to us by the "Us" spirit.

How, then, do you attack or dismantle the components of fear? How do you approach or eliminate anxiety in your life? What are your allies in this war against fear? What must you avoid, lest you fortify and perpetuate the root or seed of fear? If we succeed in our quest to know the "Us" Spirit within, we must also dismantle all fear and doubt sources. First, you accomplish this with a tool referred to as introspection. Specifically, you must bring the bondage of fear and doubt into your awareness and their root causes. It is in this space of understanding that you can till the ground. *An individual who does not take stock of what makes them who they are is a prisoner unaware of the chains that bind them.* Second, you must begin catching the thoughts swirling around in your head. Identify the narrative you speak to yourself daily. We must stand ready to thought-catch the sources of our beliefs, values, and visions, making us victorious in obtaining our legacy of greatness. To become fully aware of who God created us to be, we must shun the bondage of fear and doubt. Within this spiritual awareness resides our God-given freedom to create, love unconditionally, abide in peace always, be strengthened by joy, heal the sick, set free those held captive in their minds by negative thinking, and walk in the legacy of our greatness.

The spirit of fear seeks out the heart of doubt and enters the mind of an individual who perceives/conceives that they are alone and without options. There is no sensation like the feeling that your back is against the wall, and you think the road is a dead-end and there is nowhere to go. To *know* God is with you is to receive His Love in its fullest, His Providence, His Provision, and His Peace strengthening your heart of hope ~ Proverbs 13:12. This perfected Love casts out all fear. His Love leaves no room for fear to exist. Accordingly, we must discover and uncover how we attained these feelings of fear and doubt. Then, by force of will, we must allow the perfecting of God's love to rest, rule, and abide in our lives. According to Scripture, you live without fear when God's love absorbs you. *If fear manifests for lack of God's perfecting love, doubt establishes itself by an illusion of deceit and false pride.* Therefore, when you do not receive the perfecting of God's love, and the illusion of doubt fills you, fear and doubt consummate, creating an offspring: not enough, lack, not good enough, not smart enough, and other negative siblings veiling your greatness capability. No worries, Beloved, there is hope. "With God, *all things* are possible, if we would only believe" ~ Mark 9:23. (Emphasis mine). The Greek word for believing in this verse is *pisteuō,* meaning to "*have*

Markeithia Lavon Silver

faith (in, upon, or concerning, a person or thing), that is, *credit*; by implication to *entrust* (especially one's spiritual well-being to Christ) commit (to trust), put in trust with."[32] In other words, all things are possible if we *entrust* our spiritual well-being to Christ and *trust* in His Sovereign ability over our lives.

The presence of fear immobilizes you from moving forward in your circumstances, your ministry, your gifts, talents, acquiring a mate, finances, and your life. However, when you learn to trust God, reframe or master the alchemy of the mind, and perfect your faith, your perspective will change, allowing God's Love to enter in perfecting its calling as a prerequisite of greatness. As previously mentioned, where God's Love is present, fear cannot reside, and God's oneness shows forth as a Light that fear cannot repel.

The procreation of fear and doubt occurs when fear enters doubt, as a sperm searches for an egg in the reproduction process. Fear lurks in the shadows, awaiting doubt's appearance. When this happens, the babies of fear and doubt begin to grow. Their gestation period depends on the DNA of the parents. Fear and doubt procreate "not enough," "I cannot do it," "I cannot afford it," and more. More importantly, these babies carry a spirit that transfers to others. If your mother decreed and declared over you that you were not good enough, you will relay and impart to your children that they are not good enough. We refer to these things as generational curses. However, split them up, and you cut off the lifeline to the tares (weeds of negativity) in your life. The *Bible* tells you that faith without works is dead.

Similarly, fear, without its accompaniment of doubt, is impotent. Once fear procreates with uncertainty, it controls every level. You will question "If you are good enough, "worthy enough," and "smart enough." "I made too many mistakes; no one will love or want me," you might say. I am sure you, the gentle reader, are aware of some negative thoughts that whirl around when attempting to undertake a new adventure. Combating these thoughts with something that builds you up, not destroys you, is key to ridding yourself of them. In the art of war, you must be fierce in the Lord. Grab the mighty weapons in the Lord ~ *II Corinthians* 10:4. Fear blurs your creativity. It distorts your objectivity. It obfuscates your ability to discern any situation properly. When you are not careful in harnessing or eliminating your fear, you will be all over the place, unable to decide which way to turn. You will find yourself speaking out when you should be silent and quiet when you should state your cause. The Scripture says, "A double-minded person is unstable in all of their ways" ~ James 1:6-8. Fear will cause you to sway between two, three, or more opinions.

However, one can be bold when *knowing* God is with you. Take Jesus's display when he called Lazarus to come forth. When fear enters the space of an individual's mind, it is oppressive, debilitating your ability to make objective decisions and choking your creative talents. You may produce a product; however, it will not be your best insofar as it relates to the grandeur you would create with confidence if you *knew* that you are great on the inside. The Law of Attraction, the Law of Belief, and the Law of Correspondence will attract what you trust in, manufacturing after its kind. In other words, a rose seed will not create a dandelion. It will generate a rose.

Likewise, what we think will mirror representation within our world. When we feel we are not good enough, we will attract people and situations reflecting those thoughts. By no means am I saying challenges will not present themselves. How we respond to those challenges is critical. You can be the most positive person in the universe; however, trials will come to grow and stretch you for the better ~ Romans 8:28. We are ever learning and should embrace the lesson with joy. "In all things, give thanks" ~ Ephesians 5:20. Nonetheless, some see it as a struggle and not a joyful expression of life's way to grow, cultivate us, and make us present our best selves to the world. God customizes our trials to shape us, move

Markeithia Lavon Silver

us forward, and give us an expected end ~ Jerimiah 29:11. We take courage in *knowing* that God *knows* the way that we take and that He performs the very thing He has appointed for us, and when it is allsaid and done, we shall come forth as pure gold ~ Job 23:10-16. We can trust that His timing is perfect and that we are in His hand. ~ Psalms 31:15. *See also* Lamentations 3:22-26.

Moreover, when we allow the oppression of doubt and fear to overtake us, we open the door to procreate more babies and become possessed/gripped by them. Fears are, thus, the giver and doubt the receiver. This procreation is the substratum for bondage. Once shrouded by the captivity of fear and doubt, their many babies emerge. Their delivery manifests as shame, not enough, and all the thoughts contrary to God's promises over your life. The individual's awareness begins to diminish self, inevitably bringing self-hatred. Depression can manifest in many forms: lack of cleanliness, hoarding, lack of proper hygiene, drug abuse, sex abuse, extreme lack of responsibility, and the like because these things are nutritional by-products in your soil mind, cultivating ultimate death. When you reach this level of self-hatred, you may still be functional in your job; however, your home and personal life may lack. Therefore, we must "thought-catch" what we are saying to ourselves, pay attention to the visions we are building because of those thoughts, and seek God and His strength for breakthroughs and restoration.

Most importantly, we must bring into our awareness that God's thoughts toward us and His ways of getting us to our destination stop of greatness are not our thoughts and methods of success ~ Psalms 40:5, Isaiah 55:8-13. For God knows the thoughts (plans or purpose He has for my life), He has for us, thoughts of peace and not evil (to prosper us) and *bring us to an expected end* ~ Jeremiah 29:11 (Emphasis mine). We are His precious treasure. We can trust that He shall bring to pass what He spoke over our lives from the beginning ~ Job 23:14, Philippians 1:6. Bringing

180

Living Your Legacy Of Greatness

us to an expected end is part of the germination process because *the seed has everything inside it to produce the prescribed fruit.* This process may appear to be a deterministic view. I would ask, then, is it not the function of a seed to produce after its kind and not another? Does the type of seed not determine what fruit it will yield? Yes! Ensuring we produce after our kind as intended from the beginning! This revelation does not negate or excuse us from doing our part in renewing our minds through the Word of God and submitting to the process of God conforming us into the image of His Son. We *must* do our part! David said, Thy Word have I hid in my heart that I might not sin against Thee. ~ Psalms 119:11. If I may offer this interpretation, Thy Word, nourishment for my soul mind, have I hid in my heart that I might not sin, (allow the seeds of wickedness and corruption to alter Your righteous seed within me), so that I may produce after Your kind and not another.

As cited above, God speaks to the prophet Isaiah and tells him, "His word shall be that which goes out of His mouth: It shall not return unto Me void, but it shall accomplish that which I please, and it shall prosper in the thing whereto I sent it." ~ Isaiah 55:11. God's Word is an indomitable seed with everything in it to accomplish what He pleases. It shall sow, grow, and bring forth fruit in abundance! Why? Because He said it would! With Wisdom and Power, God envisioned the world and then spoke to it into existence. God is still proclaiming the vision, so it remains. Do you recall the "Us" Spirit made you in the image and likeness of the Creator, who has the power to send His word out, and it fulfills exactly the vision God said it would? Not only that, but it will also flourish in the thing He sent it to prosper. This creativity resides in you! Your word shall not come back void. *What you focus on is in motion to create, setting out to accomplish what it desires.* God lets us know that the power of life and death is on our tongue and "Just as I spoke and it was, so to do you speak, and it is!" Oh, gentle

Markeithia Lavon Silver

reader, this awareness is precisely why we must know what is in the seed we produce because they will create after its kind!

Moreover, when you place a backdrop of focused energy behind the words, your thoughts will manifest what you harbor in your heart ~ Luke 6:45. Again, your concepts and ideas are seeds and shall reproduce after their kind. Proverbs 18:21 says, "Death and Life are in the power of the tongue: they that love it (focus upon with certainty) shall eat the fruit thereof." Jesus said, "Out of the abundance of the heart, the mouth speaketh." Therefore, one can conclude that the tongue's power mirrors what you already spoke in your heart/soul mind. Precisely what you believe shapes your perspective and perception on a matter. These precepts and concepts develop because of your belief system, which governs how you respond to yourself and others. Let me say this another way. Your trusted belief system guides and commands how you treat yourself and others. Your reality emerges based on where you place your trust. What you believe (where you place your value) cultivates your thoughts into existence (life energy).

Jesus came that we might lay hold to abundant life, trust and conceive oneness with the Father, receive the Creator's abundance, and lay hold to our legacy of greatness. We must step into the reality of this greatness, seek it, and knock upon the door for it. It *WILL* let us in, and ask the Lord for guidance to obtain and maintain that legacy created for us. Jesus was the epitome of oneness with the Father, and he trusted the Father all the way to the cross. He explicitly told us that we could/would enjoy the same. This outlook, I believe, is what He (Jesus) meant when He said. "According to your faith, be it unto you." The operative word "it" is your thoughts, belief system, and the force you place behind them with your heart/mind.

Take a moment and consider this. If you rearrange the word belief, you get BE-LIFE. When you think a thought with intentional focus, with the same force that God thought the world into existence,

Living Your Legacy Of Greatness

you are telling your thoughts, as God did to BE LIFE or as the word proclaims, "Let there be!" And... It was! Jesus's declaration of abundant life is no small measure. The Greek word for abundance is *perissos,* meaning a sense of beyond in quantity and quality.[33] By implication, the term denotes excessiveness, preeminence, and advantage.[34] *Thayer's Greek Lexicon* defines *perissos* as over and above, more than necessary, superadded, something further, superior, more eminent, more remarkable, and more excellent. In other words, Jesus came to give us more than what we possess, more than who we are, to advance us to a place of excellence and preeminence, giving us an advantage. Can your mind imagine the vastness of what Jesus is offering if we only trust Him? Can your mind hold it, speak it, and receive it? More importantly, can you speak the life of lavishness from this position of excellence?

What thoughts did you put in motion? In part, one main reason we are in the situations we are in today is that we co-created them. First, we created our world with our thoughts and are still speaking them; thus, they remain. Again, this comment is worth mentioning: What ideas did you put in motion? To live our lives of abundance, *we must control our thoughts*. We must develop a stratagem and plan of execution for our thoughts to create the desired effect. Fear and doubt are the parents of our demise. When we want to trace why we are anxious, insecure, or otherwise contrary to God's abundance, we must ask ourselves whether we cut the umbilical cord of fear, doubt, pride, and ego. Jesus said that we could achieve whatever we want if we believe (entrust God with our well-being). Looking back does not just mean those things that are good or what we feel are pleasing but alarming and what we think is hurtful. "According to your faith—your level of trust in God—be it unto you."

Which will you choose? I dare you to choose greatness! I double dare you, as my generation used to say, to search within your mind's vast memory and trace what thoughts preclude you from your birthright of greatness. Just as God is the husbandman

Markeithia Lavon Silver

of our souls, pruning what is unnecessary so that the good may take root and grow and not the tare, we are also responsible for pruning our thoughts so the seeds of greatness will expand and grow. We are accountable for the substance of our thoughts and not God. The church taught us that God is responsible for our good and the devil for our wrongs. I submit to you that like attracts like, and when we think a certain way, we open the door for God to bless us in abundance or, in contrast, for the devil to wreak havoc in our lives. *Our situation will correspond, in a mirrored effect, to our thoughts.*

Moreover, if we believe/trust what we say, we will attract what we think, manifesting the corresponding thought. We do it all the time, unaware. We tell ourselves that we contradict the Creator's notion of what He created: not good enough, smart enough, or anything else that is the antithesis of God's word. Then, we stand in amazement when the people around us treat us how we engraved the foundation of thinking about us in our minds. We believe these thoughts and place our trust in them! It is time to tear down the high places! ~ *II Chronicles* 31:1

Challenges are going to come; I will concede that. However, how we deal with those challenges will determine the outcome. Our perspective determines how we approach a future issue, how we deal with it, and what attitude and force we are handling it.

Ultimately, we give life to our thoughts as we focus on them. A splendid example would be when my son, at age three, spent the night with his godfather. My son was running around, laughing, being his jovial self, and having an enjoyable time with his godfather. His godfather decided to tell him to settle down for a while; if he did, he would give him a cup of apple juice (his favorite drink). My son agreed to stop running and headed for the kitchen to drink his cup of juice. When he noticed it was his favorite drink, he turned to his godfather, looked him square in the eyes, and said, "You know this is a secret potion." "Oh yeah, what does it do," said his godfather, "It makes me run faster," my son said. Well, as you

Living Your Legacy Of Greatness

guessed, his godfather laughed with him and allowed him to run around a little longer. The point is that my son, in his extraordinary imagination, thought/trusted the juice to be some secret potion that gave him some superpowers.

Moreover, he was astute enough to know that his godfather wanted him to stop running and rest. I can imagine that when he figured out what his godfather was doing, he reversed it and used it to his advantage. His favorite drink used to stop running was now a super drink to continue running. The hidden treasure of trust! He believed, so it was. Jesus told us, "Except you become like one of these, you shall not enter into the Kingdom of Heaven." Just as my 3-year-old son, at the time, trusted in something as simple as a drink to make him run faster, we too must aspire to attain a child's mind, like my son, to imagine anything is possible. What thoughts are you trusting? I dare you to explore every facet of your trust!

Moreover, we can, as he did—joyfully and playfully so. Will you dare to *Master the Alchemy of Your Mind*? Will you engage life's experiences with Joy to perfect your faith? Will you allow the Lord to perfect His Love inside of you?

I double dare you!

Wholeness Defined

Allow me, before I end this chapter, to bring another story to mind involving a change of perspective, facilitating the overcoming of fear:

For an angel went down at a certain season into the pool and troubled the water: **whosoever then first after the troubling of the water stepped in was made whole of whatsoever disease he had***. And a certain man had an infirmity of thirty and eight years. When Jesus saw him lie*

Markeithia Lavon Silver

*and knew that he had been now a long time in that case, He saith unto him, "**Wilt thou** be made whole"? The **impotent** man answered, "Sir, I [do not know any man], when the water is troubled, to put me into the pool, but while I am coming, another steppeth down before me." Jesus said, "Rise, take up thy bed, **and** walk." And immediately, the man was made whole, took up his bed, **and** walked.* (Emphasis mine) ~ St. John 5:4-9.

My definition of wholeness, as I believe Jesus was asking him, is thus:

To Be Whole: The sacred communion of the mind, body, and spirit operating in the peaceful union of God's undying love. Do you desire to be whole in your mind, body (spirit, emotional, and physical), and soul? Do you *want* to *be* who God created you to be—whole wanting nothing? I am sure the answer is overwhelming and resounding, yes!

Did you ever happen upon a group discussion where the conversation was salient in your life, and your perspective changed immediately? The dialogue is so spot on that you listen attentively, hoping for some illumination into your present situation. A revelatory light manifests a different outlook, and your circumstances change immediately. When you thought you lost it all from the storm, the sun came out because your God-consciousness revealed it was there, and you drew upon the Holy Ghost's Strength to bring it forth.

John, referred to as the disciple whom Jesus loved, tells the man's story by the pool. John was a man who felt the pulse and heart of Jesus. In the virtuous pages of Scripture, we read that John often lays his head upon Jesus's breast. What a metaphor for seeking and listening to the heart of God. This type of sacred intimacy afforded him insight into powerful spiritual truths. I often ask myself if John realized how enchanting his experiences with Jesus would play out

Living Your Legacy Of Greatness

in his future self. I promise you that you will hear His heart if you meet God daily and bask in His presence!

Sometimes, we encounter something remarkable, and when we discover it, we cannot grasp the whole meaning of the experience until later in life. These occurrences were illustrated in my maternal grandmother (affectionately called "Nana") and my relationship. During our many conversations about life, she used to say, "You may not understand this now, but place it in your spiritual pocketbook so you can pull it out whenever you need it." She often explained things to me through a story with a meaningful theme. Though thrilled by her storytelling, I constantly asked, "Why is she telling me this?"

Nevertheless, she was correct in her wise assessment of *"needing it"* down the road. There were many things that I did not understand when she explained them to me, but as I matured, my understanding increased. My grandmother's wisdom elevated my thought process. I am amazed to discover that all she taught me was to return joyfully to my memory. The "spiritual pocketbook" has come in handy!

Similarly, a child's progress occurs in stages. The various cognitive development phases allow different degrees of information to be processed correctly. There are things I told my eleven-year-old son, now a grown man, that he would not understand because of his level of development. For instance, if my son said he was hungry and wanted something to eat, I would respond by telling him to go and cook himself something to eat. However, he would look at me with his beautiful light brown eyes and say something to the effect, "Mommy, I do not know how to cook, nor do I enjoy anyone cooking for me." He would *want* to cook for himself because he was hungry. However, his desire to cook did not align with his cognitive abilities. His level of mental development would prohibit him from doing so. Likewise, the man

Markeithia Lavon Silver

at the pool was arrested in his spiritual development until Jesus inoculated and advanced him with spiritual strength.

Conversely, when he eventually elevates the intellectual capacity and maturity necessary for cooking, he will boldly and confidently cook whatever he desires. Now a young man and college graduate, my son cooks for himself whenever he desires. Developmental prowess occurs at varying life stages, and we must patiently endure the process. Whether my son could cook at age three or twenty-two does not change my love for him or his position as my son. Likewise, we are God's children, no matter our level of development. We must, however, be reachable so that we are teachable. As my son, he watches me, learns from me, and humbles himself before me to learn of me. Equally, as sons and daughters of God, we must seek God to see what He *will* do. Jesus's relationship with the Father was so powerful that Jesus submitted to doing nothing unless he saw the Father do it! It unveiled the notion of sonship and oneness with the Father to us and its earth-moving power. *See* St. John 5:19, 15:5, 17:1-26, 20:21, and Hebrews 1:1-2. We can do what Jesus did, what the Father does. Amazing! *We walk in his victory, his resurrection power!*

As mentioned, I believe this advancement occurred with the man at the pool. The troubled water was a representation of barren thoughts and mental transformation. Whosoever stepped in, with the confidence of faith, was made whole. Everyone allowed the mind that was in Christ (the mind of renewal and oneness with God) to be in them, the angel's troubling of the water made them whole of whatever disease they had (straight away their conditions changed, and they were made whole, free from their ailment, and complete in God). The mind houses the most potent apparatus for change.

Specifically, some of the most powerful biblical statements concerning the thought process of the mind are:

Living Your Legacy Of Greatness

"Let this mind that was in Christ be also in you."

"Be ye transformed by the renewing of your mind."

"As a wo/man thinketh in their heart, so is s/he," and "Without a vision, the people perish."

"Greater works shall you do," said Jesus because he has given us the solution to removing the evil seeds infused into us during the Fall. We now possess the keys to unearth the seeds of destruction and death through the power of the Holy Ghost and the blood sacrifice of Christ, who removed *all* the ordinances against us! ~ Collosions 2:14-15.

If we judge these statements as factual, what, I ask, what is the process? The aforementioned gives us a systematic blueprint for obtaining the complete fullness of divine greatness. To reach this level of wholeness, Jesus implied that we first need to allow the Christ-Spirit to dwell in us richly (this indwelling is our nourishment for our mind-soil), which is the epitome of oneness with His Father. Next, we must take responsibility for renewing our minds. Once that has occurred, how we process and receive information is revolutionizing because our minds will change our thinking. Thus, what we believe we will see or envision. Dr. Jones writes in his book *Morning B.R.E.W.* on Greatness; he says:

"Greatness is your birthright… You are God's dream and who you dream yourself to be. You are God's creation and, likewise, create with your beliefs and choices. You are the result of Insistent Love and what you insist on loving daily."

I dare you to love yourself and choose greatness, as an inalienable right, as a citizen in the Kingdom of God!

Jesus saw that this man had been in this state for thirty-eight years and moved with compassion to fortify him. Jesus ardently desired to impart the wisdom of the power of will to him. He, in turn, asks him, "Will thou be made whole?" In other words, "Do you seek a genuine hunger to be whole and free from your previous state of thinking? Do you *think* yourself to be whole? Do you see

Markeithia Lavon Silver

yourself whole?" In the text, he knew the man's heart. Nothing was hidden from him because we understand Jesus and his ultimate discerning abilities. Still, Jesus asks the question about his desire to be whole. Why? I believe the man needed to hear his passion, know his desire, trust it to fruition, and *be* entirely motivated by it to change. Sound familiar? Of course, it does. God asked Adam, "Where are you?" Awareness brings deliverance!

In addition to Jesus's question, John highlights the man's disposition. He refers to him as impotent. To be impotent is to be weak, helpless, unable, and incapable of doing anything. Jesus wanted to urge him to a level of completeness and evolve him from powerlessness to potent. Did you ever encounter a friend who aspired to accomplish something, and all they needed was a little facilitation? This aid is what Jesus did for this man. He gave him a little nudge to manifest his absolute healing vision by merely asking him, "What is your earnest desire?" When he challenges his thought process, the man lets Jesus know he is ready for change. He wanted to improve and allow his fortification to take hold.

However, he met Jesus's influence in fortifying him with opposition contrary to the man's desire. In his statement to Jesus, I believe he was saying, "Just when I am on the verge of a breakthrough, fear, doubt, life's obstacles, old habits, and old ways of thinking stop me from elevating completely. Because of my thinking, I cannot make it over to the other side of my mountain. My disenfranchised self, the self I mentally beat up on for not moving quickly enough, cannot make it. The despondent self cannot make the leap when I do not accomplish what I desire. I am forced to admit I do not understand what is happening, what is precluding me from reaching my desired goal." There is hope in bringing to our understanding where we are. Consider Adam, whom I will discuss further below. As previously asserted, God could not deliver him from shame if Adam denied his nakedness.

Living Your Legacy Of Greatness

Likewise, once Adam acknowledged his place of separation, God rescued him and instituted a plan of redemption for humanity.

Christ's-Spirit within us gives us the inspiration and power to change and act upon that change. Our force of will empowers us and our earnest desire for change. *Faith is the unmovable, unshakable, planted thought within the mind—we trust it.*[2] Each time the man walked toward the pool, his thoughts would change, rendering his complete wholeness impotent. The effects would be a lack of peace, impatience, turmoil, and frustration.

Let us take a closer look at this story. Three things occurred at the pool that day. First, Jesus told the man to "Rise." Second, He told him, "Take up your bed." Finally, Jesus told him to "walk." By telling him to rise, I believe he was telling him that attitude is everything —peace is within your reach if you hold fast to your vision. No matter what you are going through, keep a positive attitude. Be tenacious, and do not give up! Please do not allow your situation to get on top of you; you get on top of it! Do not just think you can, but *see* you can also! James puts it this way, "Count it all joy when you fall into divers temptations" ~ James 1:2.

I love poetry, and as I read this passage of Scripture, I think of Maya Angelou's poem, *I Rise!* Her poem's theme speaks to the egregious acts committed upon the women of slavery, who find within themselves the ability to reach beyond the horrific acts and see their value and beauty. The title speaks volumes to anyone who has heard Mrs. Angelou's words. *I Rise* is not just for the slave woman; it is for anyone pushed down, held back, and now s/he refuses to be pushed around and held down any longer. It speaks to

---

[2] The unmovable, unshakable, planted thought within the mind is how the enemy caused Eve to *see* the Tree of Knowledge of Good and Evil from a different perspective. As many times as she viewed the Tree, she never saw it as good for food, pleasant to the eye and a desire to make one wise. However, once the enemy altered her perspective of the Tree, she activated her faith and she did eat and experience spiritual death.

Markeithia Lavon Silver

the tenacious person who says, "I will rise from the muck and the mire to a place of excellence!" It is for anyone who says within him or herself, "My past does not dictate who I am. God allows me to resurrect myself if I trust Him."

Similarly, a mentoring pastor preached a sermon once: *Your Attitude Determines Your Altitude,* underscoring the importance of fostering a positive disposition. If you maintain a poor outlook, you will be down and level with the ground, feeling (thinking) as if your back is against the wall, imagining (envisioning) no way of escape. On the contrary, if you sustain an optimistic temperament, you will "mount up with wings as eagles" and soar above your circumstances. Accordingly, by taking up his bed, the man held himself accountable for his actions and took responsibility for his thinking. Thus, Jesus is offering an opportunity for a change of perspective and rejecting the notion that he needed someone else to do what he could, encouraging him to move forward. Remember, God told Moses at the bank of the Red Sea to disregard the moaning and groaning of the children of Israel, instructing them to move forward, look to what was in his hand, and part the sea that the children of Israel may pass on dry land. *What is in your hand, beloved?!* Has El-Shaddai/God provided you with enough examples of His Providence? Of His Strength? Of His ability to Provide? Then, I, too, echo the sentiments given to Moses on the mountaintop that day, leap forward and let your faith take you to the other side, and "You *do it!*"

At the beginning of this man's story, I guess he perceived his legs (ministry, gifts, passions, and aspirations) as too weak. The bed (life's challenges) was too heavy, or he could not do it himself. However, once Jesus inoculated him with a dose of "Kingdom" inspiration, a reminder of God's blessing from the beginning to *BE FRUITFUL,* he could resist fear, reject doubt, and move from weakness to strength. Jesus's illuminating faith empowered him to the next level of his growth. If you look through the realm of

Living Your Legacy Of Greatness

history, I am sure you will find persons in your life who inspired you to resist the fear of your inadequacies and somehow propelled you forward. I know I can!

Finally, Jesus told him to "walk." By telling him to move forward, one step at a time, Jesus admonishes him in the spirit that the bridge will be there; *trust* and take a step, and then two. He told him directly, "You can attain what you say." I coined a phrase from my experiences: *"Walk and live in your space—posturing greatness!"* According to the power that works in you, whatever your space is, live in it—posture it! That space could heal your mind, body, spirit, ministry, or running your business. Whatever *it* is, call it and live in it! The *Bible* puts it this way, "Calling those things that are not as they were." Jesus handed this man a key to unlocking his healing, godly power, and human greatness in this earthly realm. He imbued him with the power to walk on top of water (life's circumstances). *HE TOLD HIM TO BE!!!*

Having a positive mental attitude (the Mind of the Christ-Spirit) and the strength and tenacity of will, the man at the pool could make it to the other side of his disease. There is no greater strength than the Creator fortifying you in your stance. There is no power but of God ~ John 19:11. Moreover, wisdom and might are His ~ Daniel 2:20. For it is God that gives us the power to obtain wealth ~ Deuteronomy 8:18. The Hebrew word for wealth is *Chayil,* meaning a force of men or other resources, strength, might, ability, efficiency, wealth, valor, and an army. Therefore, His wisdom, force, and ability, coupled with your vision, choice of will, and perfected faith, will do great exploits! Why? He gives you the *power to obtain* whatever you need! Accordingly, "He may establish His covenant which He swore unto thy fathers, as *it is* this day" ~ *Id.*

Therefore, when removing the stronghold of fear, one must begin with the things one fears outside the reverence of the Lord ~ Psalms 19:9, 111:10, Proverbs 1:7, 2:1-12. Let us review what the

193

Markeithia Lavon Silver

Lord did in the Garden. God said, "Adam, where art thou?" Indeed, an omnipresent Creator of all things *knew* Adam's exact location. God knew where Adam *was*. He wanted Adam to *know* where he was: mentally, emotionally, and spiritually. Awareness is the first step to deliverance. You obtain this knowledge by self-reflection, and understanding will lend itself to a leveling up or changing position. However, Adam and Eve chose not to self-reflect but blamed their choices. When the very thing we fear (change or otherwise) comes upon us (Job 3:25), we must remember that it is God who "changes the times and the seasons. He removes and sets up kings: He giveth wisdom unto the wise, and knowledge to them that know to understand: He reveals the deep and secret things: He knows what *is* in the darkness. The light dwelleth with Him," and we need to trust Him, for He knows His plans for us that bring us to an expected end ~ Daniel 2:21-22 and Jeremiah 29:11, respectively.

First, we know that our ally in attacking the spirit of fear begins with knowledge and reverence of the Lord, His Providence, provision, awareness of where you are (requiring introspection), joy, and humility. In the Book of Wisdom/Proverbs 1:11 and 9:10, "The fear of the Lord is the beginning of Knowledge (wisdom and understanding)." Furthermore, it would be best to incorporate a disciplined mind. Within this authority of the mind, you create an atmosphere conducive to altering your mind: changing from the old and becoming new. Mastering the alchemy of your mind commences with the renewal of the mind through the word of God. As Paul emphasized, you must bring your mind under the control of Kingdom thinking ~ *1 Corinthians* 9:27, *II Corinthians* 10: 5-6.

You must study the ministry of the Christ-Spirit as a rubric and allow it to guide you into all truth. Again, Jesus was the epitome of oneness with the Father. Accordingly, introspection is necessary to transform from death to renewal daily. Appropriately, the Book of Wisdom/Proverbs 16:18 says, "Pride goeth before destruction and

Living Your Legacy Of Greatness

a haughty spirit before a fall." The same results will persist if you remain in your darkness. Change your habits; change your results. Pride prohibits you from being you, the you that God created to be preeminent and walking in excellence. "God gives grace unto the humble, but He resists the prideful (heart)" ~ James 4:6. The prophet Nehemiah also said, "The joy of the Lord is [our] strength" ~ Nehemiah 8:10. It is something about joy ringing in every area of your life that enlarges your ability to endure, grow, and prosper. When you maintain joy like a river, you will preserve joy coming and going like a natural river. Therefore, be humble and receive His continual grace for the journey.

Accordingly, when removing the stronghold of fear, one must begin with what one fears: being alone, jealousy, anger, ashamed of who you are, inadequacy, unworthy of life's blessings, lack of resources, freedom from the opinions of others, and the like. Do you *know* what you fear? Are you willing to stop, listen in the silence, and tackle your phobias? There is a myriad of fears and doubts offspring. A person may occupy one or several children of fear and doubt. If not confronted, they will spawn more babies into the lives of generations.

Let us look at how God dealt with Adam and Eve in the garden. After the Lord questioned Adam, who said, "He was naked?" He first makes atonement for Adam's misjudgment and disobedience by killing the lamb and making clothing for them to remove Adam's fear of nakedness and shame. He ends with instructions on their living conditions.

Before I continue, I must explore Adam's notion of fear and what initiated it. We read that Eve was the first partaker of the forbidden fruit in the text. We know that fear and doubt created an open door of fleshly desires: lust of the eye and the flesh, which persuaded her to disobey the Lord and His instruction, and the pride of life, which satan imparted to her. She desired to be something more than God's creation. Eve may have feared that her husband

Markeithia Lavon Silver

and God had left her out of the Garden business. Scripture does not reveal how she assisted her husband but simply that she was his helpmeet. Eve may have felt that her husband perceived her as insufficient and chose autonomy over direct knowledge of the righteousness of God. One can only speculate why she saw the Tree as "one to make one wise."

Nonetheless, we can deduce that she felt inadequate. Eve's fear of inadequacy and not enough plagues her and opens the door to her deception by the enemy. When you read the passage, Eve, through the fear of failure, becomes confused and even changes the directives given to Adam regarding the forbidden fruit. The serpent duped her into believing she lacked what she desired: food and godly wisdom. However, one can conclude that Eve fell by deception through fear, but the enemy did not deceive Adam. He partook of his volition. From where did Adams's actions stem? Likewise, I submit that Adam, God's ambassador on earth—full of knowledge and the power encompassing the Lord's oneness, responded from a place and space on the fear spectrum before disobeying God's instructions.

Moses reveals satan's deception. However, satan did not deceive Adam. The enemy approached him from another vantage point: his love for his wife. Nonetheless, he partook of the fruit. Let us explore the possibility of why he chose to partake of the fruit and disobey God.

After partaking in the forbidden fruit, Adam's version of himself drastically changed. Specifically, Adam no longer felt safe in his environment; he began to envision a life of lack, scarcity, and shame. Unlike before, he metaphorically viewed the Lord at a distance and, thus, could not supply his every need. In fact, Adam felt afraid, naked, and ashamed. He was now vulnerable to his circumstances. His thoughts no longer upheld a vision of abundance and oneness with the Creator. He no longer trusted God to protect, supply, and meet his needs. Both Adam and Eve had

Living Your Legacy Of Greatness

succumbed to the bewitchment of the enemy's lie: if you eat of the tree, you shall not die.

Adam's focus was now on the illusion of fear, lack, and shame. God asks, "Adam, who told you, you were naked?" I imagine God asking him, "What voice is proclaiming unto you your nakedness, Adam? It is surely not mine!" If you read the prior verse, you will discover Adam decreeing and declaring this delusion of fear. He says, "I heard your voice [You, God] in the Garden, and I was afraid *because I was naked*." The Hebrew word for told is *nâgad,* which means "properly to *front,* that is, to oppose boldly by implication (causatively), to *manifest*; figuratively to *announce* to manifest by word of mouth."[35] When the Lord asked Adam, "Where art thou?" He was not inquiring about his spatial location; God is omnipresent. He knew precisely where Adam was spatially and his mental, emotional, and spiritual location. He wanted Adam to become aware of where he was to facilitate a position of deliverance. Hence, the question, "Where are you, [and who announced you were there? Who whispered in your hearing the opposite of *how I created you*—whole? Who has bewitched you, Adam?]?" God designed the question to trigger *reflection within* Adam to recognize that fear had manifested or created an illusion that he had fallen prey to. Fear announced that God's provision and divine Providence could not cover him and Eve. Fear crept in once he doubted God's protection, provision, and Providence, stealing his dream of abundance and procreating shame and nakedness. We come to understand the words of the prophet Isaiah, where he says, "Behold, God is my salvation; *I will trust and not be afraid*: for the Lord, J.E.H.O.V.A.H., is my strength and my song; therefore, with joy shall we draw water from the wells of salvation" ~ Isaiah 12:2-3. *God sustains you here in the well of salvation*; you only need to believe!

Fear is a dream stealer! It enters the womb of doubt (the soil of your soul mind). Fear and doubt emerge and procreate lack, shame,

Markeithia Lavon Silver

uncertainty, anger, resentment, jealousy, and others contrary to the fullness of abundance and greatness in Him. "Who *told* you (whispered in your ear) you were naked? Who told you (manifested fear and shame within your mind's vision) that you were naked? Who told you that I could not supply all your needs? The cattle on a thousand hills are Mine; the earth is Mine, the fullness thereof, the world, and they that dwell therein. *Who* told you that if you were sick, I could not heal? Whom did you allow to steal your vision of *Me*, your oneness *in Me*? *Who*, Adam? *Who*?" Something entered Adam's thought process (another kind), altering his thoughts and visions of the Infinite "Us" Power that once flowed through him. Let us continue our investigation into what Adam experienced that dreadful day.

So, why did Adam *choose* to disobey God? Why did he not trust the veracity of God's statement: "For the day you eat thereof, you shall surely die" ~ Genesis 2:17. I assert that he panicked when Adam looked upon his wife and beheld a change. He did not discern just any difference; he observed her fallen state. Again, the enemy did not deceive Adam. ~ I Timothy 2:14. She was "bone of his bone and flesh of his flesh" ~ Genesis 2:23. God pulled Eve from under Adam's arm and near his heart, signifying a particular position of being protected and loved. He perceived an immediate change; her demise was evident. She was no longer in a state of oneness with him—a foreigner had separated him from her. Although she stood before him, her sin alienated her from her husband in a way he did not understand. His beautiful wife now epitomized a fallen soul. She was now far from him. How could he protect and love her in her fallen state? This feeling of helplessness must have overwhelmed him as he looked at her. Adam's heartbeat increased. I imagine his brow began to sweat. He may have even begun to pace the Garden floor, trying to think of a solution. We must understand that this story is an allegory, and Eve typifies the church metaphorically. Adam typifies "the figure of him that was

Living Your Legacy Of Greatness

to come." ~Rom. 5:6,14. Therefore, the similarities between Adam and Eve and the Church and Christ are apparent. Adam sacrificed his sonship for Eve to love and protect her, as Christ sacrificed his life for the Church to redeem her unto himself. ~ *Id.*

Remember, Adam was the one to whom the Lord bestowed the wisdom of His creation. He called a lion, a cow, a bird, a tiger, and their attributes into existence ~ Genesis 2:19. Each time Adam called something into actuality, all the "things" components materialized. For instance, when Adam looked upon a lion and called it forth, the lion began to roar—it was the same for each creature he named. Adam, endowed with the godly creative power to "call those things that were not as though they were," called each animal that the Lord placed before him as he so desired ~ Genesis 2:18. He fulfilled the Lord's blessing upon him, according to Genesis 1:28. God uniquely positioned Adam as His ambassador on earth.

However, no matter his gifts and talents, he could not call her from her diminished state. She had fallen prey to the lie and *believed* it! I imagine that Adam attempted to decree life, but the stench of death remained. Regardless of his words, he could not call her from darkness back into God's marvelous Light of life. Accordingly, Adam's mind was racing to construct a formula or vision to save her. However, her sinful state remained. Where he was once prosperous in his endeavors, he perceived failure. Unbeknownst to him, only the Lord (the Lamb of God slain ~ St. John 1:29, Rev. 12:11, 13:8) could save her; however, he chose not to trust God and seek His wisdom, knowledge, mercy, and guidance. He became fearful and embarrassed of his inability to cover and save his wife. He was running away from the only One who could help him. Again, it is a hard pill to swallow when we take responsibility for our thoughts and actions; however, we place ourselves in a deliverance position headed towards freedom when

Markeithia Lavon Silver

we do. I can only imagine his pain when he saw his wife's wretched state. However, it came down to his lack of trust (belief) in God as the sustainer of his soul.

Adam had complete discernment living from and through the "Us" Spirit! Adam ascertained her fallen condition. He felt her brokenness and perceived her separation from him *and* the Lord. Eve *knew* of her nakedness, and I am positive that this fear frightened her. Eve felt disconnected and lonely as she desperately reached for her husband for her transposition. She frantically looks for Adam to hide her nakedness. I imagine her emotional state appeared insane. She may have even screamed out, "Adam, save me!" How strong and heavy must this awareness Adam had concerning her? Can you imagine? She remained in her state whenever he called life to come forth. I assert that the more he endeavored to save her from her fall from grace, the more frustrated he became. There was no change— not even a little. He loved her; she was a part of him, and he could not deliver her from her choice of results. What a ball of confusion!

I envision the enemy whispering in his ear, taunting him with these words, "You have lost your power and authority! You cannot save her unless you join her—You will be like God and can save her!" he most likely whispered many other deceptions. Then, he believed through the eyes of fear that he might be able to bring her out of her fallen state. The enemy bewitched him right out of obedience into disobedience. Additionally, I visualize how his wife's expectations of calling forth her deliverance or speaking about something other than death frustrated him. He cared for and protected her, and the trepidation he felt anticipating what she might think of him if he could not deliver her from the bondage of death weighed heavily upon his mind.

Eve's fall from grace made him feel inadequate and doubtful of his position in the Lord. Once doubt in his performance was in question and his perceived inability to save her united, it created an atmosphere of defiance. Consequently, Adam's fear deceived him.

Living Your Legacy Of Greatness

Eventually, that fear developed into a force he did not expect. Due to the enemy's prodding, Adam's emotional and psychological body was wrapped in pride. He lacked trust in *who* he was and failed to seek the Lord's assistance. I believe he thought, "If he joined her, sacrificed his sonship, his God-given power could save her, returning her to her natural state." As the story goes, Adam also partook in the forbidden fruit.

One might ask, "From where do you base these assertions?" I proclaim them centered on the ministry of Christ, his accomplishments, and the fulfillment of the Scriptures. Jesus, referred to as the second Adam, passed the tests that the first Adam did not—Christ relied totally on the Father for guidance; he adhered to His commandments and trusted God all the way to the cross, providing an avenue of reconciliation of humanity back to God. The Christ Spirit knows no fear or failure in God's love! Instead of Adam calling upon the Lord for assistance, I submit that he attempts to help her. He had the prideful, "I can do it by myself, without the Lord's help" spirit. I do not necessarily blame him; however, if Adam had besought the Lord and trusted His word, his obedience to God would have preserved his position of oneness with the "Us" Spirit.

Notwithstanding, I submit that this circumstance gripped Adam with fear, pride, and bondage to the fear of loss, and arrogance that he alone could save her caused his fall. As Adam focused on her deliverance, fear of failure permeated his being. The Love of the "Us" Spirit that covered and kept him he placed on a 'backburner.' This placement of God's love on a backburner contributed to Adam's tortured spirit. It cost him his communion and intimate relationship with the One who loved him.

Adam's position is an interesting one. He is God's ambassador on earth, full of knowledge and authority, creative powers, and incredible discernment. He was unable to call his wife from spiritual death back to life. Also, how perplexed Adam was in those

Markeithia Lavon Silver

moments before disobeying God, he knew not what soul salvation entailed.

Nonetheless, he was willing to enter this barren place to bring her out of death's bondage. How often did you, gentle reader, observe someone believing someone could change another person or believe yourself capable of that task? The individual supposed they were stronger, older, wiser than them, or more educated, embarking on a mission to create a new person. However noble this undertaking may appear, human beings will change if they choose to awaken their gifts. This example of choice is why the Scriptures state, "Whosoever will let him come." God will lead and guide you but will not override your choice. He wants you to trust Him for provision, protection, peace, and more.

Moreover, "Calling those things as though they were" cannot manifest if done in fear or doubt. Thoughts are things displayed— called with confidence, without fear and doubt, and with a joyful and grateful heart. ~ Isaiah 12:1-2. Adam joyfully called each animal into existence. He operated in his god-ness with joy and praise of the Most-High God. God's love was complete in him— fear could not dwell. However, I argue that fear entered his psyche when he lost his wife to disobedience, procreated with doubt. Then, he sacrificed his life at the loss of all humanity—and the rest is history.

Later, he hears the Lord moving in the Garden, realizes that he is naked, is now ashamed of that nakedness (exposed to the vulnerability of whatever is contrary to Kingdom living), runs to hide from God's presence, and proceeds to blame everyone but himself. Similarly, Eve takes the same stance as Adam. The Lord shows His love, grace, and mercy by removing their fear as we read the text, but doubt remains. The two are no longer self-assured in who they are. The experience has shaken them. Can you attest to this type of faith-shaken event? Has this feeling of anxiety ever happened to you where your experiences put you in a place where

Living Your Legacy Of Greatness

you do not know what to do? A place where your trust in God wanes? Instead of enduring your vulnerability alone, seek God and hope in Him! Remind yourself that He is your Light, Salvation, and Strength ~ Psalms 27. Find your confidence in His word, commit your way unto Him, and trust that He *shall* bring it to pass ~ Psalms 37:5, Isaiah 46:11.

However, I envision that they questioned themselves, wondering how they could reconcile to the place they once were in God. Thank goodness the Lord is all-knowing and never caught off guard by our choices. He always has a plan of deliverance and restoration. God says, "Behold, the man is become as one of us, to *know* good and evil: and now, lest [Adam] put forth his hand, and also take of the tree of life, and eat, and live forever." (Emphasis mine). Adam and Eve knew good and evil but could not discern it properly. Their senses were not yet perfected because the power of the Holy Ghost as a revealer had not yet come. ~ Hebrews 5:14. Then, God clothed them, made atonement for their disobedience, and gave them insight into their current state.

God prophesies over them and sets them in a place to dwell and live out their lives. The Lord does not take dominion (the ability to create what you say/think (Gen. 2:19) and to be victorious (Gen. 1:28)) from them because of their disobedience. God spoke blessings and commandments unto them. God spoke over their lives just as He spoke the world into existence. He said, *"Be!" "Be* fruitful, and multiply, and replenish the earth, and subdue it: and have dominion over the fish of the sea, and over the fowl of the air, and over every living thing that moves upon the earth" were not taken from [us] them ~ Genesis 1:28. More importantly, God never stopped coming to the Garden to meet Adam as He did each appointed time. Adam's choice did not catch God off guard, and He still came to meet him. That speaks volumes of God's love towards us, and His desire to intimately commune with us daily in

Markeithia Lavon Silver

the sacred carved-out place called the Garden in Eden! ~ Genesis 2:8.

These gifts remain, even now; however, we do not know it. We are ambassadors of the Most High God. We act as if we are beneath instead of above, the tail instead of the head. Nonetheless, God is still "mindful of us" and our success as His children. Hence, He sends examples for us to follow. Therefore, "we must strive to behave like the Spirit image you are created to be transcending calm and locked in ecstatic bliss within you"—Bhagavad-Gita.

God bestowed, among others, five gifts upon humanity. First, He told us to *be* fruitful; two, multiply; three, replenish the earth; four, subdue it (the world); and five, to experience dominion over the planet ~ Gen. 1:28. The word fruitful does not apply only to procreation; but also to every aspect of your life—ditto for multiplying and replenishing the earth. *See* Psalms 1. Accordingly, the time has come to think outside the box and punch a gaping hole through it. The Lord is vast and ever-expanding. We are to act and believe the same. "He is able to do exceedingly abundantly above all that we ask or think according to the power that works in us!" Wow! Precisely, He instructs us to ask and think lavish, large, and clearly outside the realm of smallness. God is not tiny, and we are not grasshoppers except in our own eyes. So, why do we think tiny compared to a vastness bigger than the universe, God? I submit that we are stifling the Power that works in us.

When we unleash the eternal power in us, we will see the glory of the Lord revealed. We release the "Us" power by our thought power: life and death are in the tongue/mind. We tell ourselves that we are not good enough, we cannot do it, or God cannot do it better or advance us beyond where we are. *Who told you, you were naked?* Adam allowed the enemy's whisperings to cloud his judgment, placing him in a reality that spoke scarcity and deficiency instead of abundance, failure instead of more than a conqueror, and the life of ordinances that opposed God and His creation until Christ

Living Your Legacy Of Greatness

~ Colossians 2:6-15. It is time to change the game, my sisters and brothers!

Adam felt alienated from God because of sin or any negative thought contrary to God's word for His creation, resulting in separation. When you are out of harmony with what God designed for you, you feel out of place from the world's foundational decree by God. However, when you align with the "Us" spirit, your true nature—the symphony of Love, Peace, and Joy emerges, and amazing things happen.

In *A Course in Miracles*, "fear arises from lack of love." This account does not imply that Love does not exist; however, it conveys that one is not *receiving* the Love of the Infinite Power of God to its fullest. Thus, fear can reside in the heart and mind of an individual resting in fear. However, we can abolish the illusion of fear by accepting Love. Furthermore, we must remind ourselves to "guard our thoughts carefully" and not to allow the whisperings of the enemy to hoodwink us out of our legacy of greatness.

If we choose to protect our thoughts, receive Love, trust God at His word, and invest in views sublime for the good of others and ourselves, we can rest in peace now. For instance, do you recall the story in Matthew 8:23-27? Yes! Jesus was asleep while the storm was raging. The Disciples were afraid and went to awaken Jesus. Jesus spoke, "Peace be still," and calm came over the sea. Just for a moment, close your eyes and imagine your storm. Your tempest (poverty, scarcity, sickness, or any nutrient adverse to God's intent for us.) represents the thunderstorm on the sea that day. Instead of awakening Jesus when you find him, crawl next to him and rest with him. "Peace be still" is metaphorically attempting to calm an upset within the mind. If Peace is eluding you, *know you hold power to tell it to be still*, that you may lay hold of it and rest. In Psalms 116, David says, "Return unto thy rest, oh my soul, for the Lord has dealt bountifully with thee." You choose the option of

Markeithia Lavon Silver

resting right next to Jesus. You do this because you *know* the boat will not perish if Jesus is on it.

I can recall my children coming into my room whenever a rainstorm arose. The sounds of thunder and lightning frightened them. My presence was all they needed to go to sleep. You need to know, envision, and think Jesus to be right where you are. For clarity, read Hebrews 4:3. *If you believe*, you shall enter His rest. Believe in Hebrew is *'âman,* meaning properly to **build up** or **support**; to *foster* as a parent or nurse; figuratively **render** (or **be) firm** or faithful, **to trust** or believe, to **be permanent** or quiet; morally to *be true* or certain; **to go to the right hand**: – hence assurance, believe.[36] (Emphasis mine). In other words, my trust in God puts a supernatural mortar to the back of my courage, joining them together and propelling me forward. *When I trust Him, I am supported and rendered firm.* I walk in confidence that He shall bring it to pass. Similarly, in the Greek *pisteuō* (belief) also means to trust, to have faith in or concerning a person or thing—to give credit to; by implication, entrust (especially one's spiritual well-being to Christ—to commit (to trust), put trust with another.[37] *Thayer* says, (1) to think to be true, be persuaded of, credit, and place confidence in another. A conviction and trust to which a man is compelled (meaning: Driven forward, urged on, moved by any force or power) by a certain inner and higher prerogative and law of the soul [must be ancillary to the function of the seed]. T*rust* in God through Jesus Christ can aid in obtaining or doing something. (2) to be entrusted with a thing.[38] Do we extend credit to God through Christ as the giver of trust? Do we count Him able to aid us in *all* our circumstances? The enemy wants to deceive you into thinking God will fail you, leave you in the lurch, and go back on His promises. I assure you, my sister and brother, that God is a Promise Keeper!

Knowing that the Lord *is* with you takes courage of thought and unclouded vision. Your trust in God places a supernatural cement

Living Your Legacy Of Greatness

mortar on the back of your courage that presses you forward until you reach the end of your trouble. During my grandmother's time, the Saints would sing, *"My soul looked back and wondered how I got over."* In the *Sunnah, the Second Hadith,* it says, and I paraphrase, "Oh, how beautiful a worship when you envision that God is there, watching everything you do. Even if you do not see Him, *know without a doubt* that He *is* there, *observing all* that you do." What a vision! What an opportunity to rest in His Providence, provision, and peace, no matter the circumstances!

I will close this chapter with prose entitled *Quiet Please; I am Trying to Hear Myself Think.*

Quiet, Please; I am Trying to Hear Myself Think

"Blessed quietness, holy quietness."

"Be anxious (constant unsettling mental movement) for nothing. But in all things with prayer (communication and meditation) and supplications (requests) come unto the Lord (the One who sustains, who fulfills, who lifts burdens, which quenches the thirsty soul)." In other words, "be still (quiet) and receive" a blanket of love replenishing for the soul whenever there is a need.

Quietness: A prerequisite of peace that passes all understanding to keep your heart and mind (you must bring your mind to a place of stillness to receive peace).

Quietness: A door opens to a place where one can make decisive, rational, and purposeful decisions. Take a deep breath and grab the knob.

Quietness: A place where the Lord speaks to the weary soul. He pronounces His word in a still voice to the spirit attentively listening. "He restores my soul."

When all hell (tests, trials, and tribulations) is breaking forth in your life, this quietness allows you to steal away to the door

Markeithia Lavon Silver

that leads to a place of stillness. It will enable you to visualize and access the eternal realm to gather yourself, recreating your situation.

When sought after and embraced, Stillness becomes the vehicle by which you can access your inner strength (power), transcend all adversity, embrace destiny, and fulfill your purpose. Will you enter through the door of blessed quietness?

Will you be still in the place of holy quietness long enough to reflect upon you—the [who] you are and the [who] you are becoming?

If you dare to enter this place, you will receive rejuvenation from the Most High God's Love.

If you dare to enter this place, His wisdom will fortify you, enabling you to conquer all your fears. "There is no fear in God's love."

This holy, sacred quietness challenges the soul to embrace the Light within. This quietness fulfills the requirements for building the required wick for the Light to burn.

Take the time to replenish and restore your wick (soul).

State, "Quiet, please; I am trying to hear myself think." Escape your chaos and enter a place of perpetual refreshing grandeur.

CHAPTER EIGHT

THE PROCESS OF DISCERNING AND CREATING GOD'S WILL (REALITY) FOR YOUR LIFE

"Now, Faith is the substance [THE VISION] of things hoped for, the evidence [MANIFESTATION] of things not seen ...through faith [TRUST, BELIEF, THOUGHT FOCUS, GODLY WISDOM, and KNOWLEDGE] we understand that the worlds were framed by the Word of God so that things [TANGIBLE], which ARE SEEN, were NOT made of things, which do appear [THE MANIFESTATIONS OF OUR THOUGHTS, DESIRES, AND VISIONS IN OUR MIND]." Hebrews 11:1, 3

—Paul

Often, we talk about the substance of faith and the evidence of the same, yet miss our need for other elements essential in manifesting the objects of our faith. Moreover, we never underscore a critical aspect of creating our faith's manifestation within our imagination. *Imagination, faith, godly wisdom, and knowledge of*

God's Word create the pulsating power necessary to manifest your dreams and visions. Here, the Scripture explains that the things we *see* do not create our worlds but what is behind the thoughts that formulate our reality. In other words, we manifest our thought focus and visions by what is *behind* what we perceive: Our faith and trust in God.

Moreover, faith *is* our thoughts, desires, passions, and visions, especially when they are the objects of our affection. Our ideas frame our desires and guide our aesthetics, which manifests according to our faith. I would venture to say that the necessary faith level begins with our thought focus, a measure of faith given to all humanity ~ Romans 12:3. Our faith increases in increments as we hear the Word of God. God's Word gives and sustains our lives and contributes to our spiritual growth. As we hear the Word, experience the Word, and internalize the Word, we mature from a measure of faith to perfecting our faith. This faith trajectory positions us to know God in the fullness of His splendor.

Take, for instance, the man who came to Jesus asking for the healing of his servant. This man exhibited a combination of imagination *and* faith. The man says to Jesus in Matthew 8, and I paraphrase, "I know that you are a man of authority (with expansive jurisdiction) as I am" [he could relate to Him through his imagination]. This representation is familiar. Of course, David saw God in every experience—the I Am as a Shepherd, Provider, Sustainer, Light, Strength, Salvation, Protector, and so much more. The Centurion said to Jesus, "I tell some to come and some to go, and they do as I decree. If you speak the words, I know that he will be made whole (He knew the power of spoken word under his ability and compared that to Jesus's level of authority)." In his mind, he related himself to Jesus, knowing the power of command, authority, and jurisdiction and that he could speak in a like manner. He knew that Jesus could do likewise authoritatively in the healing of his servant. Jesus's response, "I have not found *such great*

Living Your Legacy Of Greatness

[level of] *Faith!*" (Emphasis mine). Do you remember the story of David and Goliath mentioned in the previous chapter, *Expect to Do More*? We need to pattern ourselves after David and the Centurian. We forget our authority (dominion and jurisdiction) in the earth because we do not *know* who we are! Jesus himself told us that *we are as He is in this earth!* ~ I John 4:17. Our jurisdiction is vast, and our authority is endless through Christ.

Nevertheless, we still count ourselves enslaved people to sin, not children of The Most-High God. Moreover, as we continue to live our lives from the bottom up, we retard the rest of the world from developing into what God created us to be: Great sons and daughters with a co-creative ability and commanding presence in the earth. "The world yet groans and even ourselves [my brothers and sisters] for the manifestation of the sons/daughters of God" ~ Romans 8: 19-23.

Trust in God (faith), united with imagination, joy, and deliberate focus with an authoritative Christ-Mind, is great faith beyond belief. It is a knowing—an awareness of who you are! "As a wo/man thinks in their heart, so s/he *IS!*" We will do great exploits if we tap into God's *Law of Unity!* *See* Genesis 11 (The people became one (*Echâd*) unified, except their unity was not inspired nor governed by the righteousness of God—and God confounded their languages as a result). Likewise, Jesus spoke of his oneness with the Father and that he would do nothing except the Father instruct him ~ St. John 5:19, 30. Accordingly, Jesus informs us that we will follow suit ~ St. John 15:5.

Correspondingly, Paul thought it noteworthy to mention casting down negative thoughts within the imagination and bringing those meditations under the subjection of God's word. The creative mind plays an intricate part in manifesting our dreams and aspirations. We must be aware of our fears and doubts to cast them down because they go against the very essence of God's creative Spirit within us. Fear and doubt are the antitheses of perfected love and trust in God (faith). Doubt and fear did not create us. In fact, the *Bible* urges us to remember that "God has not given us the spirit of fear (like Adam received from his disobedience in the Garden) but of Love, Power and a Sound Mind." Fear and doubt are the tentacles of wickedness designed to kill, choke, and destroy the righteous seed in us! God created us from the "Us" glory stuff! The Kingdom is within! We must dare to reach within and break up the fallow ground of unbelief and fear. This confidence is the faith (the substratum) we offer God. That substance must be ready for planting, shaping, and molding, framed by Kingdom thinking and not shaped by insufficiency, lack, or otherwise. Here, the word power in Greek is *exousia.* This word denotes brute strength and conveys jurisdiction, authority, privilege, capacity, freedom, influence, force, and competency.

Sound familiar? Of course, it should! Jesus received the same power from the Father ~ St. Matthew 28: 18-19a, St. John 14:12. He then passed that power on to us! *See* Matthew 28: 18-19a again. "Therefore" is a word that logically follows the *first principle* and its supporting evidence. It concludes the matter. After Jesus tells the Disciples, "All power (*exousia*) given unto me (by the Father) in heaven and earth," he says, "Go, therefore...." In other words, I now possess complete jurisdiction, authority, privilege, capacity, freedom, influence, force, and competency in *all* matters. Now, go with this same power and teach all nations what I commanded you, for it encapsulates the *exousia* I am giving you, remembering that I am with you *always! See* St. John 14:12. Can you imagine such power? Can you envision the Father enlarging your jurisdiction and authority through Christ? God's will and testament, filed in the Probate Court of Heaven, have been read, and you are a beneficiary of His trust! Stand and take your place!

It is morning, oh, gentle reader! Thus, I hear the Spirit of the Infinite One, True and Living God, and Sustainer of all life say, "I implore you to step beyond the veil and discover, recover, and

Living Your Legacy Of Greatness

uncover the beauty of who you are in *ME*. Your smile, hands, feet, eyes, laughter, personality, and all of you are wonderful and marvelous! When you laugh, listen gently. You will hear *ME* laughing in you. When you walk, observe closely, and see *ME* walking in you. When you embrace another softly, with gentle eyes, you will see *MY* Love move from heart to heart. Look into the eyes of a newborn child, and you will see *ME* in the reflection."

Jesus said, "If you have [grasp the idea of] faith as a grain of a mustard seed, you can say unto the mountain, be thou removed from here" ~ Mathew 21:21 *See also* Mark 11:23. We consider the smallest seed, and we conclude we need faith as that size only. God calls us to look beyond the size of the seed and crack open what the "Us" Spirit *injected into the seed* when God created you in the Garden. You must engage the seed's hidden premise and implication: cultivating an atmosphere to grow it because the inner origin is a "power agent" to increase our faith. *See* St. John 12:24. If you read the parable regarding seed growth, Jesus gives examples of why a seed sometimes will not thrive in every environment. Accomplishing this notion of telling the mountain (any obstacle) to move is within the spiritual mind and heart, and the meaning behind the words you invoke when decreeing and declaring the barrier removed.

Specifically, you must be able to see it moved, trust that it will be, and see it destroyed. The same way you accomplish this act of faith is how you create affluence in your life. *This ability eludes us because we are underdeveloped in our imaginations.* Our imaginations are the fertile ground of our spiritual minds; however, circumstances will change if we train/discipline the mind to receive the seed of faith. Cultivating your tree of faith into roots and branches of knowing and trusting God will never disappoint is the conduit by which we manifest our creative reality in righteousness. We, however, must devote ourselves to the oneness in Christ, for without him, we can do nothing. Jesus holds *all power* in His hands;

Markeithia Lavon Silver

we can only obtain it through intimacy and communion with Him. *"There can be no success without commitment,"* says Al-Ghazzali. We must catch our thoughts and pay attention to the visions they are constructing. Autonomy lost us our position and authority in the Garden. We chose to learn righteousness outside of God, which cost us the transformation into another kind and transposition away from God's place of pleasure (the Garden). Jesus forever redeemed us from that loss and gave us our authority back in Him. We can live, move, and have our being of greatness if we reclaim our identity in Christ.

Moreover, we must dare to imagine and venture to dream big, so much so that the vision takes our breath away. "Is there anything too hard for God?" The answer is no! No-thing is too hard for God to help us create our reality and live a life of greatness! Our richness is not in material things but in the jewels bestowed upon us that dwell within us. Material wealth is ancillary and a by-product of the Kingdom within us. *See* Romans 14:17 and Matthew 6:33. Yet, we cannot rest upon our laurels. We must shape our imagination properly, deepening and expanding our faith (trust) in God.

First, the imagination *must* become subject to God's Word. His Word offers life, abundance, and sustainability. You must *see* the acts of the enemy as subordinate to God's Word. "I come that you might lay hold to live and enjoy it more abundantly [I come to show you the way to life and abundance]." Jesus said, "He is the Way, the Truth, and the Life…." We shall do more than him if we follow his blueprint of oneness with El-Shaddai, Creator of heaven and earth. He said so himself. Follow his way of doing things, listen to how he spoke, and *Be* Life to all we desire for the good of others and ourselves. If Jesus said, "You are healed!" you would fare well if you first believed your healing in your imagination.

Then, you must see your infirmity cast upon Christ's body. Jesus said, "Cast all your cares upon Me for I care for you" ~ I Peter 5:7. Finally, you must *see* Christ taking it away and bearing it on the

Living Your Legacy Of Greatness

cross. Although life tests us, *Christ's death eliminated infirmity's opportunity to rest in our bodies.* If we believe *and* trust that "he *was* wounded for our transgressions, *he was* bruised for our iniquities: the chastisement of our peace *was* upon him, and with his stripes, we are healed." We stand firm in our faith that the enemy casts a broad shadow of an illusion. We can arrest this deception in the spirit realm *for [Jesus] blot [ed] out the handwriting of ordinances that was against us, which was contrary to us, and took it out of the way, nailing it to his cross.* Having spoiled principalities and powers, he made a show of them openly, triumphing over them in it ~ Isaiah 53:5 and Colossians 2:14-15, respectively.

We must grasp the power of Christ's death toward us ~ Ephesians 1:17-23. He presented believers with the opportunity of reconciliation, healing, and restoration. "Jesus was despised and rejected of men; a man of sorrows, and acquainted with grief... he was despised, and we esteemed him not. Indeed, he hath borne our griefs, and carried our sorrows: yet we did esteem him stricken, smitten of God, and afflicted" ~ Isaiah 53:3. Grasping that our transgressions wounded him, our iniquities bruised him, the chastisement of our peace was upon him; and with his stripes, we lay hold to our healing, which is critical in obtaining a posture of assurance in God. In other words, *Jesus took and bore on the cross being despised and rejected, so we do not need to carry it in our emotional, physical, or spiritual bodies.* Our sorrow and grief belong to the cross. Our affliction and pain belong to the cross. Our iniquities and the punishment for providing us peace were upon *him*! His endured stripes encompassed our complete healing. His sacrifice obliterated the need for our bodies to carry these infirmities after His blood sacrifice, *but we must see it! We must envision it! Then, we must know it!* Just like Eve's disobedience gendered another kind with her spiritual body, attaching itself to her soil mind, Jesus's sacrifice provided an avenue to complete redemption and freedom from the other kind entrapped in our spiritual body from the Fall. He was there, hanging on the cross, and took our punishment without one word of remorse, complaint, or an unforgiving heart. One of Jesus's final words before declaring "*It [was] finished*" was "Father forgive them, for they know not what they do" ~ St. John 19:30 and St. Luke 23:34, respectively. What power! What strength! We now share in that power. He allowed us to *know* the hope of his calling toward us and the riches of the glory of his inheritance *in* [us] the saints. The eyes of your understanding [are] enlightened through Christ Jesus; Christ positioned us to understand the working of God's mighty power concerning His creation (His most holy thing—the saints of God) ~ Ephesians 1:18-19.

Second, you must be aware of the answer to the question: do you *believe* Him and *trust* Him, as Jabez did in enlarging his territory, protecting him from harm, and co-creating your reality into the Promised Land? If answered in the affirmative, this foundational question is surrounded by peace, immersed in love, guided by righteousness, and framed in grace. I dare you! "Taste and see that the Lord is good!" ~ Psalms 34:8. He is not slack concerning His promises. He hovers over His word, ready to perform it! Jabez trusted God for deliverance, and He granted Jabez's request ~ *I Chronicles* 4:10. Engage Him with your time and worship, and watch your world blossom beyond your wildest dreams. Simultaneously, we must give life (Be-life) to the thought that "He is, and He is a rewarder of those that diligently seek him" ~ Hebrews 11:1-6.

Thirdly, you must discipline yourself to *think like* God, governed by the essence of His Word. We are god princes and princesses, and we should live according to Kingdom principles of greatness, not earthly values of lack and not enough. We must seek to hear the heart of God. If we believe we are paupers, we will remain paupers. However, once we *see, think,* and *trust* our

Living Your Legacy Of Greatness

position in God through Christ as kings and queens, the world will change as we know it.

Take on the building of your world of abundance! Reach within your imaginative mind and pull out that God-given creativity bequeathed to you from the beginning and design well! Your greatness is but for the taking. Just as a child who joyfully reaches out at the enchanting mobile, displayed with discoveries in its new world, you can embrace all God has for you: your inheritance and legacy of greatness. You obtain this process through consistent intimacy with God. He is our Father, our Lord and Savior, our Guide, our Sustainer, our Protector, and our mind regulator. He is our Good Shephard, Maintainer of our faith, and all that you need Him to be *if we dare to seek Him and devote our heart to Him* ~ Psalms 23, 27, 37, 91, Luke 22:32, Jeremiah 30:21b. God is inclined unto the voice of His children. When you call Him, He will answer.

A child's love is an example of the epitome of reciprocated love. When they call their mommy or daddy, an observer can hear the truth of a child's love, the gentleness, trust, and unconditional affection towards the object of the child's love. Jesus said it this way, "True worshippers shall worship the Father in spirit and truth: for the Father *seeketh such* to worship him, and they that worship Him must worship *Him* in spirit and truth… and suffer the little children to come unto Me and forbid them not, for such is the Kingdom of Heaven" ~ St. John 4:23-24 and Mark 10:14, respectively (Emphasis mine).

Matthew highlights Jesus's joy concerning children. For Jesus, reflecting a child's imagination is necessary for acquiring Kingdom benefits. Jesus says, "Except you become like one of these, you cannot enter into the Kingdom of Heaven" ~ Matthew 8:3. It is not because you cannot enter in, but *because you cannot imagine yourself entering in.* Except you unlock your childlike mind utilizing your ability to imagine beyond your wildest dreams

Markeithia Lavon Silver

while harmoniously piercing the veil with childlike humility, you will not enter into the Kingdom. Children possess an innocence that transcends adult inhibitions. A child's trust is adventurous, playful, loving, tenacious, and most importantly, children are F-R-E-E. Children resist the bondage of limitation and the adults attempting to impose it upon them. No matter how often you tell a toddler not to climb on that table, they will continue to do it. They will continue to scale that table until they master it, then move on to a new adventure. *Pay close attention to the disposition of a child, and you will see just what Jesus saw.* Observe a child playing; their fearlessness and sense of adventure will enlighten you. Accordingly, a glimpse of what Jesus discerned regarding children will be evident. They feel they can conquer the world until adults teach them they cannot. We need to turn from clipping our children's wings through fear and doubt and teach them to trust God, who they are, in this loving adventure of discovering the greatness within and setting them free to soar. When we do not impart the wisdom of trusting and seeking God to them and how to recognize their divine potential, we will lose entire generations to ignorance ~ Hosea 4:6.

As a child, I recall playing several outside games with my friends: kickball, tag football, basketball, dodgeball, red-light-green-light, stickball, and anything we could imagine. Each game had its own set of rules. What is memorable are the rules for games such as red-light-green-light and stickball. Both games require the player to do something before advancing to the next level. Each player must remain until the person calling the red light or green light gives the command for the red-light-green-light game. If you moved before they made the call, you had to return to the beginning. The goal was to reach the command caller. However, you must first follow the orders of the leader to receive the opportunity to become the command caller.

Living Your Legacy Of Greatness

Likewise, during the stickball game, if you missed first base or failed to touch the first base plate on your way to home plate—and for us, children in the 70s, first base was anything we could find—you were O-U-T! The goal of both games was listening and conforming to the rules to accomplish the win. *Jesus informs us that God also has management terms.* Like the games, you must first do something to get something else. For God, seek His Kingdom and righteousness *first*; then, you will receive added gifts. This *first principle* necessarily is followed by your plans, dreams, and aspirations. Your strategy always follows God's will and goals for your life. Some of my friends reached within one stride of becoming the command caller in the games, and suddenly, they flinched and had to return to the beginning. Likewise, if you forego touching the first base or move before the call, you risk starting over until you get it right. Similarly, living your legacy of greatness requires you first to seek God, and all His intended blessings will follow.

I had the privilege and honor of watching the 2012 Summer Olympics. I was impressed by all who performed. As most of the country did, I enjoyed the women's gymnastics team, *The Fierce Five*, which consisted of Gabby Douglas, Aly Raisman, Mckayla Maroney, Kyla Ross, and Jordyn Weiber. These young women were phenomenal! During an interview on the *Late Night* with the *David Letterman Show*, David quotes McKayla when she broke her toe, saying, "What are you gonna do?" He asked her how she felt competing with a broken toe, and she said, "You ignore your pain." In other words, you push through your obstacles.

The girls all agreed, "Once you put your mind to something, you [encapsulate] a dream [hope] to work towards." However, "you must be consistent." He asked Gabby why she wanted to be an Olympian. "I desired to inspire a nation," she responded. Wow! What a vision to build upon—a "desire to inspire hope in a nation" of people you do not know. I later heard Gabby in another interview in which she gave her comment context. Again, she encouraged young people to trust God—to know that God will see them through. Wow! "Except you become like one of these." The announcer said, "Gabby needed to trust God because she had to leave home at such an early age to reach her dreams." We *all* need to trust God! I said to myself.

Additionally, they shared how they all created a vision to compete in the Olympics one day (dreaming). Furthermore, when Dave asks, "Why the *'Fierce Five'*?" They said simultaneously, "Because *we are fierce!*" What an inspiration! What a way to envision yourself! Do you *see* yourself as fierce? Gabby trusted God with her vision; she sought Him first. She consecrated her life and dreams to Him. God, then, endowed her with wisdom, knowledge, understanding, and skill to perform. Even in a gymnastics competition, *if you follow the hierarchy of God's command to seek Him first, obtaining your dreams is inevitable.* This acknowledgment of seeking God first does not mean you will not need to do your due diligence because Gabby worked hard. It is to say that placing your life in the hand of God brings all your dreams, actions, plans, and each objective you create to reach your goal under the protection of the Kingdom. He will charge His angels to watch over thee in all your ways ~ Psalms 91. This charge results from creating the essential formula according to Kingdom principles.

Creating the Right Formula

Faith is necessary to manifest your dreams, but it is not sufficient. Faith is adequate with imagination and action, as shown in the story above. Take H_2O, for instance: Hydrogen twice and Oxygen once (understood mathematically) creates water. These ingredients are necessary, do not require any other component, and are sufficient to make water. *Take away or alter one element; you no longer create water but another substance.* Likewise, this same concept applies

Living Your Legacy Of Greatness

to Adam. God made Adam from a particular substance. Once the spirit of disobedience, pride, lust, fear, and autonomy altered that body, Adam became something else! However, Christ's sacrifice regenerated the correct formula, which led back to obtaining the spiritual body intended for us from the beginning.

Similarly, the same formula applies to aspiring to know beyond faith. To create the right dynamic to bring forth your imaginative thoughts, you need one, faith [the substratum]; two, the imagination [inner vision]; three, joy [the pulsating strength behind the creation of the idea]; and four, action [the cultivation of the vision] to make it happen. You must conceive, perceive, and offer it to God (The "Us" Spirit of all Creation). What you think [meditate upon, ponder, dream about, focus upon with certainty] about will expand, just like a seed develops in the earth until it births itself into stems, branches, leaves, and fruit. ~ Matthew 7:16-20. David tells us in Psalms 1 that "we shall be like a tree planted by the rivers of water, that bringeth forth his/her fruit in his/her season; his/her leaf also shall not wither; whatsoever s/he doeth shall prosper if we delight in the law of the Lord." *See also* Isaiah 12: 2-3, Nehemiah 8:10. As we regain knowledge of our identity in Christ, our senses become sharpened, and our ability to live in the space of:

"As a wo/man thinks in their heart, so are they," purposely and for righteousness sake.

"Without a vision, the [person] people will perish." It will become our nature.

We think affirmations are of a new order. They are not unique to those who know their God. Paul admonished us with, "Finally [sisters and] brothers, whatsoever things are just, pure, lovely, of good report, virtuous, and praiseworthy, to think on these things" ~ Philippians 4:8.

What you think, *YOU WILL BEYOND THE SHADOW OF ANY DOUBT, BECOME! DO NOT GIVE UP ON YOUR DREAMS! PROTECT YOUR DREAMS; DO NOT GIVE UP!*

What Dreams Are You Dreaming, gentle reader? Take a moment to write down your dreams in your journal. The Bible says, "Write the vision and make it plain upon tablets, that they may run that read it. For the vision is yet for an appointed time, but it shall speak and not lie at the end. Though [the vision] it tarries, wait for it; because it will SURELY come, it WILL NOT tarry" ~ Habakkuk 2:2. (Emphasis mine). Then, consecrate them unto the Lord God, strong and mighty. *Placing God first assures Kingdom alliance and protection.* In other words, as you write the vision, others and yourself will see and be motivated by it. Although it is being shaped and formed by your imagination, thoughts, and actions, when fully developed, it will present itself and be faithful to the beliefs that created it—it will manifest after its kind. Take your journal and dreams into your prayer closet and *trust Him.* Commit to putting God first. Each step, action, or work product, commit to placing each task unto Him. By doing this, you bring yourself, your dreams, your ministry, your efforts, and your work product under the protection of the Kingdom because you consecrated them to Him! ~ *I Corinthians* 6:19-20.

My Dreams...

What I am Dreaming	What I am Doing to Cultivate My Dream
To desire to buy a home (5 bed/2 bath), furnishings, and the like.	I am saving my money and looking in magazines to select the home I like. I am attending first-time homeowner classes and other means associated with my dreams. I say to myself, "I shall own a home to my specifications in an area I desire for my family and me. The Lord is in the business of blessing and more."

Living Your Legacy Of Greatness

I desire to be an inspirational writer/ speaker.	I am getting an education. I am reading books on how to write and publish a book. I say to myself, the Inspiration of the Holy Spirit flows through me like a River of Living Water. I inspire others with my writing.
I desire to be a better wife/husband and parent.	I listen attentively to my family. I read books on loving others. I say to myself, I am gentle with my family. I love from a space of eternal love. I love and adore myself; therefore, I love and value others. I release my past hurts, opening myself to receive love and joy where there was pain and fear. I Agapé my family, and they Agapé me.
I desire to be married.	He that finds a wife finds a good thing and obtains favor of the Lord. I say to myself, "I attract my mate to me. The Lord is preparing them. I attract nothing but good in my life." God knows His plans for me… will bring me to an expected end. No good thing shall He withhold from me.

This exercise aims to develop a specific thought pattern in accordance with what you are dreaming about within the mind (consciousness). You can tweak these examples to your specification, transforming them into what you desire by the leading of the Holy Spirit and the grace and mercies of God. As you continue to practice these methods, you will inevitably remove the grooves and shadows (within the mind) that arrest your spirit from soaring with determined and persistent thought.

To be sure, you will face challenges in purposeful, disciplined creation. When you *know* the answer, you patiently await its arrival. While enduring a challenge in my life some years prior, I would go into my office to pray and meditate. Often, I would play *Spider Solitaire* to break up the many thoughts swirling around in my mind. I enjoy playing the game because it challenges you to

Markeithia Lavon Silver

think strategically and creatively. The *Spider Solitaire* game is like traditional *Solitaire.*

In comparison, the game of *Solitaire* uses one deck of cards with the typical four suits. *Spider Solitaire* operates as many as three decks of cards simultaneously involving twelve suits. The objective, in any case, is the same. You must move the cards around strategically to place them in numerical order. If you have played this game before, you know the challenges of winning the game. Like any other strategic game, you must think ahead. The game also gives you, the player, the opportunity, if you lose, to replay the match. If you give up and believe the game is lost, you will exit, not realizing you can win. I think you know where I am going with this. I found that playing this game, as one of my hobbies, I can win every game. Isn't that fantastic! You can put your mind to work and win every time. Specifically, knowing that a solution is on the horizon gives me hope. It allows me to see that I do not need to admit defeat or cower to the game's challenges because "where there is a *will*, there is a *way.*" I may not win the game the first, or even the tenth time, for that matter.

Nevertheless, if I keep trying and find the correct pattern of moves, I can win! It is all in how you look at it (perspective). In philosophy, the coined phrase describing perspective says, "It depends on what type of spectacles you are wearing." Knowing this allows your mind to remain open to search diligently for the right pair of glasses. Once you discover the right pair of eyewear, the creative juices begin to flow, and before you know it, you have discovered a solution to your task.

Later that night, I received an email from a close friend. I will share it with you. The email came inquiring about my night and whether it was peaceful. In my response to them, I affirmed that my night was quiet and that I had embarked upon a particular game of *Spider* that I was, at first, unable to solve. The email goes as follows:

Living Your Legacy Of Greatness

I finally discovered the correct sequence of moves for my game. It took me all day yesterday into the late morning hours. However, I realized some things.

I believe I mentioned that this game was synonymous with my situation. Since I started playing *Spider*, it has never taken this long to figure out the correct sequence. Usually, the goal in the game was coordinating the suits with each other, king through ace, respectively. This game was different.

For instance, you had to go the opposite way that the game usually takes you to win this game. After discovering the proper sequence of moves, this is what I learned:

1. Sometimes, to accomplish your desired goal, you must try a solution that may be unorthodox—go outside the box.
2. Be patient and trust the process, even though it seems ridiculous.
3. Do not give up if it does not turn out as desired. Start over, remembering what worked.
4. You did not fail just because it did not work. Failure is giving up.
5. In basketball, hustling for the ball to keep it in play makes you feel like you contributed to the win. In challenging areas of your life, you can achieve that same gratification by cultivating your vision to your specifications, encouraging yourself, being hopeful with anticipation, and being careful not to fall into the trap of frustrating anxiety (fear), which is the seed of destruction.

    This lesson reminded me of my "Nana's" ability to grow flowers. Once she planted them, she expected them *to bloom every spring and summer*. Without fail, they would blossom, and she would talk about how beautiful her labor was. Her blooms were recurring because she "worked it" and had confidence in her actions.

Markeithia Lavon Silver

6. You can achieve patience by understanding more ways to accomplish the goal you aspire to obtain. No two situations are identical; you should not treat them as such.
7. The Blueprint: Gives you the guidelines to accomplish a goal but leaves room for flexibility. All creations are subject to change. As you go along, adjust according to your good pleasure. We are all unique individuals. We relish different fingerprints, eye patterns, tone of voice, etc. We may be similar, but we are altogether different.
8. No matter the challenge, take patience in choosing the right sequence of moves to achieve your desired outcome because each move gives you a predetermined end.

Thus, perspective and perception determine how you respond to a particular circumstance. In your creation, go outside of your perspective and perception to create something beyond your wildest dreams. If you stay on the edge of the unknown, confident in your creativity, you will reflect on your creation and say, "It is good!"

These lessons reassured me that God stirred me for something greater than I could imagine. The experience fortified my thinking for several reasons. First, no matter the situation, I learned not to focus on the problem but on the solution. Second, I endeavor to ask questions and then search for answers. The answer is there; if you only trust God, it is. Third, you may need to take an approach that is unfamiliar to you. Proceed, remembering what works along the way. It may seem unbelievable, but trust God all the way to deliverance. God's track record speaks for itself. David believed in trying again and again. He sought God in *all* that he did. God regarded him as a man *after* His heart because of his demeanor and tenacity. Fourth, know, without doubt, if you put your trust in the One who created you, "There is no fear of failure in God's Love," the Holy Spirit will guide you as you walk after the things of the Spirit. "If you fall, [your circumstances will not cast you

Living Your Legacy Of Greatness

down] ~ Psalms 37:24, [for], "God orders the steps of a good wo/man" ~ Psalms 37: 23-24. In addition, know with certainty that the word of the Lord will guide you along the way, for "Thy word is a lamp unto my feet and a light unto my path" ~ Psalms 119:105. *See also* Job 23:10 and Psalms 31:3. Moreover, "the mouth of a righteous wo/man is a well of life" ~ Proverbs 10:11. Finally, speak life into your visions to the glory and honor of the Lord. He will not disappoint!

If you learn to discern the voice of the Lord, you will be likened unto a well that will not run dry; if you fall, your situation will not get the best of you, and the word of the Lord will guide you along the way. I remember the late Reverend James Cleveland's song "*God Leads His Children.* This great song displays the Loving Chords of God's Providence, protection, and provision. The song says, "If you are listening into Heaven, He will lead you."

Accordingly, when I open the game *Spider Solitaire,* I posture with the mindset, "Anything goes." You can use this concept when new challenges arrive, and you do not know what to do. Each time you encounter a unique experience, do not allow it to take you away; let the Solution guide you. Be assured that nothing is hidden from the Infinite "Us" Power of God, and no step you take surprises the Omniscient, Omnipresent, and Omnipotent Power of the "Us" Spirit. Remember, there is hope when you *know* you can win, and when the scale is tipped in your favor, you stand erect in the face of trials and tribulations. In other words, you must posture hope (rise), live in your space (take up your bed), and walk (towards your greater destiny). Finding the solution and the correct sequence of moves is your only challenge. So, go for it!

Furthermore, one must understand that, inevitably, you will gravitate toward what you think. Herein lies wisdom, one of the most significant discoveries I have ever made. Let me give you an example. Did you ever experience reading a home or clothing magazine, finding something you liked, and later looking to

Markeithia Lavon Silver

purchase the item? You are excited and set your mind to finding this item, no matter the cost. Your thoughts are now dominating your actions. Those thoughts are sending out vibrations, like a magnet attracting metal. Likewise, when looking for a solution to any circumstance, your efforts will begin to dictate the resolution. Do you recall that your thoughts are frequencies sent out into the fertile universe? Ralph Waldo Trine says in his book *In Tune with the Infinite*:

> Each [person] is building their own world. We both build from within, and we attract from without. *Thought is the force with which we build, for thoughts are forces.* Like [produces] like, and like attracts like. In the degree, that thought is spiritualized... ***Everything is worked out in the unseen before manifested in the seen,* in the ideal before it is realized in the real, and [in]** *the spiritual before it shows forth in the material.* (Emphasis mine).

In other words, your thoughts manifest things. The Bible says, "As a wo/man thinketh in their heart, so is s/he." In my experience with breast cancer, I learned that my thoughts about my disease are more potent than the disease itself. Therefore, in any situation, just as Jesus magnified this concept to the man by the pool, "You must earnestly think and see yourself whole." Your body will respond in kind by seeing yourself whole and disease-free. When we do not want to let go because of some warped sense of punishment for past sins or actions, sickness may remain. Most often, the frame of mind stems from the subconscious mind. Here, we must ask God to search us ~ Psalms 139. For no one knows the heart, save God.

Allow me to share an entry from my journal that speaks to the concept of creating your reality and what you might go through to create a narrative within your mind:

Living Your Legacy Of Greatness

While sitting in my seat, greeting people as they passed, I wondered what I would say. I reached for the program, turning it over. I began to reflect upon the time I spent at this church. My heart was overwhelmed with emotion. They had been there at a time most tender: the fight against breast cancer. I shall never forget the warm embrace of this house of worship. Although I was glad to see everyone, a parallel dimension was at play. I was separated from them, mentally and spiritually. I thought about how strategically God had fashioned me in a place that would assist me in learning the process of life's growth. The manifestation of hopes and dreams:

- Begins with desire and hope;
- Then, conceptualization within the mind;
- Followed by manifested thought and action.

We then place these upon the substratum of our faith. Desire and hope create the form or outline of a thing. The conceptualization of the object, in the abstract, of your mind makes it mentally four-dimensional (breadth, length, height, and depth) ~ Ephesians 3:18. The four-dimensional aspect of viewing an object is the vehicle that takes you from great faith to knowing in the Christ-Spirit.

Enduring the process, I learned it was more than just faith. It is a place and space of knowing. They displayed a genuine love for me. However, was it now sufficient? Was it enough for where I was going? Would I benefit them from holding on to an attachment of familiarity? A few days ago, I thought about my statement: "I am going to follow the Son: the illuminating, invigorating, pulsating, wonderful, glorious Spirit of the Lord." I thought, "Was my desire to follow the Son the feeling I was experiencing that night? I understood in a revelatory way that *I could* follow the Son and bathe in the sunshine of His love. Many people came to me and said, "You are glowing." I thought it strange because it was at

Markeithia Lavon Silver

different intervals during the night. Nevertheless, each person used the exact words when they spoke each time.

I came there crawling with a fear of walking into who I was. I had fallen many times before. I began to walk under this ministry. However, I was now confidently running. I was running into a new phase of my life; I just did not know it. As I stood there speaking words of appreciation, it seemed they took my words for granted. Were they really, or was I experiencing an epiphany? I observed them not paying attention to what I was saying. However, God was listening. God was listening, and He allowed me to see the birthing of the new Markeithia moment by moment. I stood outside myself, watching as God lifted me to another level. Then, I saw myself sitting amidst many roads. I would suppress these feelings until I could no longer bear them. That night, I needed to be there to experience my birthing into a world of endless possibilities.

Being in a place of change became overwhelming for me on Sunday. I slept off and on throughout the day. I was running from what I was feeling: the process of shedding and rearranging my life. I chose to sleep instead. After I had taken my daughter home, I stopped and purchased a sandwich. Then, I returned home and sat in my car for quite some time, thinking about my evening. I could not help feeling the Lord's impact placing a period in the chapter of my life. Where do I go from here? A part of my life ended, and a new beginning was upon me. I felt vulnerable at the moment. I ate my sandwich, trying to handle what was going on. I began to weep, not in sadness, but weep, nonetheless. Then, the question came. "What roads will you choose to write the next forty years of your life?" The Spirit of the Lord led me to look up some things I had written. I reread *Ten Things I Am Committed to* and *the Application of Receiving the Fullness of Abundance.*

I was perplexed and unsure as to which way to go. The idea of so many roads surrounding me was overwhelming. I did not know where to begin. I searched for what questions to ask. Finally,

Living Your Legacy Of Greatness

I finished my sandwich and exited my vehicle. I walked into the house, longing to identify with something familiar. I felt detached from my surroundings. Spiritually, I did not know where I was. I made significant attempts to gain my bearings.

The phone rang as I walked up the stairs. I was hoping that it was a familiar voice, and it was. "Hey, you," a gentle, caring voice said. I responded. They intuitively knew something was different. However, I could not verbalize what was occurring at that moment. I could tell them how much I loved and appreciated our friendship and how I appreciated them. I began to think, "If my life expired today, I truly learned what it means to feel loved for me." I made a couple more calls to grasp something familiar, but to no avail. Only my thoughts and mental line paper were awaiting my inscription.

How do I want to see my life unfold within the divine scheme of things? What place will my thoughts play in God's role for me? I know God's plans are an extraordinary divine destiny tailor-made for me. *What does my life look like to me*? It is more than mere desire and hope for a better life. I must be able to conceptualize it before it can manifest. It is as if the Creator said, "You now rose to a place worthy to write your own life. What do you desire and hope for in this life? What would you like to see manifested in your life? You can bring it to pass if you can conceive, perceive, and believe it. *Be persuaded in your mind!* According to your faith, be *it* unto you! Whatever you decide, it will all work for your good. I incorporated what is necessary and sufficient for your growth within your plans." I looked again at the roads, and they no longer appeared overwhelming. I began to scrutinize them one by one. As I observed each one in its importance, I saw God weave success within each pathway. The combination of different paths accomplished, in and of itself, is an achievement. Success, however, is a subjective concept on behalf of the individual. So, I did not want to focus on that. I chose to turn my attention to what God designed for me.

Markeithia Lavon Silver

Accordingly, I began to contemplate what I needed to dispose of immediately. As I reflected within the confines of my mind, I discovered that the childhood notion that I was abandoned was a farce—That I am inadequate, a charade. People genuinely love me and surround me with authentic affection. I am not deserted! I am complete in God! I enjoy people who are there to help me figure it all out. All I need to do is ask according to the Will of God, and God brings it to pass. This arrow of deceit is at the root of most issues we face. The fear of being alone to figure it all out was terrible. The irony is that I was comfortable walking alone—solitude is a best friend. This mindset, I realized, was the strength of that weakness. I now understand how fear precluded me from aspiring to absolute security in relationships. I no longer desire to carry this baggage on my journey. I can receive love, and others love me on many diverse levels. This confidence is now a reality for me ~ Psalms 27. I speak this reality to myself. The words of Isaiah came to life. "Remember ye, not the former things, neither consider the things of old. Behold, I will do *a new thing; now* it shall spring forth*; shall ye not know it?* I will even make a *way in the wilderness and Rivers in the desert…* *Keep me in remembrance: let us plead together…"* ~ Isaiah 43:18-19, 26ab. (Emphasis mine). I am keeping God in remembrance and living my "new thing, and I *know* it!"

What Are You Speaking to Yourself?

Are you ready to begin training your mind for the good of yourself and others? Are you ready to purposely plant seeds of greatness that you will harvest in your future? Are you willing to synchronize your dreams and desires with your actions and consecrate them into the right hand of the One who *knows* His plans for you? We will be more attentive to our thoughts when we realize we are working with the Laws of Cause and Effect,

Living Your Legacy Of Greatness

Correspondence, Belief, and Attraction. We shall manifest what we say to ourselves. As mentioned, peace of mind is the effect of certainty, assurance, and trust in God. Accordingly, you can obtain confidence by training the senses (your perceptive abilities) in the Word of God, trusting the experience's process, and framing a life fit for the Master's use. Just as I spent months training to become a police officer in the academy, an individual must take time to train the flowing and creation of their thoughts to become the word in the flesh. The peace of God that "passes all understanding shall keep your heart and mind, in Christ." ~ Philippians 4:7. *See also* Isaiah 26: 3.

In the Book of Wisdom/Proverbs 22:6, Solomon admonishes us to "Train up a child in the way s/he should go, and when s/he grows up, s/he will not depart from it." What did you train your mind to do? Training is fundamental in governing how we think, perceive, and approach matters in life. Whatever preparation (discipline) we receive determines and regulates how we view the world. This training includes life experiences stamped upon our subconscious mind, influencing our thinking and vision building. Appropriately, we establish our belief systems through the spectacles of our training/experiences. This be-life system, I mention throughout, is a beacon that attracts your fundamental "truths." Do you recall the cliché, "Birds of a feather flock together?" A simple yet profound statement that reminds us that we tend to associate ourselves with people who share the same values and beliefs. This statement, moreover, underscores how *you attract outwardly what you speak inwardly*—what you give life to (be-life, aka belief). Your truth may not necessarily be *the* truth, but an opinion, nonetheless. Whatever life experiences you indoctrinate upon your mind will be your reality—your truth unless you choose to change it.

For instance, if you grow up in a home filled with insecurity, mistrust, lack of love, and violence, you may attract situations, friends, and mates that solidify your "truth." Social scientists show

Markeithia Lavon Silver

that the environment *and* an individual's DNA often shape an individual's pathology, methodology, and ideology. You may weep, become depressed, and be overwhelmed due to the circumstances that befall you, continually asking yourself, "Why does this keep happening to me?" *When you do not adequately confront the source(s) of your thinking, the seeds sown by you and your collective consciousness instilled in you as a child will inevitably become the harvest in your life.*

Moreover, you will continue to speak those thoughts until you choose not to say them, resulting in a change in circumstances. Knowing what is in your mind soil will bode well in transforming your life according to the Word of God. Let *this* mind be in you that was also in Christ Jesus will take on a whole new meaning. Beloved, you hold the power to accept or reject what you learn. You can forgive the visions you create, allowing healing to saturate your mind and continue in your ascent to greatness. *Forgiveness is the act that removes the veil so you can see your future clearly.* Without it, your past continues to blind you and your ability to healthfully vision-build. Free yourself from your past and live new experiences that bring love, joy, and peace to your mind. Cast all your care upon *Me*, sayeth God! ~ I Peter 5:7.

Finally, remember to think of good thoughts or thoughts of good. Either way, feed your mind with feelings that edify you, not tear you down. "*I am who I am because I choose to be* (This is taking responsibility for your thoughts and visions)." God created me in the likeness and image of the "Us" Spirit. God is great! Therefore, greatness resides in me! My world reflects what I think and feel the most. I believe in and feel greatness! Therefore, my world is great! See it! Feel it! Taste it! Live it!

I will end this chapter with a chorus from the late Pastor James Cleveland's song, *God Leads His Children,* and prose, *Discovering Me.* "*Some go through the water; some go through the flood. Some go through the fire, but we all got to go through the blood...*

Some of us go through great sorrow, but aren't you glad? If you are listening into heaven, He will give you a song. It says, "In the night season, and all the day long... [He will lead you!]."

Discovering Me

Gazing at the reflection in the mirror, what do you see? Do you *see* Me? Do you see the gifts and talents I bestowed within you, or do the images of violent pain cloud them from the past? Forgive the inward pictures and perceptions of imperfection. Reach beyond the limitations of your mind to discover your legacy of greatness! Befriend the LOVE that created you. Embrace this Love in such a way that it frees you from the bondage of hostility and fear. It is *Morning*, little one! The night has passed over. Today, will you leave the corridors of fear in your mind, which await at each turning corner? Let Me shroud you in My Love, receding the shadow of fear, and dare to explore every aspect of My Love for you. Do you *see* Me? I DARE YOU! I AM EVER SO GENTLY AWAITING THE ARRIVAL OF YOUR PRESENCE... Take the step; I will be there!

)

CHAPTER NINE
─────────────

A NEW ME

"Be ye transformed by the renewing of your mind..." ~ *Romans 12:2.*

—Paul

"Let this mind be in you, which was also in Christ Jesus:" ~ *Philippians 2:5*

—Paul

"Stand fast in the Liberty, wherewith [the] Christ [Spirit] has made us free and be not entangled again with the yoke of bondage." ~ *Galatians 5:1*

—Paul

"They that KNOW their God shall be strong and do great exploits" ~ *Daniel 11:32*

—Daniel

When striving to change our lives, we ask ourselves, "Where do I begin?" Beginning, of course, seems to be the most challenging place. "If I could just start, I would be okay," we tell

Markeithia Lavon Silver

ourselves. What do you do if you want to commence with the art of change? Outwardly, it appears I cannot seem to get off the ground. Is it just starting at the beginning, or is there more to it than we envisage? In this instance, like many others, we disillusion ourselves into thinking the task is less of a confrontation of ourselves and more of changing our habits. However, we cannot analyze the origins of our practices without examining the "self" inwardly and confronting our structure of belief systems and the values that our methods rest upon. Supporting the notion of changing our behavior and personality traits is overrated unless preceded by a plan of introspection and the discrimination of reasoning pillars that uphold and govern our actions.

Alternatively, should we choose, we could simultaneously tackle the image of ourselves and trace the root cause of our behavior and life practices. Accordingly, this practice forces us to become in tune with who we are (our identity in God). It challenges us to live life in a more than lavish way instead of merely existing. In doing so, as neurologists suggest, we may change the manner and connection of our synapses within our brain, thus changing how we see ourselves, the world, our lifestyles, and ultimately God.

Psychologists say we all create life scripts that govern how we approach the world. These narratives predetermine our results. The grooves and silhouettes we produce with our thoughts systematically design the desired result. However, the outcome is a "Jedi mind trick" to keep us from our true selves. When we change those creases and shadows, we change the result. Mastering that change becomes a life's work. I refer to this process as *Mastering the Alchemy of the Mind*. Thankfully, we can change how we see the world and, ultimately, ourselves with the assistance of the Lord's example.

Are you ready for a paradigm shift? Are you prepared to engage in the application of the Alchemy of the Mind? When you purposefully renew your mind and refuse the bondage of your old

Living Your Legacy Of Greatness

life to entangle you, you will begin uncovering and rediscovering who you are. Then, in that exact moment, your entire world will shift. Self-discovery will cause an automatic shift in how you *see* yourself, God, others, and the world. Your connections, self-esteem, self-worth, right thinking, right perceptions, direction, favor, and open doors will all change— "Old things will pass away, and behold, all things WILL be new!" Often, we put up with things and people because we do not know who we are. We tolerate less than our worth because we are used to the ridges engraved within our minds. When we shift from the old way of thinking to a new way, our predetermined results will change who we are and, ultimately, the world. "Begin with yourself, and healing will multiply," says Mahatma Gandhi. *Today*, choose to remember who you are!

As we pursue the legacy of our greatness, we will discover the undying love, mercy, and kindness of the Infinite "Us" Power and Sustainer of all things. We will earnestly desire to become an instrument of His peace. Our pattern of thoughts of goodwill, harmony, love, and peace will not create a "new me," but it will reveal God's masterpiece, the *you* that He made from the world's foundation. The chains of fear will no longer bind you and cause you to live and become the prince and princess God destined us to be. Once the transformation occurs, you will feel the fullness of the Love of the "Us" Spirit and be willing to bestow that love upon all humanity. Essentially, we will become as Jesus is—the Word made flesh, living in the authority of our legacy. St. Francis of Assisi, in his prayer unto the Heavenly Father, says,

> Lord, *make me an instrument* of Your peace. Where there is hatred, let me sow love; where there is injury, pardon; where there is doubt, faith; where there is despair, hope; where there is darkness, light; where there is sadness, joy. O Divine Master, grant me that I may not so much seek to be consoled as to console; to be understood, as to understand;

Markeithia Lavon Silver

to be loved, as to love. For it is in giving that we receive; it is in pardoning that we are pardoned; it is in dying that we are born to eternal life. (Emphasis mine).

I love this prayer. It keeps us focused on the beautiful things of the Infinite One/Elohim/El-Shaddai, who created the world in Wisdom, Power, and Love. As we show love, love returns to us. Conversely, how can we exhibit love if we do not know it? As we come to know and love ourselves, we will know the Source of our Salvation and the Strength and Song of our existence ~ Isaiah 12:2-3. Moreover, when we realize our thoughts are seeds that will be produced after their kind, we will learn to be selective about what we think, purposeful about the visions we build, and look forward to our crop's harvesting.

Have you ever heard of a successful person thinking about failure? No. No matter the age, gender, ethnicity, or race, a successful person will ponder thoughts of success. Do you recall my blurb about *The Fierce Five*? Everything within them exudes that "something" that permeates every part of their being—their focused, positive thinking, commitment, and trust in the Infinite "Us" Power/God. Their confidence and strength spilled over, encouraging a nation. David said in Psalms 37:5, "*Commit* thy way unto the Lord; *also trust* in Him, and *He shall bring it to pass.*" (Emphasis mine).

The word "shall" is interesting. The word is a verb expressing the future tense, expressing a strong assertion or intention of inevitability.[39] In the legal sense, it is an absolute term and "generally imperative or mandatory."[40] In standard or ordinary parlance and its ordinary signification, the phrase 'shall' is a word of command that always has or must give a compulsory meaning: denoting obligation. "It has the invariable significance of excluding the idea of discretion and has the significance of operating to impose a duty which one can enforce."[41] In other words, if you follow the protocol

Living Your Legacy Of Greatness

of commitment and trust, there is no room for it not to occur—He obligates and compels Himself to perform it! That is amazing! The collateral that God will *always* honor! Gabby trusted God for her success! She trusted God for her comfort! She trusted God to bless her due diligence in acquiring the Gold! As I watched her, I prayed that the Lord would protect her in her innocence, craft, and life as she soared. *Internalizing the words of David prepares and propels us into the realm of Kingdom success.* What an injection of encouragement. Gabby's display of God's trust defends against the mind's impatience! In contrast, people display an aura about them that drains and brings them down due to negative thinking, limitations, and mental poverty. We must keep them out of our mental space until the time comes when they are open to change.

As mentioned earlier in the chapter, *Expect to Do More*, Paula Deen shared with the viewers her bout with agoraphobia: fear of exposure to unidentified danger or open spaces. In this space of fear, she created a "new" her. However, it was not the "her" she wanted to be. Petrified by her admission to this "new" state she had created, she experienced several manifestations of this fear in her body. However, she was determined to overcome this new state of mind. It was not until "she came across the Serenity Prayer" that she released her phobia. She rested in the implicit assurance of the Infinite "Us" Power of God from that moment. When she turned her mind toward God, His Peace delivered her from all her troubles. "Thou will keep thee in perfect peace all whose mind is stayed on [Him] because they trust in Him…God is an everlasting strength…" ~ Isaiah 26:3-4. Ernest Holmes says in *Thoughts Are Things*: *The Things in your life and the thoughts that are behind them:*

[Fear] is not the host encamped against you or the confusion around you that you must fear; ***the lack of confidence in the Good [God] alone should concern you***. Through an inner

Markeithia Lavon Silver

spiritual vision, you know that [God] alone is permanent and all else is transitory [fleeting]...***The Power of [the "Us"] Spirit is supreme over every antagonist.*** Therefore, you should cherish no fear **[it is a pseudo god, worthy of nothing but eviction from the mind]** ... (Emphasis mine).

Therefore, we will attract good or bad conditions into our spaces and places according to our focused thought. This wisdom is the power of the Sower! Once we *know* this fact, we can reframe our thinking to embrace our God-selves, reversing our confidence in fear and placing our assurance in the power of the "Us" Spirit. Our thoughts are seeds and contain the capacity to grow and manifest giant proverbial trees in our lives. Synonymous with this is a natural seed; when planted in fertile ground, the will, by the Power of Nature, begins to take shape until it manifests according to its kind: vis-à-vis an apple seed as an apple, a rose seed as a rose, etc. You will never see a rose seed produce an apple or vice versa. Accordingly, each source will reproduce after its kind and likeness.

However, if you grow weeds in your garden (mental fears and doubt), it may retard, delay, or even destroy your harvest. The "Us" Power/God planted (breathed into humanity) the seed of the Kingdom in us before the foundation of the world. We must immediately remove all fear and doubt to grow into greatness and claim our birthright harvest of excellence. Your successes lay in the awareness of the Infinite "Us" Power/El-Shaddai/God residing in you. If you feel it, know it, act upon it, and behave as Jesus did when he approached Lazarus's grave, you will manifest the remarkable spirit God created you to be. You will display the right action if you align the knowledge that the Source and Creation of All reside within you with your belief system. Understanding always precedes the right action. Therefore, if you create a mind of change, it will manifest in your efforts.

Living Your Legacy Of Greatness

In *Thoughts are Things*, Ernest Holmes says, "Your knowledge that the *Great I Am* is ever available gives you an increased capacity to draw upon It, and to *become inwardly aware of the presence of [His] Spirit within you...* With a penetrating spiritual vision, you can dissipate the obstruction, remove the obstacle, and dissolve the wrong condition." Apostle Paul said, "We are to stand fast in our freedom and not entangle again into the yolk of bondage (negative thinking or anything contrary to the promises of Kingdom thinking)" ~ Galatians 5:1. Living in your space and posturing your greatness allows you the opportunity to blot out the ability of every transgression (negative thought, doubt, fear, or limitation) by God's grace, mercy, and the blood covenant of Christ. We must "forget those things behind us, and reach forth unto those things that are before, and press toward the mark for the prize of the high calling of God, in Christ Jesus" (Philippians 3:14-15 *See also* Isaiah 43:18-19). Beloved, we relish the power to choose what to think. We wield it at our disposal. Elect to *be* life to greatness! Refuse to consider lack, failure, despair, or place in worship any pseudo-god that would preclude you from laying hold onto your destiny of greatness. Evict the thoughts that wreak havoc in your mind. You *must* envision the table spread that the Infinite "Us" Power/El-Shaddai/Elohim/God has prepared for you. ~ Psalms 23. David knew the glory and lavishness of the Creator. He bathed in it, danced in it, and sought after it all the days of his life ~ Psalms 27:4.

However, if there is an internal conflict between the thought (mind) and our beliefs (trust in God to bring it to pass), we will not manifest our God-selves but a drip-drop of who we are. In contrast, if you *know* God's decree of love, joy, and happiness from the world's foundation upon your life, you will fill that space with thoughts that will attract according to its kind.

As you continue to practice the art of *Mastering the Alchemy of the Mind*, you will become a master of articulation with yourself, others, and ultimately the Infinite "Us" Power/El-Shaddai/Elohim/ God, Source of All things. The more refined your thinking, the better quality of life mentally, physically, and spiritually you will experience. Consider Mother Teresa, who prayed to be an instrument of His Peace, touching many, she, in turn, became a conduit communicating a vision of goodness and a belief system assisting others to change for the better. *"Be the change* you want to *see* in this world" by discovering, recovering, and uncovering *YOU*! As you walk in the space of this greatness, the Agapé love of God will exude from within you, healing, mending, and setting the minds of those bound free.

Agapé, according to the *Encarta English Dictionary*, means non-sexual love; love that is wholly selfless and spiritual; a communal feast held by a Christian community, especially in the early Christian church, commemorating the Last Supper. *Strong's Concordance* defines Agapé in Greek as love, affection, or benevolence: specifically, ***feast upon—love feast****: feast of charity*. Wow! *I Love this!* When you rise to the level of your god-ness, you will allow others to feast upon you. This example suggests the seed of faith that will grow, allowing others to rest upon its branches ~ Luke 13:18-19. Agapé strengthens and edifies us for the journey when allowed to feast upon one another. The reciprocity function of *Agapé Love* and satiation fill, cover, and bind the wounds of those harmed.

Trust for one another is not a factor; there is no judgment, only *Agapé Love*. It is sanctioned by the "Us" Spirit when the strong bear the infirmity of the weak. You, therefore, stand before one another naked and not ashamed. This godly love intercedes, overlooks faults, seeks to meet the heart's needs, produces happiness in and of itself, and covers a multitude of sins ~ Isaiah 59:14-16 and *I Peter* 4:8, respectively. "Lord, give us our daily bread this day" at the feasting table. Each of us meets the other's needs as we become who the "Us" Spirit created us to be: the expressed image

Living Your Legacy Of Greatness

of His Son ~ Hebrews 1:1-3, Romans 8:17, I John 4:17. We feast upon one another and align ourselves with the Law of Unity at the Table of *Agapé Love* buying, eating, and drinking from the Well that will not run dry without money and price. ~ Isaiah 12:3, 55:1. Those receptive shall receive, and whosoever partakes in the feast shall eat and be nourished. Shall you look around at the table the Lord has prepared for you and not participate out of fear? Heaven forbids! Lean, oh gentle reader, into the notion of being fed, and lay down your coat, sword, and shield, for there is nothing to fear at the Master's table.

At the feasting table, all are welcome and safe from harm. You may sit in silence or converse with your fellow humankind. The holy choice is yours. However, if fear pierces the veil of your mind, it marginalizes trust, precluding one from partaking of the Feast Table. Nonetheless, we must strive to understand whom God made us, uncover our identity, and seek to incorporate the precious "Fruits of the Spirit: Love, Joy, Peace, Longsuffering, Gentleness, Goodness, Faith, Meekness, and Temperance, [into our lives] *against such there is no law*" ~ Galatians 5:22-23. (Emphasis mine). Jesus has already come to show us the way. *WALK THEREIN!*

Therefore, according to your thought focus, you MUST seek out by reflection – what kind are you? What fruits do you possess? Do not be deceived, beloved. There is a kind that is not of God ~ Matthew 13:24-30. This enemy created *another kind* that is not of God, a seed of death and not life, which separates us from Him. "Their eyes were opened" was *another creation manifested from their disobedience* opposing God's purpose and destiny for our lives. More importantly, we must carefully watch for this other kind that breeds shame, lack, and not enough under the guise of a delusion of "being *as* God." That lie trans-positioned Adam and Eve out of the Garden. That deception blurred the righteous souls of Adam and Eve right out of the Garden. This Garden in Eden was a special place carved out by God to meet Adam. It was there that

Adam received his instructions. Adam communed with God in this carved-out place, receiving His fullness and soul's pleasure. We, too, can bask in God's presence through Jesus Christ, the righteous seed. Dare to enter His presence where He will show you the paths of life, receiving the fullness of joy and pleasure forevermore ~ Psalms 16:11. *Will you do it?*

Christ's blood sacrifice repositioned us! God opened our eyes with the quickening Spirit of the Last Adam so that we might claim our dominion and power through Christ. Yēšûa (Jesus) raised our spiritual bodies with him. We sit in heavenly places with God, washed in the precious blood of the Lamb of God and transpositioned back into His presence ~ *I Corinthians* 15: 39-49. It is time to take our place! The world is awaiting our debut!

Let go and *forgive* the vision created by your thoughts of lack, not good enough, and anything contrary to the Lord's promises upon your life. God is not a man that He should lie; He is not slack concerning His promises; the Lord God Almighty is faithful to His Word (that He is still speaking those same promises since the foundation of the world). Lose the shame of the past and shake it off. The "Us" Spirit is never caught off guard by your choices, for "He calls the end from the beginning" ~ Isaiah 46:10. Forgive the vision and allow the healing virtue of the Infinite "Us" Power to make you whole and free. Then, go forth and create anew.

Ask yourself, "Why are you in the place you are today?" What doest thou here (How did you get here)? ~ I Kings 19:9,13.

"Where is your happiness, and in what does it reside?"

Additionally, "What is your despair, and in what does it dwell?"

When you discover these things, you will be well on your way to becoming not the new you but attracting *YOU*, the transfigured you created before the world's foundation.

WHERE ART THOU, OH ADAM? AND, WHO TOLD YOU YOU WERE NAKED?

He is awaiting your response. Look within and uncover, discover, and recover your legacy!

As I end this chapter, I must admonish you again that each human has a responsibility to themselves and creation to pay close attention to their thinking and vision building. Your thoughts are likened to a radio sending and receiving messages. Although you cannot see them, each system tunes in and hears the voices on the radio. When we tune in to the Infinite "Us" Power of the Universe and press into His presence, we shall receive all the messages necessary for our growth of becoming who we are, and change will occur. The Infinite Source of the "Us" Spirit sends communications and affects change within those tuned into the transmission. Likewise, when we send out our thoughts of rage, anger, lack, and the like, those of like-mindedness receive them, affecting their mental space. Remember, *your thought's first lines of defense are you.* Accordingly, when you send out thoughts of anger, they attack you first. Therefore, send ideas and feelings of harmony, peace, and love; those tuned into unity, love, and peace will receive them. Those feelings/thoughts will invoke similar thoughts/feelings of love, peace, and harmony—The "Us" Spirit shall go from breast to breast. This notion of our brother's keeper is why we must pray, intercede, and meditate on the good for all humanity, for the love that covers a multitude of sins to reign upon all humanity so that God might save us all.

A *Butterfly Effect* theory suggests that a butterfly's flapping wings in one region can affect the wind in another area. Similarly, one thought, good, bad, or indifferent, affects the entire world, causing unrest, ill will, or happiness among our fellow citizens. These are the extent of the effects of thought power. Thought power is a great gift we must respect, master, and use wisely for the greater good of all humanity. Your thoughts of excellence, harmony, and peace will accomplish what they set out to achieve and will not come back void. This standard is Kingdom living,

Markeithia Lavon Silver

and this is Kingdom thinking, and know without a doubt that the Kingdom *is within* you! "[When] much is given, much is required." So, govern yourselves accordingly.

Remember, the Strength of the Infinite "Us" Power resides in you—*you are not weak!* "With God, all things are possible to them that (trust) believe." He is ever-present. Draw from the well that will never run dry—*I am one with the Infinite "Us" Power.* Allow this thought to ring through your mind until you draw out your god-nature, live, live, and live your legacy of greatness! As you draw upon this limitless God-Power, know that it knows no boundaries, and you cannot place it in a box—*expect to do more!* It is yours to enjoy but not to hold—for it belongs to all. The all-inclusive God-Power works within us—we are a part of the Unified Consciousness of the Infinite "Us" Power/God; *remember who you are*! Do not forget to do your due diligence with thought-catching, and the visions built because of those thoughts offered up in praise and thanksgiving unto the Lord. Remember Jesus's thoughts when he went to the gravesite. "Thank you, Father, for hearing me, for *I KNOW* you listen to me *ALWAYS!*" All you must do is *BE* LIFE to the notion of your gift of greatness, trust that He has paved the way for you, seek Him wholeheartedly, and call upon Him, for He will never disappoint. ~ Jerimiah 29:11-13. Laugh often, Love much, and dare to Live your Legacy of Greatness!

Thank you, gentle reader, for taking this journey with me. It has been my joyful pleasure to explore the nature of our calling with you. I earnestly pray that you become a master of your thinking, a skilled contractor of your vision, and lay hold of the divine knowledge that gives you the power to become the prince or princess God destined you to be—perfected in your faith and God's Love. I wish you much Love, Joy, eternal Peace, and Happiness forever. I pray you experience more deeply the all-abiding love and kindness of the Eternal Father and the strength of His sustained peace each day. May you forever know that God hides you in His

Living Your Legacy Of Greatness

bosom and is the Source and Sustainer of all life. May you dwell in His presence, the "Us" Spirit, wanting nothing. Trust Him; He will never disappoint!

I will end this chapter with a verse from a popular song by Pastor Donnie McClurkin and prose entitled *I am Free. "I am walking in Authority, [living life as it is meant to be]. It is not wrong, dear; I belong here, so you might as well get used to me! And He has given me dominion, YES!"*

CHOOSE NOW, CHILD OF GOD, TO WALK IN YOUR AUTHORITY! WALK IN YOUR DOMINION! WALK IN YOUR LEGACY OF GREATNESS!

LAUGH! LOVE! LIVE YOUR LEGACY OF GREATNESS!

I Am Free

I am free.
I am free to *see* Me.
I am free to *see* what the birds see.
I am free to *be* Me.
I am free to *see* what the ocean declares.
I am free to *be* Me.
I am free to *see* what the sun proclaims, and the moon sustains.
I am free to *be* Me.
The entire galaxy marvels at my glory as I shine.
Like the stars shining in space.
Do you *see* what I see?
The Earth takes notice of My creation and bows down in honor.
I march confidently on Earth's red carpet, created just for Me.
In sync with Nature, I walk in my inheritance, singing a melody that drops like gentle rain upon my brow.
I am free, free to create Me, enjoy Me, and embrace Me.
BE WHOLE AND BE F-R-E-E!

Markeithia Lavon Silver

"Finally, my sisters and my brothers fare well! Be perfected [in your faith, living perfected in God's loving grace], be of good comfort, be of one mind [perfectly joined together], live in peace [let there be no divisions among you], and the God of Love and Peace shall be with you. Amen." ~ *II Corinthians* 13:11.

Declaration of Independence

We hold these truths to be self-evident. All of humanity has the potential for greatness. The Creator endowed us all with the inalienable rights of abundant life, creative ability, resurrected power, and the pursuit of the fullness of joy in Him.

We all generate what we ask for and have the power to change what we do not. Our Creator gives these rights and capabilities as gifts, which God will not repossess.

To obtain our actuality of greatness, we must perfect our faith. We must ascend to a place of knowing, allow the perfecting of God's love to permeate our being, strive to discipline our thoughts, and align them with what we want to create and maintain—the greatness of Love, Joy, and Peace forevermore.

"In His presence, there is fullness of Joy, and at His right hand, there are pleasures forevermore." Celebrate freedom in the country, mentally, spiritually, and emotionally. "Lay aside every weight that would so easily beset thee and run this race with patience." "Trust the Lord in all you do, even when you cannot trace Him. Know without a doubt that He guides us with wisdom, love, and power, leading us into all truth.

Be Whole! Be Free. Be Who God Created You to Be! Amen.

Living Your Legacy Of Greatness

DAILY AFFIRMATIONS

- ➤ I am one with Christ as he is one with the Father.
- ➤ Like Zerubbabel, I am God's signet ring used to His glory and honor!
- ➤ Because I am a child of The Most High/El-Shaddai, all that is Divine, the unseen Power of creation, healing, deliverance from bondage, and blessings are mine and at my disposal forever. I easily access this Power at will, live, move, and have my being.
- ➤ I have the God of the Universe on my side. His Glorious Power dwells in me and flows through me freely and richly, unhindered by opposing forces.
- ➤ I can creatively create with the Power of the "Us" Spirit who created me to help others and myself. Glory!
- ➤ This unseen Power enlightens all who encounter me, directly or indirectly.
- ➤ My mind, body, and spirit acquire this Power with ease as I enter worship of The Most High God. I seek the Source of All Power with a heart of praise and thanksgiving.
- ➤ Grace and Mercy follow me all the days of my life.
- ➤ I willfully and joyfully extend grace to myself and others.
- ➤ To the point of spiritual ecstasy, I enjoy my fellowship with God and the Spirit of the "Us" Spirit of God.
- ➤ The Source of All Power/El-Shaddai replenishes me continually.
- ➤ I attract exceptional and favorable circumstances to my life—I am responsible for the thoughts and visions I create.
- ➤ I seek first the Kingdom of God and all Its righteousness, and God opens to me the doors of success, guided by His Power to obtain wealth, and He adds no sorrow.

Markeithia Lavon Silver

- I am an excellent steward/ess of my affairs. The Lord is a lamp unto my feet and a Light unto my path.
- I am whole, complete, free, and lacking nothing in Christ.
- All my organs, cells, bones, muscles, and joints come into perfect alignment, as God created me from the foundation of the world, reinforced by the Infinite Power/El-Shaddai God. I am in excellent health, according to the word of Elohim God.
- My mind, body, and spirit perfectly align with the Power of the "Us" Spirit. No pain or sickness can dwell in my body, and God reinforces this Power in Christ.
- I am the perfect weight for my body, which operates optimally, reinforced by the Infinite Power/El-Shaddai God in Christ Jesus.
- This Infinite Power/El-Shaddai, which dwells in me, can bring sight to the blinded eyes, remove the chains of bondage in the minds of humanity, and raise the lifeless, and consciousness of humanity and set them free.
- I can recall, with ease, life's lessons to wisely apply to any subsequent challenges.
- I delight in life and all it has to offer. I am fearless in Christ!
- I make the correct choices for myself, my family, and my friends, guided by the Holy Spirit of the Infinite Power/ El-Shaddai God in Christ. These choices bring only excellent and positive results, causing no regret.
- I am a force to be reckoned with, dispelling all opposing forces that attempt to rise against me or anything associated with the Power of blood in Christ.
- I accomplish my daily tasks without struggle or frustrated tension.
- The renewing of my mind is continual without struggle, dispelling and eliminating old thinking patterns.

Living Your Legacy Of Greatness

- I can ask the question, and the answer comes freely, unhindered, uninterrupted by old thinking patterns. The Infinite godly Wisdom, Knowledge, and Skill of God guide me in all truth.
- I am motivated to change, grow, and excel to unlimited heights.
- I enjoy being a mother, daughter, sister, and friend.
- I can nurture, guide, and discipline my children with the Love and Wisdom of the Infinite Power/El-Shaddai "Us" Spirit.
- My children have all they need mentally, spiritually, and physically.
- I willingly choose, with purposeful intent, to detach myself from the negative reference points of childhood and replace them with positive renewal in Christ.
- All that belongs to the Infinite/El-Shaddai God, the unseen Power of creation, healing, and delivering from bondage, is at my disposal forever for the betterment of the world and myself in Christ Jesus.
- This unseen Power/El-Shaddai God enlightens all who encounter me, directly or indirectly. I am a beacon of light in Christ.
- When facing life's obstacles, I am calm, displaying equanimity, able to reason, and with ease, hurtled over these obstacles enabled by the Power of the Infinite/El-Shaddai.
- I am whole, free, and lacking nothing.
- I wish peace, harmony, joy, and Love upon all humanity.
- I joyfully enter the corridors of my mental past, eliminating any knowledge, thought patterns, or behavior that may hinder me from laying hold of my destiny of greatness.

Markeithia Lavon Silver

- ➤ I operate in the Breakers and Ziklag anointing according to the Word of God!
- ➤ God gives me victory at the gate of my enemies!

FOOTNOTES/BIBLIOGRAPHY

1   *Thayer Greek-English Lexicon*, G4053.
2   Cooley, C.H., "The Social Self – 1. The Meaning of 'I'",
Chapter 5 in *Human Nature and the Social Order (Revised Edition)*.
New York: Charles Scribner's Sons, (1922), p. 824.
3   *Ibid.* p. 825.
4   *Ibid.* p. 824.
5   *Ibid.* p. 827.
6   *Ibid.* p. 827.
7   Cooley, C.H., The Roots of Social Knowledge. *American Journal of Sociology*, p. 114.
8   Cooley, C.H., "The Social Self – 1. The Meaning of 'I'", Chapter 5 in *Human Nature and the Social Order (Revised Edition)*. New York: Charles Scribner's Sons, (1922), p. 824.
9   Cooley, C.H., The Roots of Social Knowledge. *American Journal of Sociology*, p. 115
10   *Ibid* p. 118
11   Cooley, C.H., "The Social Self – 1. The Meaning of 'I'", Chapter 5 in *Human Nature and the Social Order (Revised Edition)*. New York: Charles Scribner's Sons, (1922), p. 826.
12   Cooley, C.H., The Roots of Social Knowledge. *American Journal of Sociology*, p. 119
13   Mead, G.H. *George Herbert Mead on Social Psychology.*
14   *Ibid.* p. 121.
15   *Ibid.*
16   *Ibid.*
17   *Ibid.* p.163.
18   *Ibid.* p. 165.

19   *Ibid.* p.165-166.
20   *Ibid.*
21   *Ibid.* p. 218.
22   *Ibid.* p.219-220.
23   *Ibid.* p.121.
24   *Britannica*, Retrieved at https://www.britannica.com/science/metamorphosis
25   *Strong's Exhaustive Concordance of the Bible*, H2580.
26   *Ibid.*, H2603.
27   *Ibid.*, G5485.
28   *Thayer's Greek-English Lexicon of the New Testament*, G5485.
29   *Brown-Driver-Briggs Bible Concordance*, H5315
30   *Strong's Exhaustive Concordance of the Bible*, H2232.
31   Al-Ghazzali, *On Disciplining the Self*
32   *Strong's Exhaustive Concordance of the Bible,* G4100.
33   *Ibid.*, G4053.
34   *Ibid.*
35   *Ibid.*, G5046.
36   *Ibid.*, H539.
37   *Ibid.*, G4100.
38   *Thayer's Greek-English Lexicon of the New Testament*, G4100.
39   *Miriam-Webster Dictionary*, Retrieved at https://www.merri-am-webster.com/dictionary/shall
40   *Ibid.*
41   *Black Law Dictionary*, Retrieved at https://thelawdictionary.org/shall/

Coming Soon!

Living Your Legacy of Greatness, Volume One, Discovering Within the Image and Likeness of God Journal Companion.

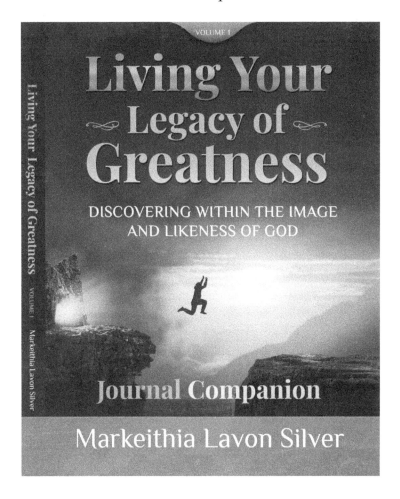

Printed in the USA
CPSIA information can be obtained
at www.ICGtesting.com
CBHW052005090824
12962CB00066B/764